PEACEMAKER

PAUL MURPHY
Peacemaker

an autobiography

UNIVERSITY OF WALES PRESS
2019

www.uwp.co.uk

British Library CIP Data

A catalogue record for this book is available from the British Library

ISBN   978-1-7868-347-20
eISBN   978-1-7868-347-37

The right of Paul Murphy to be identified as author of this work has been asserted in accordance with sections 77 and 79 of the Copyright, Designs and Patents Act 1988.

The University of Wales Press acknowledges the financial support of the Welsh Books Council.

Typeset by Chris Bell, cbdesign
Printed by CPI Antony Rowe, Melksham

Contents

List of illustrations

List of abbreviations

AEU	Amalgamated Engineering Union
AM	Assembly Member
ATTI	Association of Teachers in Technical Institutions
BIPA	British–Irish parliamentary assembly
BSC	British Steel Corporation
CLP	Constituency Labour Party
CPA	Commonwealth parliamentary association
EEC	European Economic Community
GKN	Guest, Keen and Nettlefolds
GOC	General Officer Commanding
IIC/IIDC	Independent International Commission on Decommissioning
IPSA	Independent Parliamentary Standards Authority
ISERBS	Iron and Steel Employees Readaptation Benefits Scheme
ISTC	Iron and Steel Trades Confederation
ITT	International Telephone and Telegraph
JMC	Joint Ministerial Committee
LTTE	Liberation Tigers of Tamil Eelam
MK	Member of the Knesset
MLA	Member of the Legislative Assembly
MP	Member of Parliament
NALGO	National and Local Government Officers' Association

NATFHE	National Association of Teachers in Further and Higher Education
NSA	National Security Agency
NUM	National Union of Mineworkers
OAP	old age pensioner
PLP	Parliamentary Labour Party
PPC	prospective parliamentary candidate
TD	Teachta Dála (Member of the Parliament of the Irish Republic)
TGWU	Transport and General Workers' Union
TUC	Trades Union Congress
USDAW	Union of Shop, Distributive and Allied Workers

Foreword

PAUL MURPHY is from the Eastern Valley of the South Wales coalfield where the Afon Llwyd flows from the high, bleak moorland above Blaenavon down through Abersychan, Pontnewydd, Llanfrechfa and Cwmbran to the Usk and the Bristol Channel.

It tumbles through the burgeoning communities that drew Paul's ancestors to find employment in the valley's ironworks, coalmines and factories. This is where he learned his politics and from where he has always drawn his strength. The people of the Eastern Valley moulded him into the erudite and trusted member of successive government cabinets, a man who succeeded in persuading sworn enemies to talk peace in place of war.

Much of what I know about him I learned from his father Ron, long after Paul's mother Marjorie had died in 1984, a relatively young woman. Ron was someone who, without effort, lit up any room he entered. Until he died, 11 years after his wife, he travelled everywhere with Paul and they complemented each other wonderfully, not least because of their radically different attitudes to organised sport.

Unlike Paul, for whom sport of any description held no interest whatsoever, Ron, despite his diminutive stature, had been a tough scrum-half who, after Paul became a government minister, encouraged him to accept the offers from various rugby authorities to attend international matches as their honoured guest. Ron told me of one such event in Dublin when, in a roaring, nail-biting climax to a close, hard-fought game between Ireland and Wales, he turned in excitement to find Paul sitting, oblivious to the drama, reading a book of poetry he'd brought to stave off boredom.

Both men were snappy dressers. They enjoyed good food, films and music. Paul's love of Elgar, in particular, had been nurtured in a family and community that respected and encouraged musicianship and learning. He has always believed that any society worth its name must strive constantly to provide the widest possible means of access to the very best in educational opportunities. Since his accession to the House of Lords, Paul has led initiatives to encourage school students in Wales to apply for places at the universities of Oxford and Cambridge. He is convinced that too many schools lack the knowledge and ambition required to increase the numbers of students at those centres of educational excellence from communities like the Eastern Valley.

He had enjoyed his own time as an undergraduate at Oxford in the late 1960s. The experience confirmed for Paul the truth that his parents had inculcated in him: that men and women, blessed with intelligence and imagination, could (and should) aspire to excellence, regardless of their origins and the circumstances of their early lives and education. Paul's own university experience was helped by an intellectual toughness and resilience, by his Catholic faith, by a capacity for hard work, a clarity of focus and, always, by drawing sustenance from his roots in the Eastern Valley.

That toughness was required, time and again, during his years in Northern Ireland. His key role as Tony Blair's Minister of State (later, as Secretary of State) in securing the Good Friday Agreement made him, subsequently, someone who remained much in demand for advice and guidance in troubled, violent parts of the world. He travelled widely to war-zones and peace-conferences, sharing the lessons he learned in Northern Ireland as he cajoled and persuaded individuals, militias and parties to talk to each other and to consider peace and reconciliation in place of violence and hostility.

This work didn't end with his retirement from the House of Commons. As a member of what MPs refer to as the 'other place' – the Lords – he continues to work with characteristic energy and commitment across a range of political issues. Elgar still draws him to concert halls; he remains as loyal and generous as always to his friends, and he is carving out for himself time to research and write histories.

In this volume he paints an intensely detailed picture of an industrial society that has all but disappeared and taken its politics with it. The nature of the Labour Party's relationship with the communities that created and sustained it for a century or so has changed dramatically. With that change has come doubt and confusion about what exactly the party stands for and what its purpose might be through this period of revolutionary political, technological and social change that we are experiencing currently. This is a unique historical document of a man and his times, the like of which I doubt we shall see again.

Kim Howells
Pontypridd, July 2018

Acknowledgements

THIS AUTOBIOGRAPHY could not have been written without the assistance of a great number of people.

The staff of the libraries in both the House of Commons and the House of Lords, as well as those in the National Library of Wales, have been very helpful. And I owe a great debt to the University of Wales Press, who suggested I write this book.

I also want to express my special thanks to Pam Cameron, Stuart Cameron, John Cunningham, Hywel Francis, Betty Gough, Laura Jorge Harris, Kim Howells, Anthony Hunt, John McFall, Simon Morris, Neil Murphy, Albert Owen, Margaret Paget, Jonathan Phillips, Trevor Pring, Jan Rees, John Rogers, Owen Smith, Nick Thomas-Symonds, Don Touhig and Nigel Warner.

Paul Murphy
Cwmbran, Good Friday 2019

In memory of my parents, Ronald and Marjorie Murphy

Introduction

POLITICS HAS BEEN MY LIFE – it never occurred to me that I would be anything other than some sort of politician. As a boy, I was fascinated by history and even played political games as part of Cowboys & Indians with Don Touhig, or when I joined the junior section of the Catholic Young Men's Association in Abersychan. I joined the Labour Party at the age of 15, studied history and politics at Oxford, and eventually became a councillor, MP and Cabinet Minister.

The influence of my socialist father and the political environment of my home village played their part in this development, but so did luck. I was a councillor at the age of 25, an MP at 38, a Minister at 48 and a Cabinet Minister at 50. I was, usually, in the right place at the right time when the chances came for a change of direction in my career; but the earlier years did represent an apprenticeship for more significant political roles.

When I was selected to be the Labour parliamentary candidate for Torfaen, in 1985, I said that my ambition was to serve the people of the Eastern Valley and nothing more. Events meant that that was not to be the case. I was to become a shadow Minister for nine years and, in 1997, the year of the biggest ever Labour victory, I was thrust into the Northern Ireland Peace Process, as Mo Mowlam's Deputy. Two years as Minister of State for Political Development put me at the heart of the talks which produced the Good Friday Agreement in 1998, and this led to my becoming Welsh Secretary in 1999 and Northern Ireland Secretary in 2002.

I was, as a Minister, to serve under Tony Blair and, from 2007, Gordon Brown. I was privileged to witness great events and to play my part in changing the political landscape in Northern Ireland and in Wales. For two years, I chaired parliament's Intelligence and Security Committee, which revealed to me the great debt we owe our agencies – MI5, MI6 and GCHQ. And, in my final years in the House of Commons, at the Welsh Government's request

I was to recommend ways of improving the chances of young Welsh people to go to Oxford and Cambridge.

Now, in the House of Lords, after almost three decades as an MP, I can still pursue my political interests, and take part in the public affairs of our country.

None of all this would have been possible without the help and encouragement of my family and friends and, throughout this book, I make unapologetic reference to them. I have been blessed with a loving family and loyal and close friends. And, of course, it goes without saying that my time in parliament would have been meaningless were it not for the support and loyalty of the people of Torfaen; they elected me to the House of Commons on five separate occasions, and it was always a great privilege to represent them.

Early days

I ALMOST DIDN'T MAKE IT. I was due to enter this world in the early months of 1949, but actually arrived on 25 November 1948, at Cefn Ila Nursing Home, Llanbadoc, near Usk, in the county of Monmouthshire.

Originally a moderately-sized country house, Cefn Ila had once been the home of Edward Trelawny, the adventurer and friend of Shelley and Byron, and was subsequently owned by a French marquis whose family had fled revolutionary times. It had been acquired by Pontypool Hospital, and developed after World War II as a maternity home.

I was a brand new NHS baby, but not a very healthy one. I weighed only about three pounds, and was not expected to live – I had to be given an emergency baptism by the Catholic parish priest of Usk, and my god-mother was the hospital's chief nurse, Matron Lyons, who happened to be a Catholic. I never met her, and have often wondered what became of my spiritual and religious mentor.

I remained in the hospital until Christmas, when my parents took me home to number 8, Broad Street, in the village of Abersychan, in the county's industrial Eastern Valley, some eight miles from rural Llanbadoc. My father, like most people in those days, had no car, but willingly walked the sixteen-mile round journey to visit my mother every day she was in Cefn Ila. The hospital continued to serve the local community until it closed in 1973. Indeed, my own birth was not the last occasion when my parents would be grateful for the hospital's care.

The building burnt down, less than a fortnight after the closure. Its name survived, though, in the Cefn Ila Unit, a maternity ward that was set up at the County Hospital, Griffithstown, south of Pontypool, before being controversially moved once again to the Royal Gwent Hospital in Newport. One of my first campaigns as an MP was to try to prevent the move from Griffithstown to Newport but, unfortunately, it failed.

Abersychan (the mouth of the Sychan) continued to be my home until I was well into my teenage years. The village is approximately two miles north of Pontypool and four miles south of Blaenavon.

Archdeacon Coxe, whose book about his travels in Monmouthshire was published in 1801, described the Eastern Valley as both rural and industrial. The valley (today known as Torfaen) had changed dramatically by the time my relatives arrived, more than two decades later. At the top of the valley, Blaenavon had its great ironworks, while Pontypool, in the middle, was the centre of tinplate making and the place where the Hanburys were the local squires. Abersychan lay between the two towns and was, until the opening of the British Ironworks in 1827, still a collection of small hamlets.

In the 1830s and 1840s, the population exploded. The Irish came to find employment in the ironworks, while others flocked from Somerset and Gloucestershire, and other parts of Wales. The valley was a Welsh Klondike. Until the 1860s most people spoke Welsh and they went to the Welsh-speaking chapels at Pisgah, Noddfa and Siloh. English soon took over, and "English" chapels were built in the village. Anglicans had St Thomas's church in Talywain – opened by Bishop Copleston of Llandaff in 1832. The Irish, having previously worshipped in the club-room of a public house, got their church in 1863. As the writer of a book on the Franciscans in nineteenth-century Monmouthshire put it:

> the disadvantages of [the previous] arrangement were manifold, one being that every Irishman who attended Mass thought it his bounden duty to patronise the publican who allowed the use of the room by drinking unlimited beer on its premises as soon as he could gain admittance on the Sunday evening.

Collieries followed the iron works and, inevitably, strikes and unrest were triggered by the terrible working conditions in these industries. In 1839, Abersychan Chartists took part in the march on Newport – one source reckoning that nearly fifteen hundred men in the village were Chartist supporters. Abersychan even had its Female Patriotic Association. Although the insurrection was a failure, the radical and trade union move-ment had started.

New pits were opened and most of the villagers – although the village they lived in was now really a town – relied on the mining industry for their income.

Abersychan – with a population at its peak of well over 20,000, far more than today – had its own urban district council until 1935, when it merged with the much smaller Pontypool and Panteg council to form the Pontypool urban district council.

When I arrived on the scene in 1948, Abersychan was a thriving and vibrant community. With few people owning cars in the village, two flourishing shopping centres had sprung up, in High Street and Station Street. Most men – including many in my own family – were colliers, and the whole village shut down for the annual two-week miners' holiday (traditionally the last week in July and the first in August.)

In hindsight, it was not a pretty place. There were slag tips from both iron working and the pits, but these were partially countered by the wonderful Lasgarn wood, which was on the eastern side of the valley. This was a marvellous place to walk and play in, and Abersychan children also had their own park in the middle of the village. This was adjacent to the local Co-op slaughterhouse, and one of my early memories is of watching the condemned sheep and pigs going to their deaths, and blood running down High Street.

Today, by contrast, Abersychan is a very attractive village, home to many commuters. The slag heaps have gone, along with hundreds of nineteenth-century cottages, and the chapels are not so numerous. But to me, it's still the home of my family and has kept a special place in my soul.

My father was a coal-miner at the local Blaenserchan Colliery, and my mother worked in her father's greengrocery shop in the village. My father, Ronald, was born in July 1919, and came from Irish–Welsh roots, while my mother, Marjorie, born later in January 1928, had an English–Welsh background.

My father was the youngest of seven children. The eldest, Jerry, born in the 1890s, became a soldier in the South Wales Borderers, served in the Great War and in India, but later died from malaria. Next was Dan, who moved to Dagenham to work in the Ford factory there; the next, Jack, never married and remained a miner all his life, while the three sisters Doreen, Mary and Anne all found husbands and stayed in the local area. Their father, Jeremiah, who had been born as long ago as 1875, had married Ann Whelan from Nantyglo. Jeremiah was a collier all his life, and she was an ironworker's daughter from Monmouthshire's Western Valley, whose father had been killed in the old Nantyglo ironworks. She never learned to read or write, smoked a clay pipe secretly upstairs, and in her youth worked in the mines, sorting coal on the surface. As well as giving birth to the couple's surviving children, she had apparently suffered one miscarriage in her front parlour. I only vaguely remember her, as a kindly and little old woman, who died in 1952 from pneumonia.

My paternal grandfather had been a handsome and very Irish-looking young man. I have a picture of him in the uniform of the Monmouthshire Militia c.1895. He started work, at the age of about fourteen, in the Llanerch Colliery in Abersychan. This mine was to be the scene of a major accident when, on 6 February 1890, a terrible explosion killed 176 men and boys, mainly from the Abersychan and Pontnewynydd area. A previous explosion at the colliery, on 19 October 1889, had led the mines inspector to advise the mine owners to introduce closed safety lamps. The advice was not accepted, the mine's managing director Edward Jones stating in a letter of 5 December 1889 that "we think the colliery is thoroughly well ventilated and safe to work with naked lights".

The disaster that happened just two months later was one of the worst in the country, and my grandfather escaped death only because he was made to stay home on the day in question by my great-grandmother, as he had an abscess on his arm. It was a very lucky abscess, as he would undoubtedly have been killed. He was working at Cook's Slope – right where the explosion occurred. Family legend has it that coffins were placed in the little front room of my grandparents' house. One hundred years after the disaster, I tabled an early day motion in the House of Commons, commemorating the event.

Jeremiah was to stay at the Llanerch Colliery until it closed in the 1930s. He then went to the nearby Blaenserchan pit, which had opened in 1893. He "retired" when he was about seventy – and continued to work at the Royal Ordnance Factory (ROF) in Glascoed (colloquially, The Dump) between Pontypool and Usk. I remember him coming home on the so-called dump train at half-past-five every day. Even at the time he went to Glascoed, he was still a fine figure of a man.

My grandfather had survived many accidents underground, the worst while he was relatively young when a fall of coal left his face disfigured – quite a tragedy for someone so handsome. I remember him most clearly as he was in his last years – an old, bed-ridden man, smoking his pipe and asking my father whether my wealthy Uncle Bill had brought him any whisky! He had been a hard-drinking man, thinking nothing of downing a dozen pints of cider a night in the British Legion Club in Abersychan. He was a "mountain fighter" who had to defend himself on many occasions – he had to defend his Irishness in Wales, and his Welshness in England! When his sister was beaten by her husband, my grandfather took on the offender in his own home.

Yet he was a gentle father and, returning from a night's drinking, he would serenade his children by singing "I'll take you home again Kathleen". He died in 1960 aged 85, when I was 12.

He had been the black sheep among his father's sons, the only one to go underground as a collier. Both his brothers had very good jobs – Daniel, who never married, and whom I remember as a blind old man, living with his sister-in-law, held a senior position with the local gas company. His other brother, John (with whose widow Daniel lived) had joined his cousins in New York and served as a policeman for a time. When he returned to Wales he became a colliery under-manager, but died young of cancer.

John and his wife, Margaret, had three children: Winifred, a teacher; Bernard, who worked for UNESCO in Beirut before he retired to Germany; and Eileen, a teacher who became a nun. Eileen's teaching order, the Daughters of the Holy Ghost, had fled France when religious orders were exiled by the Third French Republic in the early 1900s; they had a convent in Pontypool, in the former house of the Hanburys, the squires of Pontypool.

Eileen took the name Sister John Margaret, taught at the convent school in the town, and instructed my mother when she converted to Catholicism. In due course, she became the head of the largest Catholic primary school in England, in Luton, and eventually retired to Olney near Milton Keynes. Eileen was a lovely, generous and spiritual person, and the family would often meet up when my brother lived in Milton Keynes.

My paternal great-grandfather, another Jeremiah, emigrated from Ireland to Wales c.1865. His wife, Julia Lane, came from the village of Ovens in County Cork, and he was from what was then the small town of Ballincollig, on the river Lee just a few miles from the city of Cork.

I have visited Ballincollig on a number of occasions – twice with my father and with my friends Stuart and Pam Cameron, and once when I was Northern Ireland Secretary. Murphy is a very common name in this part of County Cork, and many Murphys are buried in the ruined mediaeval Franciscan friary of Kilcrea, a couple of miles from Ballincollig – a friary that had some significance for my family, I understood, because my Uncle John's home in Manor Road, Abersychan, was named "Kilcrea".

It's hard to be certain if my people are buried in Kilcrea, since there are so many Murphys there and so many with the same Christian names – Jeremiah, Maurice and Daniel, especially. My great-great-grandfather was called Daniel, so the chances are high that he lies there somewhere.

Just as great-grandfather Jeremiah left Ireland for Wales, so his brothers went to the USA, to Boston and New York, where some of them became policemen. We lost touch with our American cousins in the 1960s, although we know that one of them served in the American Air Force during the war in Vietnam.

So what brought Jeremiah to South Wales? Many people left Ireland in the mass migration that followed the 1845–9 Great Famine, but great-grandfather Jeremiah didn't arrive here until twenty years later. I have often speculated that he had had enough of the nineteenth-century "Fenian outrages", as they were called – Ballincollig was the home of the Royal Gunpowder Mills, as well as of a British military base, and there was Fenian activity in the town in the 1860s. Then again, perhaps he simply decided it was time to emigrate, and it's possible that friends or relatives had already gone to Abersychan.

There is a great irony to this, given what I was once told about the exploits of another of my (alleged) paternal ancestors. When I was a councillor in Torfaen, I attended a mayoral reception for Irish trade-unionists, and there was one among them who came from Cork. He recalled teachers in Ballincollig who were probably distant cousins of mine, but he also told me the story of Commandant Leo Murphy of Ballincollig who, he insisted, was of the same family. After writing to a retired Irish army officer, Commandant George Glendon, of the City of Cork, in 1992, I learned a little more about this possible relative.

Leo Murphy was a member of "A" Company of the Ballincollig Battalion of the First Cork Brigade of the "old" (1922–69) Irish Republican Army. He joined the company in 1919 (the year my father was born), and became an officer of the Ballincollig Battalion, later moving to IRA headquarters. He worked in the British military barracks in Ballincollig as a member of the civilian staff, and was thus able to provide enormous intelligence to his IRA comrades, especially the active service units known as the Flying Columns.

The battalion headquarters operated from a number of different places. On 27 June 1921, it met at O'Shea's public house in Waterfall, three miles south of Ballincollig. The Black and Tans (the British irregular troops fighting the IRA) surrounded the house, and Leo was shot dead; some years later, a limestone Celtic cross was erected close to the spot where he fell.

The military took his body back to Ballincollig Barracks, and there is a gruesome local story that, in revenge for his undercover role at the barracks, the corpse was mutilated with bayonets before his mother was brought in to identify him. The barracks is now, ironically enough, known as the Leo Murphy Barracks, and there is a Leo Murphy Square in the town.

Returning to my paternal great-grandparents Jeremiah and Julia Murphy, when they came to Abersychan, Jeremiah found employment in the local ironworks, originally owned by the British Iron Company, and first opened in 1827. In 1852, the works had been taken over by the Ebbw Vale Company. Writing in the local weekly *Pontypool Free Press* in 1868, W. H. Greene painted a vivid picture of the scene:

What a strange sight are large works like these, especially for one who sees them for the first time. The giant chimneys pouring forth their dense black smoke, the town-like buildings at their base, the bewildering apparatus, the multitude of trucks, laden and unladen, the locomotives to and fro and throbbing out white clouds, the mingled noises, the hot and sulphurous air, and those great grey mounds at once fascinate and repel by day; and, at night, when the red fires become visible in every direction, and the sky is stained deep red, there is a titanic picture wilder than any of Turner's.

This is what Jeremiah experienced on arriving in Abersychan, a different world from the one he had left in Ireland. He became a puddler, stirring the molten iron with long bars. Like so much else in the industry, it was dangerous work, and over the years he lost several fingers – which is evident in the only photograph I possess of him. He looks a stately old gentleman, unsmiling, in a formal, seated pose in the photographer's studio.

Many Irish people came to Abersychan in the same period as Jeremiah, the men looking for jobs in the ironworks. They came mainly from County Cork – McCarthys, Cronins and Murphys – living in a ghetto in the High Street area and often in great poverty. They were served as Catholics by Italian Franciscan priests. Many of them were Irish-speaking (as I suspect my great-grandparents were), and lived and worked in a community that was still partly Welsh-speaking.

The ironworks were hit by financial problems in the 1870s as industries were increasingly turning to steel, and eventually closed in 1884. My great-grandfather went to the Pontnewynydd forge, and there he stayed until retirement.

Few stories have survived about my great-grandmother, save for those that note her talent for Irish sword-dancing and her dislike of Orangemen! She died in 1929, her husband having passed away in 1917 (Jeremiah was, I suspect, a man of some standing in the local Irish community, in which he had served as Secretary of the local Hibernian Association).

My mother's paternal ancestors, the Prings, came from totally different stock to my father's. Both the Prings and the Goughs (her maternal family) originated in the West Country. There are two reasons why we know much more about the Welsh and English ancestry than we do of the Irish. Firstly, there is more archival material relating to them; many centuries of Irish family records were destroyed in the Irish Civil War of the early 1920s. With regard to my mother's family, a second major source of information comes from the meticulous genealogical work of my first cousin Trevor Pring, who remarkably carries out his research from his home in Perth, Australia, where he retired from the UK some years ago (Trevor previously lived in the Midlands, and married Tricia who came from Newport). Trevor has written two impressive historical booklets, one to chart each side of my mother's ancestors.

The earliest Pring that we can find is my ancestor Robert Pring, who lived in Cullompton, Devon, and died in the early eighteenth century; Trevor has also discovered some evidence of my branch of the Prings going back to 1626, in the Parish of Hemyock in Devon. Another Robert Pring, meanwhile, also of Cullompton, who married in 1731, appears to be descended from the Hemyock branch.

The Prings then moved to Uffculme, and their descendants went to Buckerell and eventually Nailsea in Somerset. At Holy Trinity Church in Nailsea lies the grave of Humphrey and Elizabeth Pring. Humphrey, my great-great-great-great-grandfather, was a collier in a local pit, and died in 1843, his wife having passed away in 1829. Although he is described as a "labourer", the memorial headstone would suggest a man of some means. Together, they had eight children, one of whom, John Pring, left Somerset for Newport in Monmouthshire some time before 1822. He and his wife, Mary, had seven children; one of them, Isaac, next in the line of my maternal ancestors, was born c.1823 and married Mary Edwards in Christchurch, Newport.

Isaac had a chequered life. He worked as a labourer, a mariner, a hossler and as a ship's ballast master. Mary died in 1868, and in 1870 Isaac re-married. His new bride was 29-year-old Eliza, from Breconshire. Isaac died in 1883, aged 60, in Watch Road, Pillgwenlly, Newport.

Together, Isaac and Mary had ten children, one of whom was William, my great-grandfather, born in April, 1847. He was a twin, and the two siblings were baptised at Newport Wesleyan Methodist Chapel. William married Charlotte Powell in Holy Trinity Church, Newport, in 1872, at a service conducted by the then rector of the new parish, the Reverend Samuel Fox. Later, in 1881, Isaac became captain of the steam tug *Hazard*, based in Newport Docks.

The "notorious Pring family of Pill", as one local magistrate described them, was forever getting into trouble! As my cousin, Trevor, has written: "They were a drunken, feuding, brawling family who seemed to run the docks and the large public houses in Pill, appearing in court, not only as defendants but plaintiffs and witnesses."

William died on 24 July 1884, following a quarrel with his cousin Charles. The two men had been in the yard of the Tredegar Ironworks, Pill, where William took off his coat ready for a fight, and picked up a stone with which he presumably intended to attack Charles – and promptly dropped dead of a heart attack. He was in his mid-thirties, and the Coroner's Court declared his death of "natural causes".

I had been told as a boy that William was actually a Norwegian sea captain, and that his surname had originally been Prinz. This, of course, was all rubbish, but still I confess that I wasn't deterred many years later on a parliamentary delegation to Norway from repeating the story of my alleged ancestral link to his country. The Speaker of the Norwegian parliament promptly told me his great-grandfather was a Scotsman!

William and Charlotte had four children and the youngest, born in February 1883, was my grandfather, John Henry Pring.

After her husband's untimely death, Charlotte re-married. Her new husband was Edward Charles Titcomb, and together they had two further children – one of whom, also called Charlotte, I remember vividly. She was a very small woman, usually dressed in black, and had married Arthur Kuffler – he, apparently, disappeared one night, having been last seen walking over Newport Bridge.

My grandfather John Henry Pring (always known as Jack) never knew his father, and by all accounts his stepfather was a cruel man who worked him very hard as a boy – making him push handcarts with vegetables and fruit to Newport docks, touting for business from the sailors. Once when he was ten, Jack was caught and locked up in a police cell overnight for stealing coal off a moving train!

At the same age, Jack ran away to sea as a cabin boy, to become the ship's cook and carpenter. He had never attended school, but taught himself to read and write, and eventually found work as a carpenter on the construction of the new Abersychan High School (and occasionally took a shift underground). He met Louisa Gough of Abersychan, and they were married at Pontypool registry office in June 1908. Jack was described as a "Colliery Haulier (underground)", and Louisa a spinster, the daughter of Daniel Gough "fruiterer and fish salesman". They lived in High Street, Abersychan, where by 1911 Jack was a greengrocer – he remained a greengrocer all his life, with shops in Union Street and Broad Street, Abersychan, as well as running a greengrocery round from a horse and cart, and at one time owning a fish and chip shop.

Louisa and Jack had two sons – William (1909–70) and Godfrey (1911–87) – as well as a daughter, Muriel, who died aged three of diphtheria. In time, the family would flourish: Jack owned a Model T Ford, one of the first motorcars in Abersychan, and he was also the first to own a gramophone, which he bought in Newport. He used to play Caruso on it while walking through Abersychan! But as the Depression worsened, he allowed too much credit to the families of striking miners and was left in great debt.

I never knew Jack, but I was always aware of him as an amazing man. He had a natural gift for playing the piano – and he had never been taught – and he was a great practical joker and well-known character in the village. When I became MP for Torfaen in 1987, it was almost four decades after his death, but I found people would continue to tell me stories about Jack Pring for many years. The only photograph I have of us together was taken when I was a baby, and he took me to the Twyn-y-Ffrwd public house for refreshment!

My maternal grandmother's family, the Goughs, were agricultural labourers from Thornbury, Gloucestershire. The earliest record we have of them relates to Thomas Gough (1730–98), my great-great-great-great-great grandfather. His son Joseph (1756–1823) married Sarah Cossham (1755–1837), the great-aunt of Handel Cossham MP. So, through Joseph, I share ancestry with the only other MP in the family: Handel Cossham, MP for Bristol East between 1885 and 1890, having been Lord Mayor of Bath between 1882 and 1885. He was born in 1824, in High Street, Thornbury, and named after the composer Handel; he worked in Yate Colliery, and eventually became the owner of the Kingswood and Parkfield Colliery Company. As a Nonconformist, a Liberal and a strong believer in Home Rule for Ireland, Cossham was a philanthropist of note and donated Cossham Hall to the people of Thornbury; the Cossham Memorial Hospital in Kingswood was dedicated to him. In April 1890, he was taken ill in the library of the House of Commons, and died the following day; it was estimated that 30,000 people lined the streets at his funeral.

Joseph Gough's son George (1793–1871) married Jane Everett; their son Henry (who died 1849), married Sarah Bell of Thornbury (1811–71). Henry moved from Thornbury to Abersychan sometime in the 1840s – there was family talk that he had been involved in the Newport Chartist Rising in 1839, although the dates don't match (he must have been living in Thornbury at least until 1842, as the third of his five children was born there in that year).

Daniel, another of Henry and Sarah's children, was my great-grandfather. He was born in Abersychan in 1847 and, following his father's death in 1849, Daniel's mother Sarah re-married in 1855. Her new husband was named Shadrach Flower. Sarah died "of apoplexy" it is said, in the workhouse.

My great-grandfather Daniel married Elizabeth Parfitt, of Clutton, Somerset. She was born in 1851, and we can trace her ancestors back to north Somerset in the seventeenth century. Her father had been a baker, but the main employment in north Somerset at that time was coal-mining, and there is little doubt that a recession in the North Somerset Coalfield caused many miners and potential miners to move to the Eastern Valley of

Monmouthshire. The Goughs crossed the Severn for the same reason – literally tens of thousands of West Country folk flocked to Monmouthshire at this time, and names from Somerset, Wiltshire and Gloucestershire are very common in south-east Wales.

My grandmother told the story of her parents walking to the old Llanvihangel Pontymoile church, her mother in a pretty bonnet, on the occasion of their marriage in 1867. Daniel was first a miner, then a fishmonger, and publican of the Live and Let Live public house in Old Road, Abersychan. But, by 1891, he was once more simply a fishmonger. By 1901, he was living at an address in High Street, employed as a greengrocer and florist, with a number of shops in the village that were run by his daughters.

In total, Daniel and Elizabeth had 13 children, two of whom died in infancy. In 1887, Daniel decided to emigrate to the USA, and sailed with his eldest son George, aged 19, from Liverpool on the SS *Indiana*, arriving in Philadelphia in September of that year. Elizabeth and nine other children followed on the SS *Lord Clive*, which berthed in the same city on 18 December 1887, and it appears the family later moved to Shamokin in Montgomery County, Pennsylvania, a mining community that attracted many Welsh colliers.

There is a family story that tells of Louisa, one of their daughters (born in 1887), dying during this period in North America. Pennsylvania burial records indicate that a Louisa Goff [sic] died in 1888, and that she was buried in the Montgomery County community of Bala Cynwyd (a place-name that reflects the fact that the area was settled by Welsh immigrants). Other records, however, indicate that when most of the family returned to Wales in 1889, a Louisa was among them. This Louisa's sisters believed she had been born in the USA but without being registered at that time, and that she had been given the name and assumed the identity of her dead sister. It was this Louisa, who came with her returning family to Wales, who married Jack Pring in Pontypool in 1908.

Another of Daniel's and Elizabeth's sons, Joseph, went west to Salt Lake City in 1905, but he too eventually returned to Britain. Daniel, meanwhile, continued shopkeeping in Abersychan, but became an alcoholic and went blind through diabetes (a family trait), dying on 23 January 1913 at 47 High Street, Abersychan, aged 62.

Elizabeth took the shop and her youngest daughter, Rosetta (known as Tet, born in 1894), lived with her and helped her mother in the business. Tet was very pretty and bright, and became increasingly friendly with her brother-in-law, Jack Pring. At the age of 44 in 1927 Jack left home, supposedly to settle outstanding accounts with wholesalers in Newport, but never returned. He had eloped with Tet, who was then aged 33, and they went to

Derbyshire where he worked underground. Together they had two children: my mother Marjorie (born in 1928) and Betty (born in 1932). The family lived in a converted railway carriage in Chesterfield.

Louisa, abandoned by Jack, was devastated. She decided to move to Birmingham (living on Coventry Road) to open a fruit and vegetable shop. She moved on to Coventry in 1932, and took another shop near the city centre on the Queen Victoria Road. Her sons William and Godfrey (known as Goff) were already living in the city, both working for the Triumph Motor Cycle Company, and they eventually became involved in the fruit and vegetable wholesale business.

During the Second World War, Godfrey enlisted in the Royal Artillery and served in North Africa and Italy; he married Lydia May North, and they had two children – Ruby, who died as a young woman of breast cancer, and the aforementioned Trevor (born in 1937). After the war, William joined the Geest banana company, a business that he expanded over the next twenty years; he married Evelyn Shaw, and the couple had one son, Robert, who tragically died in his mid-sixties.

Jack Pring left Tet in 1931 or 1932, and returned to his wife, Louisa. Again, he opened various greengroceries, and in 1937 started a business called *The Quality Shop* at 196 Binley Road, Stoke, Coventry. It was located close to the large GEC telephone works and a new housing estate, and the business did very well.

What about Jack's two daughters? Well, when Jack and Tet parted ways, my mother Marjorie went with her father to live with Louisa (Jack's wife and Marjorie's aunt) – it was a traumatic experience for my mother, aged four at the time, who didn't really understand what was going on. The younger daughter Betty stayed with Tet, and they went to live in Birmingham, in considerable poverty, and later moved to Coventry.

When the war came, my mother stayed with Jack and Louisa when they returned to South Wales to open a shop at 6 Station Street, Abersychan. Marjorie had been preparing to attend grammar school in Coventry, but with the move to Monmouthshire she went instead to Abersychan Grammar School, where Roy Jenkins (founder member of the Social Democratic Party, the SDP, in 1981) had been educated. But Jack would not pay the school fees, and after a period of time Marjorie had to transfer to Twmpath Central School in Pontypool.

I still have some of my mother's school reports. The earliest is from Stoke Council Junior School, Coventry, dated 21 December 1938. Marjorie was then almost eleven years old, and her best subject was "reading". She was described as "very satisfactory at times, but . . . sometimes inclined to hurry and write very carelessly" – just like her elder son!

In 1941, at Twmpath school, she was top of the class in French, Science and Algebra, and second overall – her worst subject was Civics. She recorded good attendance, although she had missed some days because of bad weather.

The blitz bombing of Coventry on 14 November 1940 had a huge effect on the family. The house where Godfrey lived was completely destroyed, as was the house where Tet lived with Betty. Betty was nine at the time, and has written vividly of that terrible night – their home was gone, and she recalls avoiding falling shells and buildings as Coventry and its cathedral were set alight.

Tet and Betty returned to Abersychan – to Talywain – where they ran a shop during the war, making enough money to move to Cardiff into the post-war years. Tet lived into her early eighties and died in 1975. Goff went into the army, while his wife and two children were evacuated to Abersychan. My mother, in Station Street, was helping to run her father Jack's shop – she was still a "Midlands girl", and the local children always wanted to hear her speak because of her strange accent (she eventually lost the accent although, when she was with her brothers, it always returned).

Jack Pring had been directed to work at the Rogerstone aluminium factory, but the authorities realised he would be of more use to the war effort if he continued as a greengrocer. He actually produced more fruit and vegetables for the good people of Abersychan than was strictly legal – he smoked his own herrings, boiled his own beetroot, and provided fish from Newport market. At the end of the war, he was famous for putting on great street parties in Station Street, celebrating VE and VJ nights, occasions still remembered by the (very) old people of the village.

It was in the final years of the war that my parents met. Ronald was a collier and very handsome – he looked, as people said, like the film actor Ronald Colman. He had a baritone voice and was often asked to sing at local dances. His favourite song was Cole Porter's *Begin the Beguine*. It was at one such dance, at the Catholic Hall in Manor Road, that he first set eyes on Marjorie Pring, she still in her late teens and he in his mid-twenties. Their courtship was precarious – Jack Pring didn't approve. Ron Murphy was a Catholic of Irish descent while Marjorie was Anglican and the daughter of a shopkeeper, and the couple had a tough time maintaining their relationship against such odds in those days. They had to rely on various relatives to pass messages between them. Initially, Jack had refused to attend the (Catholic) wedding, but eventually relented and would become a great friend to my father.

Ronald and Marjorie were married at St Alban's Catholic Church, Pontypool, on 4 April 1947. As my mother was a non-Catholic, the wedding was very bare and cold, although family friend Sheila Casey was allowed to sing *Panis Angelicus*. My parents, after living for a very short time in "rooms" in Pontypool, found a house at 8 Broad Street, Abersychan, which was a three-storey cottage over the Sychan brook. It had one bedroom, one living room, and one kitchen/toilet room. The house has now been demolished. After a couple of years, they moved into 6 Station Street, and there they helped my grandfather in the shop (he was apparently declared bankrupt in 1949, and the business was now in Louisa's name – although my mother did most of the work).

Jack Pring died of thrombosis, in the Royal Gwent Hospital Newport, on 5 May 1951, aged 68. My father continued to work at Blaenserchan Colliery, and my mother's shop was relatively successful. She sold grocery and greengrocery mainly, but sometimes fresh meats, faggots, hearts and fish too. As a young boy, I would occasionally serve behind the counter, and one of my customers was the local MP, Daniel Granville West, who lived in the Old Lane.

When I was three, I was sent to the local nursery school, Brynteg, which was also in the Old Lane. I have some memories of the school: of having to go to bed in the afternoon; of my mother quarrelling with the headmistress because she had hit me; and of playing on the nursery's outdoor equipment. It was at that school that I first met Don Touhig, who has remained a lifelong friend – there's a photograph of Don and me in the school's playground, with nothing to suggest that we would both become MPs, Ministers and Peers over the next sixty years! Don's ancestors had come from Ireland and Belgium, and his parents Mike and Kate were friends of my mother and father, Mike and dad working together underground.

When the Irish came to Abersychan in the mid-nineteenth century, they were ministered to by Italian Franciscans. Naturally, the local church, which was built around that time, was dedicated to the founder of the Order. My paternal grandfather attended the church in the 1880s, as did my Protestant grandmother. My father was a pupil at St Francis school in the 1920s and, remarkably, when I myself went there three decades later in 1954, I was taught by Miss May Murphy (from Youghal – pronounced "Yawl" – in County Cork) who had also taught my father. She was by then in her late fifties or early sixties – she had one leg, and walked on crutches (it would seem that an infected nail had led to a poisoned leg, and the limb had to be amputated).

Miss Murphy was an excellent, if tough, teacher who taught me the basics of reading and writing. She lived opposite the new Catholic church, also St Francis, in Talywain. She would attend Mass at nine on a Sunday morning, and see which of her class was there, and would look out of her window to check who was at the eleven o'clock Mass. Woe betide those bold children who missed Mass on a Sunday! The school headmaster was a

Mr Dennehy, soon replaced by the gentler Vince McCarthy, whose wife was also a teacher at St Francis (they had come from Merthyr Tydfil, and were both fine teachers).

The school had a distinctly Irish atmosphere. Also from County Cork, along with Miss Murphy, was the monk-like parish priest Father Skelly, who came from Skibbereen. We celebrated St Patrick's Day with probably greater gusto than St David's Day, and we sang "Hail Glorious Saint Patrick" most weeks.

I eventually went to Mrs Davies's class – she was a Touhig, a cousin to Don, and was a first-class teacher with a rigorous approach in all subjects. We learned our bible stories and our catechism with her, and she probably gave me my first interest in history. It was at this time, too, that I joined the Abersychan Library. We had few books in our house, and for me the library was a real treasure trove.

As well as Don, I had some other good friends in the school – especially Susan Cremins, for whom I had a very soft spot. Her father, who had lost a leg at Dunkirk, was a friend of my father, and the family lived quite near to us. Susan and I would play together in the evenings. Susan's grandmother, old Mrs Cremins, lived with her, one of those remarkable characters that the valleys produced.

Susan lived opposite another friend of mine, Christine Goodwin, whose parents were also great characters. Christine's mother, Lil, was a pianist and natural comedian – she had a pet sheep called Herb, with whom I once caught her dancing! Lil's husband Stan, or "Digger" as everyone called him, was another comedian. He wore a huge hat and spoke in very early Abersychan dialect, now long died out, a unique mixture of Anglo-Welsh and West Country.

As well as our friends, our extended family (save for our Coventry relations), mostly lived in Abersychan or elsewhere in the Eastern Valley. On my father's side, his sister Anne had married Jack Rosser, and I regularly played with their son John. Meanwhile, Aunty Mary lived with Uncle Ivor Powell and their daughter Rosemary, in Pontypool; Aunty Doreen had moved in the 1930s to live in Bournemouth; Uncle Dan, as I've said, had gone to work in Dagenham; and my uncle Jack was a bachelor and miner.

There was a huge number of relatives on my mother's side, mainly because of the large Gough clan. I've already mentioned, for example, that of Daniel and Elizabeth's children, eleven lived into adulthood: eight became shopkeepers, all of them specialising in fish mongering, greengrocery and flowers, as well as making wreaths. One of my earliest memories is of my various great aunts intricately weaving flowers onto the wreath wires. Aunty Ede Hodge had a shop in High Street. Her three daughters – Marie, Lena and

Phyllis – were all close to my mother, as were the daughters of Aunty Flo (Peake) – Doreen and Maud. Aunty Lol (Cullis) had a shop in Pontnewynydd, as did Aunt Beat (Collins).

Great-uncle George Gough was a fishmonger. George's grandson Lyle had a wholesale greengrocery business in Coventry Market, and Lyle's brother Dick was a cattle dealer in Monmouth. Uncle Joe, George's second-eldest brother, moved to Bournemouth and had a number of shoe shops (from which he made a small fortune), dying in 1935 and leaving his money to his sisters – apparently cutting out his wife.

My mother inherited the family's business acumen and, had she not been taken out of grammar school, I believe she would have gone far in business. My brother, too, is a natural businessman, and, as I shall later describe, he made a considerable mark in the British pharmaceutical world.

I have no doubt that had my father been given the chance, he would have prospered in a different way. He was exceptionally intelligent, writing memorable prose and poetry; he enjoyed music and literature, and had a deep interest in politics and trade unionism.

The economic situation in the early 1930s, however, meant that he was forced to go underground when he was 14. He often told me how he wept on his first day at Llanerch Colliery as he descended into the pit. There were stories of rats and ponies and comradeship, and exceptionally hard toil as a collier, all of which he expressed in a moving poem he wrote many years later.

Slagtips
by Ron Murphy

Like sentinels, sombre and gray, grim reminders of bygone days,
Of pits whose shiny seams of coal first gave men work and then the dole,
Of men and boys, slag and stone, early graves and broken bones.

Sweat and toil in headings, stalls, feared of gas and dreaded falls,
Working hidden out of sight in another world where it's always night.

No moon nor stars are seen down there, just total darkness everywhere.
No city lights to show the way, no sign to tell if its night or day.

No birds there sing or fly on wing, no crocus grow to welcome spring.
No scented rose on summer breeze, no autumn leaves to fall from trees.

No winter snow or sun or sky, the changing seasons pass them by.

Their world of darkness underground where nothing changes all year round.
Where nature's beauty never treads, they spend their lives in fear and dread.

Oil lamps dim with tiny flame, lifeline, numbered, miner's name.
Spikes and chalk, moleskins, yorks, bread and cheese, tea-jack, corks.

Mandrills, shovels, clamps and wedge, hatchet, bar and heavy sledge.
Pairs of timber, props and flats, hornets, black bats, hungry rats.

Horses with impressive names like, Royal, Roman, Easter Flame.
Windroads, airways, double doors, brattice sheets draped to the floor.

Big vein, black vein, drams raced high, journey ropes that kick and fly.
Rippings, slag and drams of muck go up the pit to waiting trucks.

Engines, hooters, whistles blow, trucks are full and off they go,
Down the line for slag tip bound, carrying muck from underground.

Bloodstained stones, and slag and shale, broken timber, bent up nails,
Brattice sheets all torn and ripped all went hurtling down the tips.

Waiting there in bitter cold, men and women, young and old,
Fingers, bodies numb to bone, picking coal from slag and stone.

But now the tips are grassed and green, its slag and stone lie there unseen.
No sign of blood, of pain, of grief, that lies there buried underneath.

Nothing. Nothing to show unless you know of those sad days so long ago.

I remember how my father would so often come home from the pit, exhausted and sometimes injured. He experienced a number of coal falls, or accidents – the sight in one eye became permanently blurred as a result of one accident. After a particularly distressing incident underground, when he witnessed the tragic death of one of his "butties", as they were called in Wales, my mother insisted that he quit coalmining.

I recall living in Station Street, Abersychan, very clearly. Our home was next to the Eastern Valley railway line, and I remember the steam trains and then the new diesel multiple units. We were just a few yards from the railway station and, more often than not, used the train rather than the bus for transport. I went to grammar school by train. The line, like its equivalent in the county's Western Valley, was closed to passenger traffic on 30 April 1962 – almost a year before the wide-ranging closure proposals in the now notorious Beeching Report were published.

Our house at number 6 Station Street had in the nineteenth century been a public house, the Colliers' Arms, but it was subsequently converted into a shop. The toilet was in the so-called back yard (a covered toilet, which was a luxury at that time when so many were open to the elements). There was no bathroom – we used a zinc bathtub, which hung on the kitchen wall when it wasn't in use. A geyser provided our hot water, and there was no central heating, of course. I can recall how, in the winter, we often found frost inside the windows.

My "grandmother" Louisa (that's what I called her – I used to boast that I had three grandmothers!) was bed-ridden in what had once been the club-room of the old pub. It was in that room I saw her die on 4 June 1956, at the age of 69.

I was rushed from Station Street by my Aunty Anne, who had to inform Louisa's sister Ede of the death. My mother was devastated – she had lived with her "step-mother" for 24 years, and had nursed her for at least ten of those – and she suffered a nervous breakdown. Her GP, Dr Jarman, suggested that she might have another child to assist her recovery – a somewhat drastic remedy, but it did work.

So, my brother Neil Ronald Murphy was born on 4 July 1958, at the same Cefn Ila Maternity Hospital where I had taken my own first breath ten years before. Neil was a big, bouncy baby, weighing in at 8 pounds, and I held him in my arms in the taxi when he and my mother returned to Abersychan.

During the time my mother was in hospital, I wrote to her:

Dear Mummy,

I hope you and the baby are alright, and I hope you don't mind having a baby boy. Isn't it funny that Neil was born on the Fourth of July, American Independence Day, mummy. I'm glad it is all over, and I'm sorry you had such a bad time . . . Miss Fields said are you having enough food?

All my love,
Your son,
Paul

My great-aunt Flo lived opposite us in Station Street. She had been bed-ridden for almost twenty years (she had broken her leg and she stayed in bed thereafter, cared for by her devoted daughter, Doreen) and was more than a little cantankerous. She knew everybody's business despite being in bed, and fell in love with the toddler Neil.

Susan Cremins and I used to take Neil in his pushchair for long walks to the Old Trevethin church and, as he grew up, he was regularly to be seen around the village playing on his scooter. He eventually went to St Francis school. When he was about two, he suffered serious burns in an accident which could easily have proved fatal, after colliding with my father who was carrying boiling water for his bath. Neil was rushed to Chepstow Burns Hospital, and happily he recovered – although he retains a scar on his shoulder to this day.

For holidays away from home, we always went to Bournemouth, where we stayed with my Aunty Doreen and her husband Dan (coincidentally also a Murphy), who was a plumber. We could be sure of a good holiday with them in Southbourne, a suburb of Bournemouth. Like so many other families, even as the 1960s dawned, we still had no car and would make the journey from Abersychan either by bus or by train.

During other school holidays, we played in the local Glansychan Park, and on Saturdays Don and I and other friends would travel by bus to Pontypool for ice-cream and lemonade in Fulgoni's café.

The Fulgonis were part of the famous Welsh-Italian community, most of whom originated in the north Italian towns of Bardi. In Abersychan, we had a number of families of Italian origin – the Bracchis (who owned the fish and chip shop) and the Bellis (who ran the café, or "Temperance Bar" as it was usually called). At Mass on Sunday mornings, I would listen to them speaking to each other in Italian, and I studied with their children at St Francis.

Monmouthshire, in those days, still operated a selective form of secondary education, and children had to sit the old Eleven Plus examination. I was well taught and, I suppose, was a studious pupil, and lucky enough to pass the exam in 1960.

Still, even at that time, I felt uneasy. It was a terrible system – to decide a child's academic future at the age of 11 made little sense, and many youngsters who lost out in this process felt a sense of failure and shame. When I taught in further education, many of my students had failed the Eleven Plus, and came to college for a second and very often successful chance.

Anyway, I had passed and my parents were thrilled. I had a choice of three schools: West Monmouthshire Grammar School for boys, in Pontypool; Abersychan Grammar School, which was just a few hundred yards from my home; or the new Croesyceiliog Grammar School in faraway Cwmbran.

I decided that West Mon, as it was always called, was the one for me: when my parents and I went to the open day, what impressed me most were all the books in the school library.

Roy Jenkins (who, before leaving the Labour Party to be a co-founder of the SDP, had been Home Secretary and Chancellor of the Exchequer) often pondered with me why he himself had been sent to Abersychan School and not West Mon. I told him it was because his father, Arthur, had been the local alderman and chairman of governors of the school, and he had felt obliged to send his son there. Who knows?

West Mon

I N SEPTEMBER 1960, I became a first-former at Jones's West Monmouthshire School, Pontypool.

West Mon had been opened in 1898, a "Haberdashers' School" built out of money left in the early seventeenth century by William Jones, a merchant adventurer and Haberdasher, who came from Newland in the Forest of Dean. Jones died in Hamburg in 1615 a very wealthy man, and left nine thousand pounds in his will (an equivalent to millions in today's money) to establish a school and free alms-houses in the town of Monmouth. Over three hundred years, the charity administering his bequest had accumulated so much money that the charity commissioners ordered a large part of this income to be devoted to the building of Monmouth School for Girls, and another school, subsequently designated a boys' school, west of the river Usk in Monmouthshire.

The site of the latter was chosen by competition between the relevant communities – Pontypool's victory was no doubt influenced by the fact that Squire Hanbury of Pontypool had offered to donate the necessary land.

The new school was opened by Lord Tredegar and catered for both boarders and day boys, with teaching provided by headmaster Mr Priestley, along with four staff. Under its next head, R. Ivor Jones, in 1935 the school became a member of the Headmasters' Conference, and so, nominally, a "public school", sending many boys to Oxford and Cambridge – including Ivor Bulmer-Thomas, from Cwmbran, who went on to become an MP and Minister.

In 1954, West Mon left the Haberdashers' family of schools (mainly because the company's income was badly hit by its wartime loss of property during the London Blitz) and became a boys' grammar school under the Monmouthshire County Council. In its time as a Haberdashers' establishment the school had produced eminent surgeons, civil servants, academics, actors (Anthony Oliver and Sir Anthony Hopkins) and politicians, including Lord Chalfont.

In 1958, Roy Wiltshire, a Rhondda man and former education administrator with a double-first from Cardiff University, became the fourth headmaster. And two years later, I arrived!

By this time, the school had over six hundred pupils, mostly from the Eastern Valley and Usk, and the staff comprised about twenty five masters. Each year group was divided into three classes, imaginatively called "W", "M" and "S". The 1961 issue of the school magazine, *The Westmonian*, observed in form notes for my class "1W" that "Murphy is especially fond of History". I was not fond, however, of mathematics or sport, and until I entered the sixth form and could say goodbye to both these distractions, my weeks revolved around negotiating those classes and avoiding sport of any kind.

Until the Great War, the principal team game at West Mon was soccer. However, well before I went there it had become a great rugby school, producing Welsh internationals such as Ken Jones and Bryn Meredith. And two near-contemporaries of mine at West Mon, Terry Cobner and Graham Price, went on to play with distinction for Wales from the mid-1970s. None of this, however, changed the fact that I was definitely not good at playing rugby, and in that respect I was a huge disappointment to my father who had himself been a fine rugby player. He used to finish work on a Saturday morning and rush off to play for Abersychan RFC, where he captained the team and in later life wrote an account of how the club had acquired new grounds in the years of the Depression.

History, however, was my great love, and during my school years I concentrated on this subject more than any other. Our teachers were mainly young men, and sometimes older teachers who had fought in the Second World War. Among the latter, for example, was Major Williams, who taught us Mathematics, and was a master of what might politely be called "irony". And there was Major Room who, in his unique style, introduced us to German.

As a school which sent boys to Oxford and Cambridge, we had a "third year sixth" (called "7X") and a "fast stream" for brighter lads. I was fortunate to be in that stream, which meant we skipped the fourth form, and went directly from "3W" to "5W", and then sat our "O" Levels one year early. I took mine in 1964 and did very well in arts and humanities, but very poorly in the sciences. Overall, however, my results were good enough for me to enter the sixth form to study History, English Literature, and Economics.

My History teacher was Ken Roderick, who came from my home village of Abersychan. He had himself been a pupil of the school, had gone on to Jesus College, Oxford, to read History. He returned to West Mon as a member of staff and was, more than any other, the master who inspired me to apply to study History in Oxford. I was also taught History by Len Morgan, the deputy head, who was a kindly and helpful man. Alan Bath taught me Economics, and later British Constitution. A native of Abertillery, he had studied at the London School of Economics: he was to drop dead in the school a few years after I left. *Post hoc sed non propter hoc.* English, meanwhile, was taught by Mr Burroughs, an exile from Southern Rhodesia as it was at the time, and he was very right-wing (a fact which generated some interesting debates between us).

Another inspiring teacher was Graham Harris, an Oxford classicist who taught Latin and was the school's librarian. He also held lessons simply called "Ideas" where we exchanged thoughts about everything under the sun – I'm not sure today's curriculum would allow such flexibility.

Headmaster Roy Wiltshire was, despite his rather harsh exterior, a very caring man who presided over a school that produced impressive results. Like others, he applied corporal punishment, a practice I detested then as I do now. I suppose it was symptomatic of the age, but it was in my view an unnecessary and brutal form of discipline.

The school had a good many societies which, unlike sport, attracted me. With Adrian Babbidge, who became a distinguished archaeologist and museum curator, I formed the Local History Society. We organised trips to places of historical interest and even set up a small museum for the school. As one might imagine, I joined the Debating Society and the Classical Music Society, which was where I began what has become a lifelong friendship with John Rogers from Pontnewydd. The two of us also sang in concerts, as members of the school choir, and I recall singing Fauré's *Requiem* (the choir rehearsals being directed by Dorothy Adams Jeremiah, the county music organiser, who had fostered the great sopranos Gwyneth Jones and Margaret Price), with Charles Farncombe (a celebrated professional musician who lived in the county) conducting the combined choir and county youth orchestra in the public performance.

School was a place to make friends, and I made many in the sixth form particularly – Graham Morgan, who became a solicitor; David Bassett and Roger Vaughan, both of whom went into industry after university; and Peter Taylor, ultimately a professor in Sheffield.

Another special friend was Richard Lewis, who lived in Cwmbran. His father worked in a senior capacity for the National Coal Board. Richard and his girlfriend, Ruth Oliver (later his wife, and another great friend –

I was best man at their wedding), both went to Swansea University. Richard read History, and Ruth read English; he graduated with first-class honours and, later, a doctorate in Welsh Labour History, and eventually moved to Middlesbrough becoming a senior lecturer in History at Teesside University. We've been friends for more than 50 years.

Richard and Ruth were Labour Party supporters, and this created a natural bond between us. We were in the Young Socialists together, and after leaving university we all involved ourselves in local politics.

I had joined the Labour Party in Abersychan in early 1964. I clearly recall the occasion when Don Touhig and I met Eddie Thomas, the local Labour county councillor for Abersychan, in Glansychan Park. He encouraged us to become members, which we did, and I still remember the first party meeting I attended. It was in the Co-operative Hall in High Street, Abersychan, in a meeting room lined with books on Labour and Co-operative history, and everybody sat around a very large table. The Chairman was Councillor Wilf Chivers, who was one of three local councillors on the Pontypool urban district council; the two other councillors were Em Robinson and Vi Gullick (whose brother had been Labour MP for Bristol Central).

Don and I were soon deeply involved in the ward party's activities, becoming delegates to the Pontypool local Labour Party and the then Pontypool Constituency Labour Party General Management Committee. I am still a delegate to the same CLP, more than half a century on!

The village was overwhelmingly Labour-voting and, to date, has been the home or birthplace of seven Labour MPs: Arthur Jenkins, MP for Pontypool; Roy Jenkins, MP; Will Coldrick, MP for a Bristol seat; Don Touhig, MP for Islwyn; Daniel Granville-West, MP for Pontypool; Nick Thomas-Symonds, MP for Torfaen since 2015; and me. It has been quite an achievement for a relatively small place with a population of just over seven thousand in the 2011 Census.

Local government in Abersychan was also Labour. In fact, candidates standing for other parties were so rare that there had been no need for elections for a county councillor in the area since 1935!

My first canvassing experience was at the 1964 General Election when I was sent to knock on doors in Ffrwd Road. At the very first door, the lady of the house greeted me with the words, "Don't worry about that business, we're all Labour here. How's your Mam?" In those days, election literature had to be put in envelopes with hand-written names and addresses. Don and I travelled to play our part in this huge job at the election HQ in Pontypool, which was run by Ray Morgan, election agent for Leo Abse, the constituency MP at the time. Ray was the TGWU convener in the great

Girling factory in Cwmbran, and was to be my first election agent more than twenty years later.

Abse, a Cardiff solicitor, had been the MP since a 1958 by-election. He succeeded Daniel Granville West, who had represented the constituency from 1946 to 1958, and had been made one of the first life peers. As a child, I remember Granville West alighting the train from London wearing a bowler hat and coming to buy fruit from my mother's shop.

Abse was Jewish, and was a colourful and flamboyant character. His work as a solicitor and councillor inspired him to devote his energy as an MP to social issues and family law, a focus reflected in the many private members' bills he was to sponsor during his Commons career. His life and mine became increasingly intertwined over the decades – I found him larger than life, and I was very much in awe of him. He once awarded me a prize on Speech Day at West Mon and, in his address to the school, pondered whether one of the pupils at that gathering might one day succeed him.

As well as being members (and soon respectively secretary and chair) of Abersychan Ward Labour Party, Don and I formed the Eastern Valley Labour Young Socialist Branch. We quickly built up a reasonable membership – including Jennifer Hughes, Don's girlfriend, who was to marry him in 1968. The branch met in Sebastopol Labour Hall, a few miles south of Pontypool, holding socials and attending conferences, and helping out at election times. We were never really on the far left of Labour politics, which was unusual in a young socialist branch!

Within the Eastern Valley Labour Young Socialist Branch, we felt no resentment from the older members of the party. On the contrary, we were given great encouragement and help. My cousin, Ken Woolfe, who was a leading trade unionist at ROF Glascoed, spoke up for us at the CLP, and we even received a grant! Some of the most influential local Labour figures became my friends, and were to play a big role in my later life – people like Mabel Lee, Phyllis Roberts, Dennis Puddle, George Day, to name just four.

In the year I joined the Labour Party, my parents started thinking seriously about moving from Abersychan to Cwmbran, a big decision arising from financial necessity coupled with the aspiration to live in a new and modern house. My parents' shop was losing business rapidly because of the growth of the new supermarkets, and had to close in 1962. My father had by this time left the colliery and was now working at the British Nylon Spinners (BNS) factory at Mamhilad, a few miles outside Pontypool – it was a move he hated at first, but as soon as he became a TGWU shop steward things took a great turn for the better.

My mother also decided to look for work. She found a job in the Fine Fare supermarket in the developing Cwmbran town centre (I remember I was with her in the store on the day President Kennedy was assassinated). She eventually left to become the manageress of the newly-opened Merrett's Bakery shop in Pontypool, a job she much enjoyed.

Some time later, my mother transferred when Merrett's opened another shop in Cwmbran, and that was the catalyst for us finally to move. My parents applied to the Cwmbran Development Corporation for a rented home in Fairwater, the newest part of Cwmbran, and thanks to their status as key workers, we became the tenants of number 42 Wiston Path, Fairwater, Cwmbran, within three weeks of applying in 1965.

My mother's boss in Merrett's was Ken Humphries, the sales manager for the group. He and his wife Betty became great family friends; Ken had been in the Welsh Guards during the war and had experienced huge privations in a German prisoner of war camp. On the day we moved to Cwmbran, many of our smaller items made the journey to our new house in the back of a Merrett's Bakery van!

For the first time, we had a bathroom, and even central heating and two toilets (both inside). Dad, of course, when he was working as a collier, would have used pit-head showers, but domestically the new facilities were transformational – I remember my father taking a bath and marvelling at this novel experience, quite a change from the kitchen bathtub of old.

I remained at West Mon, but the bus journey was now much longer; Neil, meanwhile, changed school from St Francis in Abersychan to Our Lady of the Angels in Cwmbran (another Franciscan foundation). And, of course, our parish changed. It was quite an emotional and difficult break, but our physical lives were considerably improved. We continued to visit our friends and relations in Abersychan and, quite improperly, I continued to attend the Abersychan Ward Labour Party despite the fact that I was now a "New Towner"!

Cwmbran, in the south of the Eastern Valley, had been a small town; coalmining and foundry-working (at GKN), along with the Girling brake factory and the local biscuit factory, had been the main employers. Pontnewydd was the other large village in the area. But everything was to change when the 1945 Labour government named Cwmbran as the site of what would be the only New Town in Wales – like Harlow, Basildon, Stevenage and all the other New Towns, Cwmbran was to expand enormously.

People flooded in – mostly from the valleys, but also from West Wales, as men came to find jobs in the new Llanwern steelworks in Newport. Tens of thousands of houses were built, and from the mid-1960s particularly the town centre quickly began to expand. Factories were constructed on the industrial estates, and the population rose to 55,000.

We had to find new neighbours and make new friends. Alun and Eiddwen Roberts were very special. The couple were from Hendy in West Wales and were Welsh-speaking, with Alun coming to work as a manager at ROF Glascoed. My brother Neil made new friends easily at school and in the local streets.

My closest Cwmbran friend (although technically, as I've already noted, he lived in Pontnewydd) was John Rogers. From the time I moved to Cwmbran, we regularly found ourselves travelling on the same bus to school, and our parents also became friendly. John's father Wilf had been a radio operator in the Merchant Navy during the war, and his mother Enid was a sister at Cefn Ila maternity home (where my brother and I had been born, of course). Wilf worked at STC (Standard Telephones and Cables, eventually part of ITT) in Newport, and he drove a little A35 car. John was (and still is) witty and very intelligent, and to this day we go to concerts together, from Cardiff to Oxford and Malvern and, over the years, to the great Three Choirs Festival held in Gloucester, Hereford and Worcester.

My interest in music came originally from listening to my mother playing the piano. She had learned with 'Madame' Freda Martin, who taught the internationally renowned opera singer Dame Gwyneth Jones. I remember my parents asking me if I'd like to have piano lessons, an invitation that I foolishly and arrogantly declined, one of the greatest mistakes of my life. Still, it didn't stop me enjoying music. I like jazz and big band music of the 1930s and 1940s, but my real love is classical music – with the exception of contemporary classical music, I like it all!

My great favourite is Elgar, and I've been a member of the Elgar Society for many years. I was for a time a trustee of the Elgar Edition, which was formed to publish all of Elgar's printed works. And my life has been enriched by Elgar – his choral music, particularly *The Dream of Gerontius*, has sustained me throughout difficult times. Chopin is another of my favourite composers, and I was introduced to the Chopin Society by the late Lady Eirene White. I am now privileged to be an honorary member of the society. West Mon school played a vital part in developing my interest in music – it's often the extra-curricular activity in schools that has the most lasting impact upon pupils, and I was no exception to this.

Local history was always another passion. From an early age, I was a member of both the Monmouthshire Local History Council, and the Monmouthshire and Caerleon Antiquarian Association. In the sixth form, I started to do some research and writing, and was able in 1966 to publish an article in the journal of the Local History Council, *Presenting Monmouthshire*. The article was a short account of Catholicism in Gwent from the time of the Reformation to the 1680s, and it took me some time to research.

I relied heavily on material at the Newport Public Library, and my article recounted the story of the people of Gwent who chose to remain Catholic (recusants) and who, in consequence, often faced persecution. I was very proud to have had my research published, and I followed it up with other articles in later years. In the 1971–2 edition of *The Severn and Wye Review*, edited by the Chepstow historian Ivor Waters, I wrote of the Jesuit College at the Cwm, Llanrothal, near Monmouth, which flourished in the seventeenth century. Writing again in *Presenting Monmouthshire* in 1970, I continued the story of Gwent Catholicism covering the period from the end of the seventeenth century to the restoration of the Catholic hierarchy in 1850.

I sat my "A" Level examinations in 1966, and could have done better. I earned a B grade in History, and decided to stay on for a further year in "7X" to sit another two "A" Levels in British Constitution (for which I earned an A grade) and Economic History (B). With these results I was offered places to read History and Politics at university, at Manchester, Swansea and Sheffield.

But I wanted to go to Oxford. I viewed Oxford as the best university in the country to study History, and it was the place to practise Politics, so I decided to take the Oxford Entrance Examinations in Modern Studies (Politics, Philosophy and Economics). Opting for the PPE route gave me the chance to sit a paper in Politics. It was a shame that I wasn't able to read Modern History and Politics, but it wasn't a degree option in 1967 (although the joint degree is available today).

Applying with me to go to Oxford were two of my closest school friends. The first was Stuart Williams from Usk, an exact contemporary, whose father (like mine) worked at BNS. Stuart has always been very intelligent and personable. He decided to apply to Magdalen College, and as a linguist sat the Entrance Examinations in German and French.

The other friend was Stephen (Efstathios – Stathis for short) Gauntlett. Stathis came from Abersychan (Talywain, to be precise), and his father was a local boy who worked in the Girling factory. He met his Greek wife in Greece, during the war, and when he brought her back to Wales she spoke very little English. Stathis grew up speaking Greek fluently and, encouraged by the Classics teacher, Graham Harris, he took the Oxford Entrance Examination with a view to reading French and Modern Greek at Oriel College. He eventually graduated with first-class honours degree and a D.Phil. – and he also graduated with a wife, Maria, who was a Greek Cypriot working in Oxford. They would later emigrate to Melbourne in Australia, where they had two lovely daughters and Stathis became a professor in the city's university.

On leaving Oxford, Stuart Williams pursued a Master's at the School of Oriental and African Studies in London University. He worked as a professional linguist and German translator. He later switched career to become a barrister, and eventually the senior employment tribunal judge in Wales. Stuart married Lindsay, and they had a fine son and daughter.

Casting my mind back more than fifty years, I remember the day when Stathis, Stuart and I all went to Oxford for our interviews in December 1967. It was a nerve-wracking experience. I had applied to Oriel College and the interview panel consisted of Dr J. W. Gough, Dr W. A. Pantin (an eminent mediaevalist) and Mr H. T. Lambrick (a retired and kindly former Indian civil servant, who wore a monocle). They were interested in my local history publications, and in my political involvement.

Billy Pantin, chairing the panel, said that I should get hold of some past examination papers of first-term exams, which I took as a strong hint that I had been accepted at Oriel. I was right: the acceptance letter popped through the letterbox a few days later. My parents were overjoyed, and my life entered a new phase.

During 1967, I had entered the European Schools Day essay competition, organised by the Council of Europe. It invited school students in European countries to write test essays on the subject of European Unity, and I was fortunate enough to be one of the winners from Britain. Another successful essayist from Wales (not to mention my good friend John Rogers, who had won in the same competition in the year before) was Rhodri Walters from Merthyr Tydfil, who was later to become a very senior clerk in the House of Lords, and our paths wouldn't cross again for another thirty years.

The British section of the European Schools Day Organisation had, as its president, Sir William Hayter – a one-time ambassador to Russia, and later Warden of New College, Oxford. I was to meet him and his wife 30 years on too, when I visited Vienna as treasurer of the Anglo-Austrian Society.

A total of 181 students from all over Europe had been winners in 1967 – about a dozen from the UK – and for the prize-giving ceremony we all travelled to Rome by train in late July 1967. It was my first time abroad, and the journey took 34 hours. We were in Rome for five days, and stayed in what had been Mussolini's sports stadium! It was desperately hot, over 100 degrees Fahrenheit (that's 38 degrees Celsius in new money), and I was daft enough to walk to the Vatican in the middle of the day! But the walk was worth it. On 26 July 1967, I received my prize-winner's certificate from the Italian Minister of Education, Professor Luigi Gui, in a ceremony at the famous Capitol Palace. As well as taking part in discussion groups, we were given a tour of Rome and taken to a performance of *La bohème* at the

Caracalla Baths. (The venue became known to a worldwide audience more than 20 years later as the setting for the first of the famous *Three Tenors* concerts, featuring Luciano Pavarotti, Plácido Domingo and José Carreras.) Seeing the opera was a great experience, although tainted by a memory of being charged a fiver for a can of Coke!

At the end of our visit to Rome, we had received a letter of congratulation from Pope Paul VI, and for the next stage of the journey we were split into groups for a further week studying another European country.

Rhodri Walters and I were put in a group of ten students that travelled to Belgium – two students from the UK, two from Austria, and one each from Germany, Italy, France, Denmark, Norway and Luxembourg. Over the last fifty years, I have kept in touch with Luigi Brambilla from Italy and Heinrich Rumpfhuber from Austria, and also maintained correspondence with Veronika Baier from Munich and Søren Ehlen from Copenhagen until we lost contact – I often wonder what happened to them.

The group spent nine days in Belgium and we covered virtually the whole country – not too difficult considering its size! Our guide and mentor was Leon Decouveur from the Belgian Ministry of Education – a small man with excellent English, and rarely unaccompanied by his ample Irish mistress!

The programme was well-planned and comprehensive, taking us to Nivelles, Mons, Tournai, Cambrai, Ypres, Ostend, Bruges, Ghent, Antwerp, Liege, Malmedy and, of course, Brussels – an experience that gave me a lifelong interest in Belgium and its past. I specialised in Belgian history when I was at Oxford, and many years later became a member of the parliamentary All Party Group on Belgium.

School days were well and truly finished – my seven years at West Mon prepared me well for the future, and my interest in history as a first-former had developed to the point where I was about to begin reading the subject at the University of Oxford. The teaching at West Mon had been good, in some cases outstanding, and I had made lifelong friendships. Oriel now beckoned!

Oxford

I WENT UP TO ORIEL COLLEGE, Oxford, in October 1967, and from that point on my life was to change dramatically.

I had chosen Oriel because of some school connections, and because I saw it as a "History college". The Regius Professor of History (Hugh Trevor-Roper at the time) was a Professorial Fellow at Oriel. In previous years, the college had produced many famous historians, including A. J. P. Taylor and Kenneth O. Morgan (now Lord Morgan), although neither of them had much enjoyed their undergraduate years.

Oriel is the fifth oldest college in Oxford and was founded by a royal civil servant, Adam de Brome, in 1324. It was re-founded two years later by Edward II. Its official name is "House of the Blessed Mary the Virgin in Oxford", but it became colloquially "Oriel" after 1329 when it was given a piece of land which was the site of a large house called "La Oriole".

Most of the college's buildings date from the early seventeenth century, although the very imposing library and senior common room date from the eighteenth. The Rhodes Building is Edwardian and was funded by money given to the college by Cecil Rhodes, who has himself become a subject of some controversy in the twenty-first century.

Famous alumni include Thomas More, Walter Raleigh, Beau Brummell, Gilbert White, as well as the Nobel Prize winners Alexander Todd (Chemistry) and James Meade (Economics).

Probably the most important part of the history of Oriel was in the early and mid-nineteenth century, when it was regarded as the top intellectual college at the University of Oxford. It was the home of the so-called "Oxford Movement", and numbered among its fellows Cardinal John Henry Newman, Thomas and Matthew Arnold, Richard Whately and John Keble. Two great reforming provosts transformed Oriel – John Eveleigh and Edward Copleston, the latter subsequently becoming Bishop of Llandaff (and being responsible for the building of St Thomas's Anglican Church in Talywain, in my future constituency).

The college was a middle-sized foundation, and the last in Oxford to admit women (which happened in 1986). Today it has about 40 fellows, 300 undergraduates and 160 graduates, and is probably the top rowing college in Oxford.

The first week in university is always nerve-wracking. I was fortunate to have my school friends Stuart and Stathis with me – Stuart was in the new building at Magdalen, while Stathis and I shared rooms at Oriel. We both had unheated bedrooms, but we had joint use of a very fine sitting room with seventeenth-century panelling in the First Quad, above the Porter's Lodge. Bathrooms, of course, were not provided en-suite – we had to walk two quads to reach them. What a great privilege it was, however, to take our meals in the beautiful hall, and to eat dishes that I had never encountered – jugged hare, or pigeon!

The college's students were overwhelmingly southern English, with a majority of public-school undergraduates. There were closed scholarships to Harrow and other schools, and to a working class lad like me from the valleys, the upper-middle-class English accent was a novelty. I have to say that I was in no way daunted by this – I had obtained my place on merit and I was as good (or as bad) as anyone from an English public school. I never felt out-of-place, and in fact many of the friends that I made in Oxford were English and former public-school boys.

I made lifetime friendships at Oriel – Paul Brown, a linguist from County Durham; Anthony Campbell from Liverpool, a historian like me; Alan Duffin, a lawyer from Barnsley; Clifford Payton, a mathematician-turned-lawyer from Reading; Peter Siddall, a chemist from Barnsley; Nick Whelan, another lawyer, from London; and Brian Wilson, a mathematician from Lewes.

One of my closest friends at Oxford was Bill Redmond. Bill came from Bootle, and had been educated at St Edward's College, Liverpool. His father had been a headmaster but died at a young age. Bill and his brother Anthony had been raised by their mother, Mary, who was also a teacher. Anthony was in his third year at Oriel when I arrived – he was reading PPE, and was to become a local government finance officer and, later, lectured widely in the subject. Bill, meanwhile, was reading French and Spanish at Oxford, and we both had a love of music. He was a skilful organist and pianist, and I once (very inexpertly) turned the pages for him when he gave a piano recital at Oxford's famous Holywell Music Room.

We were both Catholics and attended the university Catholic chaplaincy. The chaplain was Fr Michael Hollings, a legendary priest and former Guards officer, assisted by Fr Crispian Hollis, the future Bishop of Portsmouth. Bill and I became great friends and, on one occasion when he visited my home in Cwmbran, my mother asked if he had ever thought of going into the priesthood. He blushed, and said that he did indeed plan to be a priest, but that only the university chaplaincy knew his of intention. He rightly wanted to lead a normal undergraduate life, and I was the only one of his contemporaries who was aware of his vocation at that time.

After leaving Oxford and completing a teacher's diploma, Bill went to Upholland Seminary and then on to Rome and Jerusalem. He became an expert in Old Testament Studies, and could read French, Spanish, Italian, German, Latin, Greek and Hebrew. His talent led to his becoming a lecturer at Ushaw College, Durham, but his health was never the most robust and, in time, he had to move to a small parish in Warrington. He eventually became a parish priest in Widnes and, again, Warrington, and was ultimately appointed Canon Theologian of Liverpool Archdiocese. I was privileged to be present at his induction. Bill was a clever, very funny and compassionate friend and pastor, and we holidayed together almost every year for more than three decades.

His health, however, deteriorated and he was forced to retire. Shortly after retiring, in December 2015, he fell down the stairs at the Presbytery in Warrington where he was then living, and tragically died. It was a great blow to me, and he is always in my memories and prayers. Two archbishops, three bishops and dozens of priests were present at his funeral – it was a fitting testament to a very special human being.

Academic life at Oriel was very different from what I had known at school. Here, we were left on our own to get on with work. Although we had to attend the famous one-to-one Oxford tutorials and occasional seminars, lectures were not compulsory. Still, we would have been foolish to miss them, especially as they were often delivered by some of the country's leading historians.

Listening to Hugh Trevor-Roper on Gibbon and Macaulay, or to A. J. P. Taylor on Beaverbrook, for example, was fascinating. Taylor would speak for an hour, without a note, to a crowded audience in the examination schools. There were others who were not as famous, but were still experts in their specialisms – like Frederick ('Freddie') Madden of Nuffield on Commonwealth constitutional history.

My Oriel tutors were distinguished within their own field. My "moral tutor" was Dr Billy Pantin, who, as I've said, had chaired my interview panel. He had written the standard work on the history of the fourteenth-century English church. He came from a wealthy background to study at Christ Church before spending his entire academic career at Oriel. He was the

Keeper of the Oxford University Archives. In her book *Oxford*, Jan Morris paints a memorable and accurate picture of Billy in his rooms.

A tutorial with Dr Pantin was eccentric but rewarding. His rooms were full of books, records, papers and heaven knows what; and tea and cakes (and on one memorable occasion a pint of beer) would be discovered behind piles of mediaeval manuscripts! He bought his clothes from Carnaby Street and loved taking his students into the Oxfordshire countryside to visit mediaeval churches, and afterwards, to dine in some country inn. He once gave me a tutorial when he was in bed, recovering from a cold!

Billy was a devout Catholic and a lay Benedictine. He was in his mid-sixties when he taught me and on the verge of retirement. He collapsed and died in 1973, walking in the cloister of Corpus Christi College, and was succeeded by another fine mediaeval historian, Dr Jeremy Catto (who died only recently in 2018).

When I was in the Northern Ireland Office, I attended a reception with Cardinal Basil Hume in Archbishop's House Westminster. We had a very serious conversation about the Guildford Four, but conversation eventually turned to Billy Pantin. The Cardinal's eyes lit up as he reminisced about being taught by Billy many years before, when the latter was a young Don.

Dr Robert Beddard, who taught early modern British history, was one of the younger Fellows. He was an excellent tutor who had graduated from London University and Cambridge, and was an expert in late Stuart history. He was very different from the older Dons, even down to addressing you by your Christian name rather than your surname, for instance.

Christopher Seton-Watson, the college's vice-provost and Politics tutor, who taught me modern European history, came from a distinguished family of historians. His father, R. W. Seton-Watson, was an expert on Eastern Europe and advised the powers at Versailles in 1919; his brother Hugh, meanwhile, was the acknowledged authority on modern Russian history. For his part, Christopher had won the Military Cross in Italy during the war, and had developed a great interest in modern Italian history. His book *Italy from Liberalism to Fascism* became the standard reference in English on that period in history. Some years later, he was to supervise the son of my predecessor as MP, Leo Abse, when Toby Abse was studying for his PhD in Italian History at Cambridge.

We students of History were also farmed out to other Oxford historians, depending on what we were studying. As a result, I was taught by Michael Brock (vice-president of Wolfson and later Warden of Nuffield) on British Constitutional History; by Agatha Ramm (of Somerville) on Modern Diplomatic History; and by (later Professor Sir) Brian Harrison (of Corpus

Christi College), a really brilliant tutor who taught me Modern British History and was later to become the editor of the *Dictionary of National Biography*.

In 2004, I was invited to attend a dinner in Brian Harrison's honour. I couldn't get there because of my duties in Northern Ireland at the time, but he wrote to me saying he hadn't made the connection "between the Paul Murphy who is now Secretary of State for Northern Ireland and the Paul Murphy whom I taught from Oriel in the late 1960s". He kindly added that I had been "a responsive, energetic and lively pupil, with no fewer than ten essays successfully completed in one term".

I was obliged to sit preliminary examinations in the first year, mainly in foreign languages, but after that no formal examinations were held until the end of the third year. We had internal college examinations, called collections, and we were interviewed each year by the provost. In my time, the provost was Kenneth Turpin, who had been a university administrator and for some time private secretary to Clement Attlee. Turpin was also the university vice-chancellor for most of the time I was at Oriel, which included 1968, the famous year of university uprisings and disruptions. I recall the university's administration building being occupied by students – they had my full moral support!

The Modern History course was pretty wide-ranging, but very "English". We studied the whole of English history, from the Romans right up to 1939, as well as a period of modern European history (in my case nineteenth- and twentieth-century). In addition, we had to study courses in political theory, and modern British and Commonwealth constitutional history. A major part of the study involved a special subject, and I chose "British Policy and the Making of the Ententes 1898–1907". It was a gripping subject, dealing with the diplomatic world in the run-up to the First World War, and I had to study diplomatic documents in French and English in great detail.

Much as I enjoyed the academic work, another welcome feature of Oxford life was the number of marvellous opportunities to explore all kinds of wider interests. Though I was most definitely not a sportsman, I was certainly interested in politics, music and the arts, and the college boasted a number of societies devoted to music and discussion. I regularly attended all sorts of classical music concerts around the city, and was also a member of the Greek Society, the Archaeological Society, the United Nations Society and Oriel's Bryce Society, which dealt with historical and political issues.

I didn't join the Oxford Union, but did occasionally go along to listen to visiting speakers. I remember listening to one speech by Richard Crossman, for example. Contemporaries of mine who ran for office at the Oxford Union included William Waldegrave, Edwina Cohen (later Curry) and Christopher

Hitchens. I did, however, join the Labour Club (which changed its name to the Democratic Labour Club), at an annual member subscription of six shillings (or 30 pence). Other contemporaries who were members of the Labour Club included John Spellar and Roger Liddle, and guest speakers included Vic Feather (General Secretary of the TUC), Roy Jenkins, John Mackintosh, Dick Clements (editor of *Tribune*), Ralph Miliband (father of David Miliband and Ed Miliband), Bill Rodgers, Barbara Castle and Tony Crosland – a fine selection of Labour stars of the times!

Activities at the Catholic chaplaincy took up much of my time. As well as attending Mass every Sunday, I would go to events in the Old Palace, where the chaplaincy was based. Sermons at Mass would be given by visiting preachers, including clergy from the Church of Scotland, the Church of England and the Free Churches, as well as by monks, missionaries and bishops! In November 1969, Cardinal Heenan spoke on the theme of "The time has come . . ." but, I fear, I can't remember exactly whose time had come! I also became, with Bill Redmond, a member of the St Vincent de Paul Society.

They were heady days for Catholics – the Second Vatican Council, which closed in December 1965, had changed the religious landscape for Catholicism in a way that none of us could have imagined. The idea of a woman Baptist minister preaching at a Catholic Mass was novel, to say the least. I recall attending Mass in the chaplaincy one Sunday morning, then an afternoon service in a rural Methodist chapel, and finally Evensong at Oriel chapel. I would often attend the university sermon held on Sunday mornings at the university church of St Mary the Virgin, which was Newman's old church, just across the road from Oriel), to listen to such famous clerics as the Russian Orthodox Bishop Anthony Bloom. On other varied occasions, I listened to sermons by Michael Ramsey, the Archbishop of Canterbury, and by Malcolm Muggeridge.

The Newman Society gave us the opportunity to engage with the likes of Sir Isaiah Berlin and Father Herbert McCabe.

For my first two years in Oxford, I lived in college. In my second year, I had a room on my own, still in the First Quad. Of course, our fees in those days were paid by the local education authority, and we had a substantial maintenance grant as well. My parents would send me a pound each week (which was a lot in those days, equivalent to a third of the weekly rent at home – my mother earned just eight pounds a week). In the final year, we were obliged to find lodgings, and Nick Whelan and I lodged together at Divinity Road, with Mrs Doris Hillier, who always gave us a good start to the day by serving up a hearty breakfast. Her golden Labrador provided us with much-needed entertainment!

The college's social life was very full, and tutors would regularly invite students to dine, or to take sherry before dinner. One such occasion took place at Boar's Hill, when Mr Lambrick had an "At Home" with beer and cheese in June 1969. Not having public examinations in the second year meant that the long and beautiful Oxford summer of '69 could be enjoyed without pressure, and I took full advantage – punting on the Cherwell, even watching university cricket in the Parks.

The third year, however, concentrated the mind. Examinations loomed, and students had to start thinking about a career. I contemplated research into Catholic influence on the Labour Party, but decided instead to go into business; I was interviewed by GKN, Lucas, and by Ranks Hovis McDougall (who did, after a weekend of interviews, offer me a position). I chose ultimately to apply to the Co-operative Wholesale Society (CWS), an option that seemed to me to combine business and politics, and I was successful in securing a position as a graduate management trainee.

The Oxford terms were very short (just eight weeks), which meant that I still spent much time with my family in Cwmbran. We had no telephone, so when I wasn't at home I would write every week and my father or mother would reply. I still have many letters we exchanged – my mother concerned for my everyday needs, my brother giving me the latest news of school, and my father offering wise advice. I had started to smoke a pipe, and from time to time "tobacco money" would arrive from home – usually ten shillings! My brother Neil was now a pupil at West Mon, although he was getting quite a hard time from older pupils whom I had put into detention back in the day when I was a prefect there! My mother continued as manageress of the bakery store, Merrett's, in Cwmbran, and dad was still working shifts at ICI Fibres (the latter name of BNS).

This was the age of proper letter writing. As well as my family, I exchanged long letters with John Rogers (mainly on music and plays) and with Don Touhig (mainly on politics).

Occasionally, my parents would come and visit me in Oxford – I remember a lovely occasion one summer, when family friends Bill and Norah Smith drove my parents and Neil to Oriel. We met up with my Uncle Goff and Aunty May, and Trevor and Ruby came from Coventry with their son and daughter. Our great family friends Ken and Betty Humphries also came up with Mam, Dad and Neil when I graduated, both as BA and later as MA.

The final examinations in the summer of 1970 were gruelling, all held in one week. I left Oxford in time to campaign in the 1970 General Election. We all believed Labour would win, but we were all proved wrong when Ted Heath surprised the country and himself!

I took a holiday job with the Electricity Board, measuring commercial premises in Monmouthshire for tariffs. Richard Lewis and I spent some interesting weeks at this work, and we became members of the Electricians' Union.

I had to ring the university for my exam results from a telephone box on a wind-swept housing estate in Newport. I had been awarded a Second Class Degree, which meant I was now Paul Murphy BA (Oxon).

Happily, my association with Oriel and Oxford didn't finish with finals in 1970. I returned to College to attend "Gaudies" (dinners with your contemporaries, held every decade or so) and to go to the "Oriel Weekends", organised by the excellent Oriel Society. I was to make new Oriel friends at these events, among them eminent QC Sir Peter Gross.

I also built up a firm friendship with Ernest Nicholson, the provost of Oriel, and his lovely wife Hazel. Ernest was from a Northern Ireland Anglican working class family, and had studied Theology at Trinity College Dublin. He became an Anglican priest, and was to go to Glasgow and Cambridge universities before coming to Oriel as Professor of the Interpretation of the Holy Scripture. He was a Fellow of the British Academy who held three doctorates, as well as being a famous Old Testament scholar and author of many books and articles.

Ernest took a great interest in my political career, especially my time as a Northern Ireland Minister, and he and Hazel visited me in Hillsborough Castle when I was Secretary of State.

Ernest wrote to me in November 2000 with the news that Oriel had elected me an Honorary Fellow of the College. I was very moved by this, and I return to the College frequently. At his retirement from Oriel, when he was succeeded by Sir Derek Morris, another fine provost, Ernest wrote to me saying, "Your friendship and support over the years has meant more to me than I can adequately express." He died before his time in 2015.

The successor provost to Derek Morris was Moira Wallace, the first woman to hold the post.

I have visited Oxford on many occasions to speak to various societies, including the Labour Club and the Newman Society. I have had the privilege of speaking at the Oxford Union on four occasions – once to speak on devolution (with David Trimble); twice to defend the government in the "No Confidence" debates (with Michael Heseltine, Ed Vaisey, Alan Duncan and Ben Bradshaw); and once to oppose the motion that "This House believes that its politicians shouldn't do God" (with Matthew Parris, Stephen Timms and Lord McNally).

I also returned to preach! In 1999, when I was Northern Ireland Minister, I gave a sermon in Oriel College Chapel entitled "Peace and Reconciliation in Northern Ireland". Three years later, as Welsh Secretary in 2002, I had the privilege of delivering the University Sermon. I entitled it "Christianity and Politics: a Personal Perspective" and, as I climbed the stairs to the pulpit in the university church, my mind turned to J. H. Newman who had delivered his famous University Sermon from the same spot 170 years before.

In 2006, I accepted the opportunity to become a Visiting Parliamentary Fellow of St Anthony's College, Oxford. There are two of these fellowships, each lasting twelve months and first awarded in 1994. The recipients each year are parliamentarians, one from the government party and one from the opposition, and as well as giving talks in the College during the Hilary Term, the fellows organise a series of seminars and work with the two academic conveners (who were Dr Alex Pravda and Professor David Marquand in 2006).

My colleague Parliamentary Fellow was Charles Kennedy, former leader of the Liberal Democrats. I had always liked Charles and we had visited Jordan together on a parliamentary delegation. He wrote to me in February 2006, asking if I was aware of the coincidence of our having the same birthday. He went on to say, "We must make fun of that at St Anthony's in due course", and so we did. We also collaborated very closely on the seminars, and I thoroughly enjoyed working with Charles, whom I had known since entering parliament. He was great company and highly intelligent; he and I were both Catholics, and often attended Mass together in the Crypt Chapel in Westminster.

The theme that Charles and I took for the seminars was "How can democracies cope with minorities?" We had varied speakers, such as Denis MacShane MP, Lord Roger Liddle, Baroness Falkner, Archbishop Peter Smith, David Trimble, Mark Durkan MP, Michael Portillo, David Steel and Professor Roy Foster; subjects included faith schools; South Africa, France and Spain; multi-culturalism; national minorities in the UK; and the Northern Ireland experience.

That year was fascinating. I made some very interesting new friends at St Anthony's, like the Russian expert Professor Archie Brown, and learned a great deal during my fellowship.

In February 2003, Lady Jennifer Jenkins wrote to thank me for my correspondence on the death of her husband, Roy Jenkins. Roy had been Chancellor of the University of Oxford, and I had developed a late friendship with him. I have already noted that he came originally from Abersychan, the same village as me, and that his father was once MP for my own con-stituency. Roy himself had wanted to become MP for Pontypool in 1946, on the sudden death of his father, but his attempt to be adopted as the Labour candidate was unsuccessful. Roy was to visit the valley many years later as Home Secretary, but Leo Abse, my predecessor as MP, fell out with him when Roy left the Labour Party as one of the Gang of Four who formed the SDP in 1981. I had been very angry at Roy's move, too, which I believe played its part in Mrs Thatcher's election victory of 1983.

I have also already noted the occasion on 11 September 2001 when Roy visited Abersychan to unveil a plaque to some of the MPs who had lived in the village. It gave us an opportunity to talk about old times and about Roy's father, Arthur Jenkins, and it soon became clear that Roy and I had much in common. It would not be long before we were to meet again, but that day in 2001, marked in history as 9/11, was in retrospect a strange occasion in view of what was taking place simultaneously in New York.

Andrew Adonis (now Lord Adonis) was at that time working in No. 10 Downing Street, and was writing a biography of Roy Jenkins. He invited Don Touhig and me to have lunch with Roy, to bounce thoughts and memories off one another. It was a great idea. When I reminded Roy that Obadiah Evans, the miners' agent who succeeded his father, was related to me, it prompted Roy to order a further bottle of Claret!

I drank another bottle of Claret some time later when I was invited to one of Roy and Jennifer's famous Sunday lunches, at his home in East Hendred, Oxfordshire. It was a lively and convivial occasion, which ended with Roy showing me the study where he wrote his books. He gave me a copy of his *Churchill* to keep – the American edition, because the quality of the paper was better!

If things had been different, I often wonder whether Roy would have led the Labour Party – it's ironic that Tony Blair's New Labour would become the sort of party that Roy had argued for before forming the SDP.

The influence that Oxford had on me was beneficial, and it has informed the rest of my life. I hope my undergraduate years at Oriel and my continued connection with the university have made me a more fair-minded and liberal person – which is something, however, for others to judge!

Apprenticeship
1970–1987

I STARTED WORKING for the Bakery Division of the CWS in the summer of 1970. I was a graduate management trainee, and still lived in Cwmbran because there was a Co-operative Bakery in neighbouring Pontnewydd. I divided my time between the bakery, the bigger one in Taff's Well to the north of Cardiff, and the Headquarters of the CWS in Balloon Street, Manchester. I went on lots of different visits and courses, and also learned to drive – passing my driving test at the first attempt. I acquired an old Ford Consul, which lasted for only a few months, and kept breaking down. Having experienced the vagaries of its 3-speed gearbox and its unpredictable vacuum-driven windscreen wipers, I had no regrets whatsoever when I upgraded to a blue Ford Anglia, NW0 14F, a retired police car!

The Bakery Division of the CWS was sold to J. Lyons, and I had to make up my mind whether to stay with the new company or go to Manchester to work in personnel management. I decided to do neither after spotting an advertisement for the position of assistant lecturer in History at the North Monmouthshire College of Further Education in Ebbw Vale.

Although I had no teaching qualifications (which weren't necessary in further education in those days), I was selected for interview and got the job.

The position had been held by one Neil Kinnock, although he never took it up, soon becoming instead a lecturer/tutor for the Workers' Educational Association (WEA). I often reminded him that, had he played his cards right, he could have become a senior lecturer at Ebbw Vale!

I was to start in the autumn term of 1971 on an annual salary of £1,300 (which was £200 a year more than I had been getting at the CWS). I would naturally have to drive from Cwmbran to Ebbw Vale, a journey that, despite being a distance of only 20 miles, took 90 minutes. Fortunately, by the time I finished working there sixteen years later, new roads had cut the journey time in half.

My job was to teach "O" and "A" Level History (including one evening class for "A" Level) as well as Economic and Social History for various secretarial classes. My time as a lecturer began unremarkably – I was given the syllabus and told to get on with it. Many of the students (who came from North Monmouthshire and South Breconshire) had failed the Eleven Plus examination, and for them the college provided an invaluable second chance. Others had decided to enrol instead of staying on for sixth form at their schools, while others simply wanted to gain extra qualifications as more mature students. Indeed, one of my first evening class students was in her late sixties, and had lived through many of the events that I was teaching her! It was a very rewarding job – I really felt I was doing something worthwhile, and that the students were genuinely committed to getting on.

As the years went by, I taught British Constitution (or Government) at all levels, and many of the part-time students in particular went on to university to study politics. Steve Thomas, later the General Secretary of the Welsh Local Government Association, joined one of my "A" Level classes. By my final years at Ebbw Vale, I was teaching the children of my first students!

The college was very hierarchical – presided over by the principal, Vernon Hewlett. He was an interesting man, a great expert on Mozart, but he was very much of the old school. He and I were to clash many times after I had become deeply involved in the lecturers' union ATTI (later renamed NATFHE, and now the University and College Union) – to which I was parliamentary adviser in the Commons many years later.

My head of department was Cyril Walby, a very large, chain-smoking man, who had been a Tredegar Labour councillor – very witty, but again old-fashioned when it came to managing his department.

Some years later, they were both succeeded by more modern educational managers – Frank Evans as principal, and Ty Rich as head of department. Ty, and many of my teaching colleagues too, became good friends – Paul Morgan (Geography and Management), Clive Davies (commercial subjects), Walter Simms (Accounting), Peter Halligan (an Irishman who taught English and Psychology), Bill Rutter (a Baptist minister who taught Sociology), and Stan James (management and commercial subjects). We were a close-knit bunch, and their comradeship and support made my job even more satisfying.

Steel had dominated the college in every respect. With the run-down and eventual closure of the Ebbw Vale steelworks, which had been the area's main employer, the college had to find new ways of giving opportunities to the people of North Gwent. Computing, engineering and catering were just some examples of areas in which the college diversified.

In more recent years the original college buildings, like the steelworks, have been demolished, and a new "Learning Zone", one of the campuses of Coleg Gwent, has been built on the old steelworks site.

Many years after I had left Ebbw Vale, I joined the Prince of Wales in my capacity as Secretary of State for Wales on a visit to the college. Back in 1971 when I became the most junior member of staff there, I could never have dreamt how my career would change!

Naturally, returning to Monmouthshire (as it still was then) after my Oxford days, I was quickly involved in local politics again, first as ward branch secretary of the Fairwater Labour Party. This was a new branch, set up to mirror the huge expansion of housing in South West Cwmbran, and it was where I was to begin my friendship with party members who were to play a big role in my life.

Glyn Parry, the chairman of the ward party, hailed from Bargoed. He had been a professional soldier, and would later study for a History degree at Cardiff University as a mature student. It was he who invited me to become secretary. On the left of the party, Glyn later became a member of the borough council with me.

Brian Smith, a professional photographer, was a young, able and charismatic member of the urban district council, and he too was to represent Fairwater on the borough council. Along with his wife Jean, Brian was a great friend – witty, intelligent and a very resourceful politician with a keen judgement.

Fairwater and Henllys ward sent four members to Torfaen Borough Council – myself, Glyn, Brian and Dave Lloyd. Dave was the oldest among us (in his late forties when he became a councillor), and was a skilled tool-maker at Girling's brake factory in Cwmbran. He was a solid and wise trade unionist, and a native of Henllys, while his wife Phyllis came from north Devon. Dave was also a talented pianist, accompanist to Shirley Bassey in her early career.

The member of Gwent County Council for our ward was Ron Wellington, who had moved to Cwmbran from Blaina. His brother Robert was to become a Fairwater councillor, when Glyn retired from the authority. Robert – Bob – has been a good and loyal friend over the years, along with his wife, Shirley. He became chairman of the Economic Development Committee of the council, and eventually leader of the new Torfaen Borough Council. In addition to his council duties, Bob chaired the Welsh Local Government Association, for which he rightly received the CBE, before stepping down from the council in 2017.

Another leading member of the branch was Gethin Williams, who had come to Cwmbran to lecture at the Gwent College of Higher Education, where he was ultimately appointed principal. He and his wife Eileen were fine amateur musicians, and both became great friends of mine. Gethin was a fervent devolutionist and a considerable economist.

The branch was lively and rooted in our local community. Every year, we organised a Christmas social for pensioners at St Joseph's Catholic Social Club (of which I was to become a Trustee), and the ward consistently returned a full complement of Labour councillors at the local elections – even in such difficult years as 1976.

I had first joined the general management committee of the Pontypool CLP in 1965, and on return to the Eastern Valley I was to be a delegate once more, representing Fairwater ward (as its secretary). I have remained a member until today, and I suppose must be one of its longest-serving members. The agent and secretary was Ray Morgan (who became my own agent in 1987). However, the combined job was too onerous for one person, and the party decided in the summer of 1975 to split the posts; Ray continued as Leo Abse's agent, and I took over as secretary (I had previously been assistant secretary). I was to hold that office for twelve years, until I was elected the valley's MP.

The job of secretary was not easy, but it was both influential and rewarding. I had to convene meetings, liaise with the ward parties and the trade unions, and oversee local government selection meetings. All correspondence was dealt with by me, and generally I had to hold the party together.

The duties of the post also meant I had to work very closely with Leo Abse as our MP, and over the years this experience proved to be highly valuable.

Sometime before I became CLP secretary, Leo found himself in a great deal of trouble with the local party, because with Roy Jenkins and others he had defied a three-line whip requiring him to oppose the Conservative government's "decision of principle" in 1971 to join what was then the EEC. This was the only occasion when Leo was seriously threatened with de-selection. Don Touhig and I, as officers of the Eastern Valley Young Socialists, put forward a compromise resolution to the party, which rapped Leo over the knuckles and asked for his undertaking not to vote with the Tories on subsequent EEC legislation.

Leo was instrumental in obtaining major speakers for the CLP. We listened to Tony Benn on Energy, Robin Cook, Tony Crosland, George Thomas, and many others. Leo was himself a towering figure – in contrast to his physical stature! He was a brilliant and passionate speaker, and his parliamentary reports were riveting. Sometimes, after a CLP meeting on a Friday evening, Don and I would join Leo for dinner at a local hotel, and the gossip was fascinating.

In common with some ward branches, the CLP also organised social events. At one New Year's dance, I burnt a hole in my new suit jacket by putting my lighted pipe in the pocket! We also conducted countless campaigns – over the ReChem toxic waste plant at New Inn, over plans for reorganising secondary education in the Eastern Valley, over the closure of hospitals, and so on. Although always serious in purpose, these campaigns often had their lighter moments, and in that context my very good friend John Rogers recently offered me the following recollections of an incident from nearly fifty years ago:

> I remember an occasion in the early 1970s, during the fight to persuade the County Council to speed up the planned introduction of comprehensive education in the upper half of the constituency. As part of our drive to secure public support for the campaign, we visited various places in the affected area, inviting people to sign a petition we had launched. On one memorable day we were in Blaenavon, in the very north of the valley, hoping to gather many signatures. The weather was not auspicious: snow, initially light, grew steadily heavier, the clouds lower and passers-by more infrequent. Undeterred, and with the enthusiasm of youth, we persevered. Then, out of the stygian gloom, trudged a male figure with, one on each side, clutching his hands, two toddlers. Sensing that here was someone who would be certain to have the best interests of our youngest citizens at heart, we confidently asked if he would care to sign our petition. "No, I wouldn't," he growled, "I hate ruddy kids." So saying, and still with his two charges in hand, he plodded grimly away.

The most important role for the local Party, however, was to return a Labour MP for the (Pontypool, and later, Torfaen) constituency. During my time as secretary, there were General Elections in 1979 and 1983. We were also faced in 1981 with the problem of the parliamentary boundary review.

Pontypool had been a parliamentary constituency since the First World War. Before the war, the valley had been part of the old North Monmouthshire division, represented finally by Reginald McKenna, the Liberal Chancellor of the Exchequer and Home Secretary. By the end of the war, the South Wales miners had converted to Socialism, which together with the change in the franchise, meant that the new constituency of Pontypool returned a new Labour MP, Tom Griffiths, a steelworker from Port Talbot, who became a government whip. But he never lived in the constituency (which didn't seem to matter much in those days). Eventually, however, he was effectively de-selected by the local party, making way in 1935 for Arthur Jenkins.

Significantly, in a constituency with many collieries, the new MP was the local miners' agent.

Arthur became PPS to Clement Attlee the Labour Leader, and a junior Minister, but he died in 1946. His son had hoped to be adopted as the new Labour candidate, but lost out to Daniel Granville West, a Newbridge solicitor, who held the seat until 1958 when he was made one of the earliest of the new Life Peers.

Hugh Gaitskell, the then Labour Leader, tried to parachute the steelworkers' General Secretary into the seat, but this was deeply resented in the constituency and the local Party selected Leo Abse. Leo was to become one of the great parliamentarians of his generation, and went on to introduce more Private Members' Bills than any other MP.

No one seriously thought that the constituency boundaries would ever change. The Eastern Valley was a natural social and political unit and, after 1973, had its own local authority – Torfaen Borough Council. But the Boundary Commission recommended its dismantlement, and the valley, like Gaul in Julius Caesar's time, was to be divided into three parts, and the constituency was to disappear. All hell broke loose! The MP and the council led a campaign to save the seat, and I was heavily involved as party secretary. A public inquiry was held at County Hall, Croesyceiliog, Cwmbran, and the former Solicitor General, Sam Silkin MP, led the fight against the change. We won, and the Commission changed its mind. The constituency was saved, and was to be known as "Torfaen". The first election to be fought for the new division was in 1983, when Labour held the seat but with a reduced majority.

Much of my work as CLP secretary was taken up with local government and in organising selection meetings for local council candidates. In 1972, I had myself been chosen to stand for the new Fairwater and Henllys ward of Torfaen District Council. Along with Brian Smith, Glyn Parry and David Lloyd, I presented myself to the people for the first election that I contested in the spring of 1973. The Conservative administration in Westminster had reorganised local government in England and Wales in the previous year (although the changes did not take full effect until April 1974), and Wales now had county councils and district (or borough) councils. My local county council was Gwent; consisting of the combined areas of Monmouthshire and Newport, it had responsibility for education, social services, the fire service and other major areas of provision.

Our district council (which was later to become a borough, with its own mayor) comprised the former urban district councils of Blaenavon, Pontypool and Cwmbran, and part of the old rural district councils of Pontypool and Magor and St Mellons (and Henllys – in my own ward). The new council was to be a "shadow authority", running alongside its

1. CEFN ILA NURSING HOME

2. KILCREA FRIARY

3. STATION STREET, ABERSYCHAN *(above)*

4. JEREMIAH MURPHY *(right)*

5. GRANDFATHER AND ME *(opposite)*

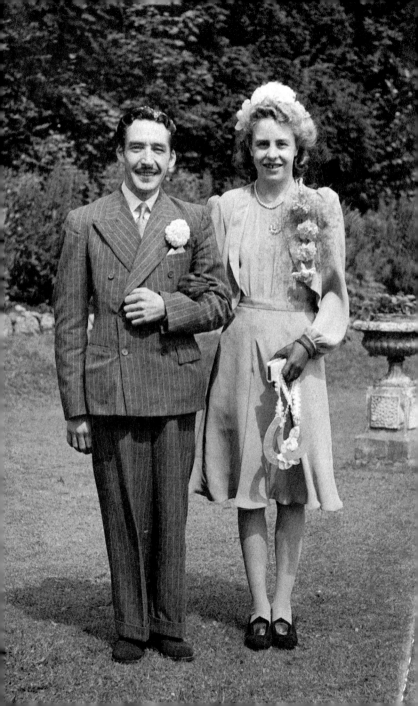

6. MAM AND DAD'S WEDDING, 1947 *(opposite)*

7. MAM AND DAD, AND DON TOUHIG'S DAUGHTER KATIE *(below)*

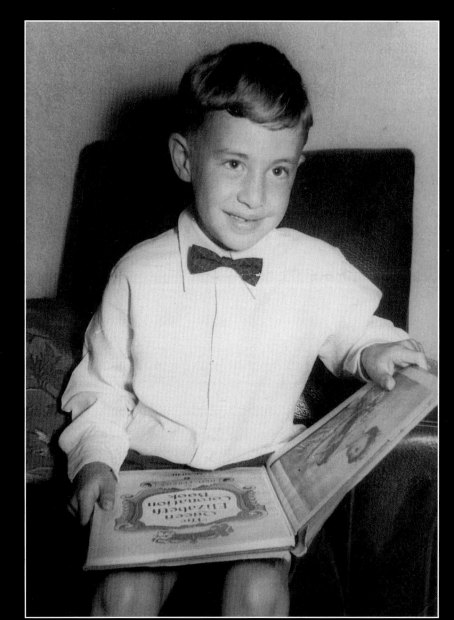

14. WITH DAD AND DANIEL AT THE 1987 GENERAL ELECTION *(left)*

15. JUMPING OVER THE VOTES, 1987 *(below)*

16. WITH DAVE LLOYD AND BARRY JONES *(opposite)*

20.   WITH ROY HATTERSLEY IN WALES *(above)*

23. WITH KIM HOWELLS, HYWEL FRANCIS AND DON TOUHIG
    AT THE WALES OFFICE

24. WITH NEIL KINNOCK AND ROMANO PRODI IN SWANSEA

predecessor for one year, while it set up its new structures and personnel. During those twelve months, we appointed new chief officers, and of course new political leaders. The leading members of this new body, which was unsurprisingly strongly Labour, were George Day from Pontypool, Bryn Richards from Cwmbran, and Dennis Puddle from Blaenavon.

Inevitably, I was a very junior member of the council, as was my contemporary Jon Vaughan Jones, a highly intelligent and able Cambridge graduate who was employed by British Steel. It was therefore a singular honour for me to be put onto the Establishment (Personnel) Committee.

I was also made a member of various other committees, and so began my apprenticeship as a councillor. My council membership had some impact on my full-time teaching job, but I was able to arrange my teaching timetable so that most of my college work was done in the mornings.

The expenses regime for councillors in those days was based on the so-called "ten pound allowance" claimed on a daily basis. It proved deeply unpopular with the public, with the result that at the next council elections in 1976 Labour, as the ruling party, was badly hit. We only just managed to retain control.

I began to specialise more in local government finance, an area that I really hadn't expected would interest me. I had never been any good at maths, but this was different. Analysis of the council's budget was much more interesting than it perhaps sounds, and, of course, you would have oversight of everything the council did. The other advantage was that most councillors shied away from this area, and so there was hardly any competition!

I became vice-chairman of the council's Finance Committee. My chairman was Colwyn Little, who represented Abersychan and Garndiffaith. By trade he was an electrician, and ran a local business – he was a bright and effective councillor, and it was a real pleasure to work with him. Colwyn and I had become friends when we both went on a planning visit to Germany – the first time I had ever flown!

The council's treasurer was Ernest Keeley, a Southport man who had held the same job with the old Pontypool urban district council. He was very much an old school chief officer, but none the worse for that, and we worked together until his untimely death some years later. His deputy, who eventually succeeded him, was Garth Edmunds, a younger man who came originally from the Rhondda, and who had been town clerk of Blaenavon urban district council. Innovative and clever, Garth came up with money from all kinds of sources, and we were able to finance some very different projects like the Big Pit Mining Museum in Blaenavon.

In 1977, I became chairman of the finance committee, a position I held until I was elected MP for the valley. It was, in itself, a fascinating and sometimes very challenging job. Under the Thatcher government, when finance was scarce, the decisions we took were more difficult. I had to ensure that the Labour group concentrated on the priorities for the authority, and this sometimes meant making very hard choices. But this was the very stuff of real politics and, for me at least, it was invaluable experience for when I was to become a Minister (which would include being a Finance Minister) many years later. Indeed, serving as a councillor is a wonderful apprenticeship for any MP – you learn how to deal with casework, with issues affecting your ward, and the whole business of representing people in a local democracy.

The annual budget-making exercise was very thorough and ended in my presenting the budget to the full council. It was with the Labour group that the big decisions were made and, of course, I had to work closely with the council leader.

The first council leader I worked with was George Day from Pontypool, a trade unionist who had a brilliant wit and a shrewd intelligence. He was succeeded by Bryn Richards from Cwmbran, who was the AEU convener at the Girling brake factory in Cwmbran. A Welsh-speaker originally from West Wales, he was a bright and very able councillor with enormous experience in local government. Another leading figure was Dennis Puddle from Blaenavon, who was a miner and a long-standing councillor. He was to become leader of the Welsh Local Government Association.

Brian Smith, who was appointed Bryn Richards's deputy, had a particular interest and talent in housing development. He became the chairman of the Housing Development Committee. After a short interval when Ian Jackson was leader, Brian, who had been deputy for Ian as well as Bryn, took over the leadership of Torfaen in 1984, and remained in the role until he died tragically of a brain tumour in 2004.

The Labour councillors I worked with were dedicated and reasonable people who took great pride in representing their constituents. Some were miners, others were steelworkers and engineering workers, while others still were teachers and shopkeepers.

Long before all-women shortlists were introduced in the Labour Party, the Pontypool CLP had produced many notable local women politicians. One great example was Mabel Lee from Pontypool, who was the town's registrar of births, marriages and deaths. Mabel had been a teacher, and became a Pontypool urban district councillor in the 1950s. She was already widowed by the time I knew her, and she was a formidable and effective operator. She was another who had a great interest in housing, and became the mayor and was a leading light in the Labour Women's movement in the valley. Other notable women included Millie Dean from old Cwmbran, one of the great characters of the party; Anne James from

Pontnewydd, who knew everyone in Wales; and there was Phyllis Roberts from Blaenavon. Phyllis has been a great friend to me for well over forty years. The daughter of a leading member of the old South Wales Miners' Federation, she joined the Labour Party in the 1940s. She became a JP, a Blaenavon member of the town, borough and county council, and was deservedly awarded the British Empire Medal when she was 90 for her great work with older people's charities!

I first became aware of Phyllis when I was in the Young Socialists, and she gave us a filmed account of her time as chair of Blaenavon urban district council. In time, we became council colleagues, and she took on the role of being my vice-chairman on the Finance Committee. She succeeded Fred Gifford, who had joined the Cwmbran urban district council in the 1930s and brought great wisdom and experience to the job. Fred had attended West Mon, half a century before I was a pupil there myself!

Phyllis's great friend, especially after she lost her husband Tommy, was Bernice Price. Bernice was a Blaenavon town councillor and the chairman of Blaenavon's twinning committee (the town being linked with Coutras, near Bordeaux). She and Phyllis were also great friends of my father and, for many years, the four of us went on holidays together to France.

The Labour Party and the people of the Eastern Valley owe a great debt to the likes of Phyllis and others who spent their lives in the service of men and women the length and breadth of Torfaen.

The years between 1973 and 1987 saw big changes in my family life. My father completed 25 years with ICI Fibres in Pontypool, and took early retirement in 1981. This allowed my parents to buy their development corporation house. Dad took a porter's job at Boots the Chemist in Cwmbran, which he much enjoyed, and my mother also changed jobs eventually to become a general assistant in the Home Economics department at Fairwater Comprehensive School. She was a star in this role, earning the nickname "Aunty Marj" from the pupils. My brother Neil left West Mon, having completed his "A" Levels, and became a management trainee with Marks & Spencer in Swansea, before taking a sales job with Crookes Anestan, a subsidiary of Boots, where he helped to introduce the new pain-killing drug Nurofen into the UK. This job later took him to the Boots headquarters in Nottingham, and would lead to even more senior positions in the pharmaceutical world.

Life was reasonably comfortable for all of us, and my parents and I became more adventurous in our holidays, travelling to Austria and to Ireland, where we did some ancestor hunting in the county of Cork. Meanwhile, my mother passed her driving test and acquired a car, which gave my parents new horizons and opportunities.

Our last holidays together were in 1983, when we travelled by coach to Sorrento in the summer, and to Bournemouth in the autumn. But, by now, the clouds were gathering.

My mother began to experience breathing problems, and she was diagnosed with lung cancer. Within weeks of diagnosis, she had died at the terribly early age of 55. We were all devastated, but my father was destroyed. He never really got over losing my mother. Her funeral took place on 10 January 1984, in the new Catholic church in Fairwater, and she was buried in the cemetery at Panteg, near Pontypool. Hundreds attended, and a large sum of money was donated to cancer research. It was the most horrific part of my life, and my brother (then 25) and I (aged 35) felt particularly deprived of what should have been an enduring relationship with her for many years to come.

A happier occasion was the wedding of my brother to Claire Sly on 8 April 1985, when I was the best man. Claire was from a well-known Cwmbran family and worked at the Midland Bank in the town centre. The couple owned a relatively new house in Cwmbran. They were later to have two children, Daniel and Rachel.

I also extended my circle of friends in these years. As well as those already mentioned, many new friends were political colleagues, like Jim and Isa Mullin, who came from East Kilbride in Scotland. Jim worked at ICI Fibres, and became first a town councillor, and then the county councillor for Fairwater. Jim was another who died too early, at the age of just 60.

Richard Lewis and his wife Ruth lived in the Coed Eva district of Cwmbran. Richard was completing his PhD at Swansea University, and was very active in local Labour politics (becoming treasurer of the ward party), and Ruth was teaching English at Fairwater School. They moved to Middlesbrough, where Richard lectured in History at Teesside University; Ruth took another teaching job, and became a JP and county councillor. They were to have two children, Jennifer and Daniel.

Meanwhile, Don and Jen Touhig settled into married life in Griffithstown, near Pontypool, and had four children – Matthew, Charlotte, James and Katie. Don was elected a Gwent county councillor, eventually chairing the council's Finance Committee.

During these years, I became very friendly with Stuart Cameron and his wife Pamela, as well as with their four children – Louise, Katherine, Rachel and Allen. Stuart was a year older than me, and worked as the mayor's assistant on the council. He had been an industrial photographer at ICI Fibres, before the research facilities were moved to Harrogate. He came from an established family of butchers in Cwmbran; his father, grandfather and uncles had all entered that trade. After Stuart's father's death in 1994,

I got to know his mother Yvonne and sister Sue very well. Stuart and I shared an interest in chess, a game we often played after council meetings (and which I invariably lost).

John Rogers continued to be a good friend, and we kept up a steady series of visits to classical music concerts. It's now more than four decades since we began to join the audiences every year at the Three Choirs Festival, and in that time, as already noted, other venues have been added to our list. Sadly, John's mother Enid died in 1980, having been diagnosed with breast cancer in the late 1970s; John's father Wilf was to re-marry, some years later, to Nell, his first wife's best friend. After a long and active life, Wilf died in 2003 aged 88.

In 1980, Stuart, Don and I went on a "Euro tour", sponsored by the European Community and the Labour Party. In what was termed "An Information Visit of members of the South East Wales European Parliamentary Constituency", we took in Brussels, Luxembourg, Trier and Antwerp. Among the tour highlights was a drinks reception with the then president of the European Commission, Roy Jenkins. Roy, as I've already mentioned, was an Abersychan boy and keen to hear news from the valley, but he declined to answer Stuart when asked what he intended to do after he left Brussels. It was a memorable – if boozy – occasion!

As far as my personal life was concerned, it was the case that with nearly all my friends married I decided to stay single. Opportunities didn't seem to offer themselves in a turbulent and busy political career, and I have often pondered what life would have been like with a wife and children. I sometimes wonder if the full-time politician, especially in Westminster, can sustain a happy family life – most do, but many marriages fail. I was never to find out!

I shouldn't pass by the early 1970s without mentioning Manu Mehta, a Ugandan Asian barrister who had been forced to flee Malawi during a political crack-down by President Hastings Banda. In 1971, Manu was appointed the town clerk of Pontypool Urban District Council, and then of Torfaen Council. He was a dedicated official, who was to play a significant part in Welsh local government, for which he deservedly received an OBE. A good friend, Manu became the partner of my cousin Diana Telling, who was herself a Torfaen councillor for some time.

Torfaen was a leader among Welsh councils in a number of ways. There were more OAP warden schemes built than in any other Welsh local authority. Economic development played a big part in the council's priorities, and in 1980 I helped secure European Coal and Steel Community funding for the valley (the first time a local authority had ever received such a loan).

The council had put forward a case for a grant for recreation and leisure projects to increase tourism and industrial development. The loan was dependent on our giving jobs to former steelworkers, and it would be at a much lower rate of interest than other loans the council had.

Three of us – Colwyn Little, Garth Edmunds and I – went to the Belgian capital at the suggestion of the South East Wales MEP, Allan Rogers. Ensuring the best chance of securing the money meant making the case directly to the relevant EEC officials. We toured the offices of the European institutions over a couple of days, and met the director-general of the EEC's Regional Fund – I described the meeting as "one of the toughest I had ever experienced".

In April 1980, we learned our bid had been successful, and we obtained a £200,000 loan at an interest rate of 9 per cent (low for the time!) over 25 years. *The Free Press* called it a "scoop for Torfaen", and said that "Torfaen Council is to be congratulated on a piece of fine initiative".

We had to return to Brussels the following year, when we met officials from the directorate general of Regional Policy, Employment and Social Affairs, Information and Economic and Financial Affairs as well as the European Investment Bank. In my report to the council, I concluded that "there can be no doubt that Torfaen Council has made its impact on the EEC and that many contacts have now been established. As long as we remain members of the Common Market, we believe it is imperative that we try to obtain maximum benefits from our membership."

Membership of the council played a hugely important part in my life, and I have never regretted the 14 years I was a local councillor. I fervently believe our democracy is founded on local government, and I pay tribute to all those who contribute to the day-by-day delivery of vital local services.

Cwmbran, of course, was a New Town and had a development corpora-tion. After 1949, the town was developed and expanded over half a century, and my own council ward, Fairwater, grew hugely in population and hous-ing stock. For most of my time as a councillor, the corporation was chaired by Fitzroy, Lord Raglan, a Labour hereditary peer who took the Labour whip in the House of Lords, although he later joined the SDP. He was strongly committed to Cwmbran, and I got on with him very well.

I represented Torfaen on the New Towns Committee of the Association of District Councils, a fascinating job which kept me in touch with New Town councillors from all over England and, when the CDC eventually transferred its assets to the local authority, it enabled me to compare what was happening in Cwmbran with how transfers had taken place elsewhere.

With membership of the council came the opportunity to be a school governor. I officially joined the combined governing body of the three comprehensive schools in Cwmbran at the early age of 22, and once was shown into the room for shortlisted teaching job applicants when I was actually one of the interviewers. I was also a governor of my local primary school, and later of the separate governing body of my local comprehensive school, chairing the governing body for a year. Norman Lease had been the first headmaster of this new high school; he was a member of the Labour Party, and introduced the teaching of Russian at the school, quite a novelty in those days, and many future academics benefited from his decision.

My ambition was to enter parliament, and I had tried to become the candidate for Monmouth (the neighbouring marginal Tory constituency) and for Caerphilly, a safe valley Labour seat. Indeed, I was beaten for the Co-operative Party nomination in Caerphilly by Ednyfed Hudson Davies, the former MP for Conwy, with just one vote separating us. Although Davies had only this single nomination, he went on to be selected. He was another later defector to the SDP.

I had seen that the Wells constituency was looking for a Labour candidate. At 29 years of age, I threw my hat into the ring, and in 1978 was selected. The party official overseeing the election was Jean Corston, who would later serve with me in the Commons as MP for Bristol East, and is now a colleague in the Lords. I was to challenge the sitting Conservative MP in Wells, Robert Boscawen, an old Etonian and government whip, who had been badly injured during the war. The Liberal candidate was Alan Butt Philip, another old Etonian and a university lecturer.

The Wells constituency was huge, an area of more than 300 square miles, and in 1966 Labour had come within 3,500 votes of winning the seat. The constituency was eventually split into two, but at the time in 1978 it covered the towns of Wells, Frome, Street, Bruton, Wincanton, Glastonbury, Shepton Mallet, Castle Cary, and all the hundreds of villages in-between. The campaign was tough going, although the towns all showed reasonable levels of Labour support.

Street included the Clarks shoe factory. The main trade union in the area was the National Union of the Footwear, Leather and Allied Trades (NUFLAT), and its office in the town was to become my General Election HQ.

The party chair was Henry Fair, who had retired to Somerset from London. He had worked for the Woodcraft Folk, a Co-operative version of the Scouts, was a fine socialist and kept the flag flying – especially in his home town of Bruton. Other notable members included Walt Pinnions, who was a TGWU member and town councillor, and Percy Targett. My first agent was Simon Hamilton, who ran a bookshop in Bruton. To drive from Cwmbran to the constituency took almost one and a half hours and I did the journey frequently, but I was young and enthusiastic, and was supported by a committed and loyal party.

Campaigning can be great fun, and I bombarded the local media with stories covering trade unions, family life, the economy and agriculture.

I was brilliantly aided by members of the parliamentary party – including Leo Abse, Joan Lestor and Neil Kinnock – while Lord Fred Peart, the Lord Privy Seal and former Minister of Agriculture, was my guest at the Wells CLP's annual dinner in Wells Town Hall. Prime Minister Jim Callaghan, in a message to the local Party, said: "I know in a constituency such as yours, it is no easy task fighting the Labour cause, but you have in Paul Murphy a young and able candidate with his roots deep in the Labour movement".

Bearing in mind it was covering a rural and Tory constituency, the Wells party was very active and quite well off, although it had only a few local Labour councillors. Members were kept busy raising issues that affected the countryside, and they even produced a party magazine, *Labour Review*. They organised a rally in Bruton, with Joan Lestor and me as the main speakers, and we marched through the East Somerset town led by the Wincanton Silver Band. We were heckled on our way by boys from the local public school! The Bruton party had probably the most active branch, and Henry Fair (who, in addition to his constituency role, was the Bruton branch secretary), received the Labour Party's national award at the annual conference in Blackpool in 1984.

Like all Labour PPCs I made my way to the party's 1978 Blackpool conference. It was the first time I had attended the annual event, and I remember being deeply impressed by Jim Callaghan. That autumn, we all thought Jim would go to the country, but the election didn't happen and we were then faced with the Winter of Discontent. I think Jim should have held an election – Labour might have won – but hindsight is easy. All local parties were on election alert, but it wasn't until 3 May 1979, after the defeat of the Labour government by one vote in a confidence debate in the House of Commons, that the election finally came.

I had fought two council elections in the 1970s, but this was the first time I had contested a parliamentary seat. It was fascinating and often highly enjoyable. I knew I wasn't going to win, but I was carrying the Labour flag and doing my bit to help re-elect a Labour government. I stayed in Somerset for the three weeks of the campaign, and travelled for miles and miles during that time. My agent by this time was Sid Wilshaw from Wincanton, a Midlander who had moved to the South West.

Some months before the election I was involved in a car accident near Milborne Port – I was travelling from canvassing in Wincanton on a country road at dusk, and crashed into an unlit combine harvester crossing the road into a field. The car was a write-off, but, happily, my seat belt saved my life. I was put up for the night by the treasurer of the Wells CLP, Graham Cole, and his lovely wife Pat. Graham, originally from Coventry, was a manager at Westland Helicopters in Yeovil, and a hugely intelligent and able businessman who was eventually appointed both managing director and chairman of Westland, as well as a director of GKN. We became great friends.

The election campaign was lively, touring town and villages and unusually – even then – speaking at public meetings all over the constituency. Our slogans were "Into the Eighties" and "The Labour Way Is the Better Way". My election address read:

> Labour brought Britain successfully out of a crisis in 1974 and has controlled inflation, improved living standards, cut taxes, improved the balance of payments, increased benefits and pensions and acted on prices. It has helped the dairy industry, given more protections to working people, assisted the disabled and handicapped, abolished tied cottages, improved the status of women, and given the British people the final say on our membership of the Common Market.

Some of my campaigning time was spent at factory gates, such as Clarks in Street, or touring factories. On one such occasion, I visited the Morlands sheepskin factory in Glastonbury. It was quite an experience, and very moving to see my campaign stickers attached to the machinery. The owner, Mr Morland, was a Labour supporter, married to a Jewish German who had fled the Holocaust. He lived in a fine house, overlooking the town, and it was the duty of every Labour candidate to take tea with him and his wife, after which a large cheque was given to boost the campaign!

However, the country was in no mood to give Labour a boost, even though many people held Jim Callaghan in high regard. Mrs Thatcher was elected, and was still in office when I became an MP many years later.

I came third behind the Tory and Liberal, with 10,025 votes, which was 16.9 per cent of the total. By the time of the next election in 1983, the constituency boundaries were changed. Much of the old seat became the new Somerton and Frome constituency, with Robert Boscawen as its MP. The new Wells seat was to be represented by David Heathcoat-Amory, another old Etonian! In 1983, as a consequence of the boundary changes, Labour's share of the vote in the revised Wells was squeezed to just 7.8 per cent.

Much of my political career has been tied up with the issue of devolution in Wales – it dominated my time as Secretary of State for Wales, and still plays a big role for me in my capacity as a Welsh peer. My "Welshness" has been a matter of some discussion over the years. I once remarked in a Welsh Grand Committee debate that I didn't look into the mirror in the mornings to see if I was a Welshman – I knew I was Welsh and didn't have to prove it to anyone. Similarly, when I was first appointed as Welsh Secretary, my press officer told me that the Welsh press was asking if I was going to learn to speak Welsh, and I told him to say "no" because I was a Welshman.

I am an English-speaking Welshman, born and bred in Gwent. My Welshness is of the South Wales valleys. It is both radical and proud. Our "talk tidy" accent and dialect is known the world over. We support Welsh rugby, vote Labour and sing. There are a million of us, almost a third of the Welsh nation.

Although Monmouthshire was, perhaps, the most Anglicised of the Welsh counties, the Welsh language with its distinctive Gwent dialect could still be heard there into the twentieth century. And now, of course, there has been a revival of the language, mainly through education and the introduction of Welsh-medium schools.

Welsh was rarely taught in Monmouthshire and, if anything, there was some hostility towards the language. Until 1974, the county was, technically, English, although "South Wales and Monmouthshire" was often used as a term of reference.

The Eastern Valley was peopled by men and women whose ancestors were mostly migrants – from Ireland, Somerset, Gloucestershire, Wiltshire, Staffordshire, and mid- and West Wales. It was an amalgamation of cultures and traditions. The English language was the common denominator, and working-class solidarity was more pronounced than cultural identity. Aneurin Bevan, perhaps our most famous Welshman, was patriotic but cool on any sort of devolution. He once told the Commons: "There are sheep on the Welsh mountains and there are sheep on the mountains of Westmorland and Scotland, but I do not know the difference between a Welsh sheep, a Westmorland sheep and a Scottish sheep."

My successor as MP for Torfaen, Nick Thomas-Symonds, writes, in his fine biography of Nye that "[w]hile Bevan was shaped by the common industrial struggles across the South Wales coalfield, he was a distinctively 'Monmouthshire' figure, a representative of the English-speaking Welsh Valleys, and a proud Welshman".

The issue of devolution began to emerge seriously when the Welsh Council of Labour and a number of Welsh Labour MPs such as John Morris and Cledwyn Hughes began to promote the idea of a Welsh parliament. The Welsh Office had been created in 1964, and this partly addressed the matter. But as the 1970s approached, pressure from devolutionists continued. The Labour government set up the Crowther Commission (later the Kilbrandon Commission) in 1969, and its report in 1974 recommended the establishment of a Welsh Assembly. In the previous ten years, Plaid Cymru had been making progress, with Gwynfor Evans becoming the party's first

MP by winning the 1966 Carmarthen by-election, the party almost taking the constituencies of Caerphilly and Rhondda West in by-elections later in the decade, and gaining two further MPs – Dafydd Wigley in Caernarfon and Dafydd Elis Thomas in Merioneth – in 1974. By 1977, the Labour government had also lost its majority.

In the meantime Labour's anti-devolutionist Welsh Secretary George Thomas had been succeeded by John Morris, a fervent supporter of a Welsh Assembly, when the party returned to power after the Conservative administration of 1970–4. The government brought in a Scotland and Wales Bill in 1976, and this heralded a bitter struggle within Welsh Labour.

The Welsh valleys' Labour MPs were deeply opposed to the creation of a Welsh Assembly, and six MPs assumed prominence – Leo Abse (Pontypool), Neil Kinnock (Bedwellty), Donald Anderson (Swansea East), Fred Evans (Caerphilly), Ioan Evans (Aberdare) and Ifor Davies (Gower). As early as 1975, Caerphilly CLP had started to campaign for a referendum on devolution, which was at that time opposed by the government and by Welsh Labour.

Rebel MPs decided to form the "Labour No Assembly" campaign – Ifor Davies MP became the campaign president and Elfryn Lewis from Gower was the secretary. Neil Kinnock phoned and asked me to be the treasurer, and I gladly accepted the job! In the campaign literature, I was introduced as "a young lecturer in history and government at the North Gwent College of Further Education, Ebbw Vale". The introduction went on, "He is Secretary of the Pontypool Constituency Labour Party, Chairman of Torfaen Borough Council's Finance Committee and Prospective Parliamentary Labour Candidate for Wells in Somerset. He has been a member of the Labour Party since the age of 15."

My job was to coordinate the fund-raising efforts of the campaign and to keep the accounts. We set up an account with the Co-operative Bank, and raised thousands of pounds all over Wales. Looking back at the records today, I can see donations from Pontllanfraith, Amanford, Cardiff, Neath, Penarth, Caernarfon, Wrexham, Newbridge, Aberystwyth, Pontypridd, Rumney, Briton Ferry, Abertillery, Swansea, Llanidloes, Newport, Roath, Bristol, Gorseinon, Port Talbot, Blackwood, Mumbles, Aberdare, Cwmbran, New Tredegar and Blaenau Ffestiniog – opposition to the Assembly proposals was clearly not confined to the Welsh valleys, and Welsh local government too was often vehemently against devolution.

The campaign set out a detailed case for its position. It produced a ten-point manifesto called "Facts to Beat the Fantasies", which argued that devolution would cost £20 million; it would diminish local government, fracture the UK, put at risk a majority Labour government, and would be a sell-out to nationalism. A press release of 7 December 1978 opened with:

Throughout the Labour Movement in Wales, there is strong rank-and-file opposition to the proposals of the Wales Act, 1978, to establish the Assembly. That opposition reflects the opinion held by vast numbers of Labour supporters that the proposals are a costly, risky and unnecessary attempt to appease Nationalism, which has nothing to do with the real social, economic, political and cultural problem of Wales.

The release went on to defend the rights of Labour Party members to disagree with the party line, and argued for everyone to respect "honest disagreement on moral and constitutional matters". It emphasised that the campaign relied financially on "voluntary effort", and continued "we have no major public or private organisational funds from either side of industry at our disposal".

The campaign was very well organised, with coordinators in each Welsh county. Neil Kinnock wrote to all supporters urging them to give press interviews, attend meetings and write letters to the newspapers. I did my bit by writing to the *Western Mail*, outlining the potential costs of devolution, and the *Western Mail* editor headed the letter: "Better ways to spend £20 million".

Meetings were held all over Wales and attracted hundreds of supporters. I particularly remember a meeting in Abertillery when the local MP, Jeffrey Thomas, stayed away while nearly all his CLP members attended. The meetings held in Torfaen were very lively events. Leo Abse specialised in the "threat", as he saw it, of a "Welsh-speaking elite" dominating Welsh politics. I spoke myself on a number of occasions and highlighted not just the cost of the Assembly but also the danger of having devolution confined to Wales and Scotland. If, I argued, devolution was about democracy, why then did we not want devolution for the English regions?

In parliament, Neil Kinnock and Leo Abse managed both to get a separate Welsh Bill on the devolution proposals and to secure a referendum on the matter. When the referendum was held in 1979, with the Labour government under Jim Callaghan campaigning for a "Yes" vote, there was a "No" vote in every Welsh county. In Torfaen, the vote against devolution was overwhelming. Devolution was, for the time being, a non-issue in Wales. Plaid Cymru withdrew its previous support for the government, which was then defeated on a vote of confidence in the House of Commons. Labour lost the resulting General Election, and we were to endure eighteen years of Tory administration.

As time went on, people changed their minds. The reality of almost two decades of Conservative rule, especially in Wales where there was still a majority of Labour MPs, had an effect on people's view of devolution. More, the rise of the quangos – quasi-autonomous non-governmental organisations, unelected public bodies which ran many services in Wales

– was deeply resented, especially since they were staffed by Tory appointees. Even in the valleys, views on devolution changed – including my own!

The experience of being a parliamentary candidate in 1979 had been exciting and valuable. So I embarked on the milk-round of seeking another – winnable – constituency to contest at the next election, which took place in June 1983. The closest I came to selection was Farnworth, near Bolton, which was a safe Labour seat held since 1979 by John Roper. John joined the SDP, and later became a member of the House of Lords. The resulting vacancy was advertised in *Labour Weekly*, and I wrote to the local party. Local party activist Steve Hutchinson worked tirelessly for me, but I lost the nomination by just one vote to Terry Lewis (whom I got to know well when I entered the House of Commons). Terry was elected in 1983 for the new constituency of Worsley, with a majority of just over 4,000.

I persevered, and applied for other seats – Oxford East, Gower, Woolwich, Bristol North East, and Cardiff North; I also put myself forward for the European parliamentary seat of South East Wales, which was eventually held by Llew Smith.

In the end I never managed to stand at the 1983 General Election and, by 1985, had started to look for another opportunity. I applied for the Bridgend constituency, but withdrew my name in September 1985 when my own MP, Leo Abse, announced that he was to retire. Leo had represented the constituency for more than 27 years, and had been a hugely successful and distinguished Labour back-bench MP. The legislation he initiated through his private members' bills changed the law on a large range of social and family issues – including homosexuality, divorce and adoption. As a national figure, Leo would be a very hard act to follow.

As I had spent my adult life in Torfaen and had been so heavily involved in local politics, it was obvious that I should try for the seat.

My first task was to secure my shortlisting for the candidacy. I wrote to all party and trade union branches in October, emphasising my local connections and the work I had done in the party and on the local authority. I also referred to my time as a parliamentary candidate. I appealed to the trade unionists and to the women in the party, writing about my mother and her membership of USDAW, and of my grandmother, noting the struggles that both of them had faced in their time: "I have no other ambition than to represent our people to the best of my ability." My closing comments stated: "Together, we must work towards a Socialist Commonwealth which has been the hope of all working people – men and women – of this valley since they first sent Tom Griffiths to the House of Commons almost seventy years ago."

The battle for the nomination was to be extremely tough and often bitter. Selections in safe Labour valley seats occurred very infrequently, and the competition would be fierce. While I benefited from my deep roots in the constituency, a local candidate can often suffer because of local battles in the party, and I was to prove no exception to the rule. One year earlier, the Labour group on the council had split because of leadership issues and, inevitably, this impacted upon the selection process. In the end, only three candidates were shortlisted – myself, Jon Vaughan Jones and Joan Ruddock.

Jon was a very able and talented Cambridge graduate, and was my assistant secretary on the CLP. He was popular with the members and was a very effective county councillor, chairing the authority's finance committee. We were friends and we respected each other's interest in the seat. Jon was the research officer for the Wales Labour Party, and eventually joined the National Audit Office; he was to die at a very young age.

The other shortlisted contender was Joan Ruddock, the talented and well-known chair of CND. She was a Pontypool girl who had gone to Imperial College, London, and certainly had a legitimate claim on the seat. Her main support came from those in the local party who did not want to see me as their MP.

I organised my own shortlisting campaign on military lines. My chief strategist was Ray Morgan who, as well as having been Leo's agent, was a vastly experienced trade union fixer, and his expertise and knowledge were invaluable. We gathered a great team around me – Don Touhig, John Cunningham, Stuart Cameron, Brian Smith, John Turner, Terry Davies and many others – and concentrated on getting nominations and support from party branches and trade unions, and on canvassing all members of the party's general management committee, which would make the final choice. It was hard going, but only meticulous attention to detail would give us the victory. Meetings of branches were critically important and, as was the case for all candidates, I had had to speak at them. I received the largest number of nominations, and Jon, Joan and I learned of the outcome on Tuesday, 3 December; the formal selection meeting would be held on Friday, 6 December, at St James's Hall, Pontypool.

The meeting was the most stressful I had ever attended. The stakes were high and the previous two months had been hectic. We had done as much as we could, and it was now up to me to give the speech of my life. I still have my notes for the speech – it lasted about ten minutes. I talked of my experience as a parliamentary candidate, and emphasised the need for a local person to fill the role; I referred to life under a Thatcher government, and concluded by quoting Clement Attlee, who told the party in 1945 that "[w]e must go out for political power so that we might have a socialist government to reconstruct Britain and to play our part in bringing about the universal brotherhood of man." The speech was well received, but I'm not sure what difference it made; literally all 110 party members in that room had by this time made up their minds.

I won on the second ballot – Joan Ruddock was the runner-up, and went on to become the MP for Deptford and, later, a successful Minister in the Labour government.

When I returned to the hall to be told of my win in the ballot, I was given a very moving and tumultuous reception, with some members standing on their seats and applauding. I now had under two years to nurse the constituency, and also to heal the party rifts that inevitably arise when selection processes are rare.

I had many letters of congratulation, including one from councillor Peter Law from Blaenau Gwent, who said: "I have for a long time felt that we in these valley constituencies should give more opportunities to our local people, particularly those such as yourself . . . there are all too often too many 'carpet baggers' around . . .". It was a portent for the future, when Labour in the Blaenau Gwent constituency would fail to select Peter as their parliamentary candidate, a move that led to the Party's losing the seat.

The eighteen months between my selection and the General Election were very busy – learning the new skills I would need as an MP. My council experience was invaluable, but there was still much to absorb! I visited Leo in the Commons, attended his constituency surgeries, and involved myself in a host of different local activities. I listed some in a report to the CLP: "Opening Cwmbran Trade Fair; attending Pontypool RFC matches; attending the Annual Social of Pontnewydd AFC, the TGWU Annual Dinner, Torfaen District Scout AGM, the Cwmbran Gymnastics Annual Presentation, the retirement service of the Rector of Cwmbran, Armistice Parades and the Cwmynyscoy Homing Pigeon Society's annual presentation . . .". I was also involved in local campaigns, visiting factories and OAP groups in the valley.

Even though Torfaen was considered safe Labour ground, I was privileged to have had a number of leading party figures visit the constituency – Michael Foot MP; Gerald Kaufman MP; Barry Jones MP; Jo Richardson MP; and Llew Smith MEP.

Just before Christmas 1985, at the start of my time as PPC for Torfaen, Gareth Hill of the *Free Press* interviewed me, and kindly headlined the article: "Socialist with 'My Valley' at Heart". It was a sympathetic piece, and reading it again, thirty-odd years later as I write this book, is a strange experience. In the interview, I stressed my local links, discussed the effects of the miners' strike which had ended earlier that year, defended Neil Kinnock on his handling of the Militant Tendency, and aired some views on Catholicism. When Gareth asked me where I stood politically, I explained that when I was on the shortlist for Gower I was regarded as a candidate of the left, and when I was involved in the selection for Cardiff North I was seen as a candidate of the right!

Although Labour had a majority of just over 8,000 (very modest by normal standards in the constituency) at the 1983 General Election, Torfaen people were essentially loyal to the party. During the miners' strike, there was huge sympathy for the colliers and their families, and as chairman of the finance committee I did all I could legally to ensure our community didn't suffer.

When Mrs Thatcher called the election for 11 June 1987, we were ready in the Eastern Valley. I was fortunate that Ray Morgan was now my own agent, continuing the role he had performed for my predecessor, and he and his team worked tremendously hard – we treated the constituency as if it were a marginal seat. The Liberal candidate, Graham Blackburn, had achieved a relatively high vote in 1983, and he seriously thought he could win this time. We put out literally thousands of posters, knocked on thousands of doors, organised a huge car cavalcade down the valley on the Saturday before the election, and held a rousing pre-election day rally at St James's Hall in Pontypool, where Leo spoke and we all sang *The Red Flag* led by mayor Dave Lloyd on the piano.

I became the fifth Labour MP for the Torfaen area in 69 years, and as the *Free Press* said: "The Eastern Valley emphatically lives up to its reputation as a Socialist stronghold." Compared with the result in 1983, we doubled the Labour majority with 17,550 votes. The Liberals lost 3,000 votes, the Conservatives dropped 1,000, Jill Evans for Plaid Cymru picked up only 600, and the Green candidate managed just 450 votes – it was a triumph for the Torfaen CLP. During my speech after the count, as I reflected on the national result, I blamed the Lib-SDP Alliance for splitting the anti-Tory vote and for letting Mrs Thatcher back into Downing Street.

Our pile of ballot papers stretched more than half way across the leisure centre's main hall by the time the count was over, and I jumped over them – a reckless act, to be sure, but caught on camera! Elsewhere in my speech I referred to the ballot papers, which I said were "not just pieces of paper, but people waiting to go into hospital, people who don't have jobs or hopes for jobs, people who don't have homes".

Unfortunately, the result in Torfaen was not repeated across the country, and the Tories returned to power with a majority of 102.

The following week, the director of education for Gwent, Geoffrey Drought, wrote to me: "Thank you for your letter dated 15 June 1987, informing me of your decision to resign from your lecturing post at the Ebbw Vale College of Further Education. I accept the unusual circumstance which has caused your hurried departure."

Opposition
1987–1997

IT WAS LIKE STARTING in a new school. New rules, new offices, new people, new job. The triumphant M4 group of new South Wales Labour MPs – Alun Michael, Rhodri Morgan, Paul Flynn, Win Griffiths, Alan W. Williams and I – all went to London on the same train. A BBC film crew travelled with us, gathering footage for a documentary, *Journey to Westminster*. We sang *The Red Flag* on Newport and Cardiff station platforms, and all six of us walked into the House of Commons at the same time. We took our oaths, sat for the first time on the famous green benches, and then went back to our constituencies – only to return for the Queen's opening of parliament on 25 June 1987. We were six out of 120 new MPs.

We then had to get down to practicalities, acquiring an office and a secretary. For weeks, I hand-wrote letters in the House of Commons library, and stored my essentials in a locker in the dining room corridor (which I kept for almost thirty years). I now have a similar locker a few yards down the same corridor, but in the House of Lords. The Labour whip responsible for allocating offices was Sir Ray Powell, MP for Ogmore, who was a parliamentary legend and very kind to his fellow Welsh MPs. Some new MPs had to wait a long time for offices (including Ken Livingstone, who had referred to "provincial" MPs in a less than flattering way), but we were lucky. Alun, Rhodri, Paul and I were given a large office in Old Palace Yard, adjacent to Westminster Abbey and opposite the House of Lords. We were joined by John McFall, Elliot Morley and Eric Illsley. So, seven of us shared this one office and, for private telephone calls, had to make do with a telephone box outside. I have now returned to the same building three decades on!

Although we were in a crowded office, mutual proximity proved to be beneficial. We learned the job together and from each other's mistakes, as well as of our small parliamentary triumphs. We were good friends and dined, laughed and gossiped together, and were never lonely in the Palace of Westminster – which can often be the experience for new MPs – and we were nearly all Welsh!

I quickly made friends with John McFall, the new MP for Dumbarton. John had been a deputy headmaster in a large comprehensive school in Glasgow, and had taught my namesake and later the Scottish Secretary Jim Murphy. John was a chemist (a vocation that, coincidentally, he shared with Vernon Hewlett, the principal of the college where I myself had taught), but he had other degrees in education too. Eventually, John was appointed a shadow Minister and, in government, parliamentary under-secretary at the Northern Ireland Office (NIO) and later still became a very distinguished chair of the Commons Treasury Committee. His wife Joan was a primary school teacher, and my father and I enjoyed our visits to John and his family in Scotland. Other friends from those early days included Doug Henderson, a Scots Newcastle MP who was to become a Foreign and Defence Minister; and Mo Mowlam, the charismatic MP for Redcar (of whom more anon). Locally, Roy Hughes, MP for Newport East, was also to be a great friend. Roy was a Pontllanfraith boy who found work in the car industry in Coventry, where he became a TGWU official, before returning to South Wales as MP for Newport. My other Gwent neighbours were Neil Kinnock (Islwyn) and Michael Foot (Blaenau Gwent), both in their time leaders of the Labour Party.

I needed an office in the constituency. Leo had never had one, but parliamentary allowances would pay the cost. I acquired a base at Bristol House, Pontnewynydd, and later, at the Clarence, Pontypool, before ending up at the local TGWU office in Trosnant, Pontypool. I also gained a new secretary, Irene Fowler. Irene, who was of Italian descent, proved to be both able and very popular in the valley. She would be helped by Bev Miller and Pam Cameron in the years ahead. Computers were the new thing and we obtained one of these fascinating devices – as well as a fax machine, which we showed off to party members, who marvelled at its magical qualities.

Only a couple of years into my first parliament, my agent, the hugely competent and hard-working Ray Morgan, died. His untimely end was devastating to all – he and I had been great friends and fellow trade unionists, and I gave the eulogy at his funeral. Ray was succeeded by another friend, John Cunningham, a councillor for Upper Cwmbran. John had contracted polio as a child, and throughout his life has done much good work for our disabled citizens, for which he was deservedly awarded the MBE. John was to become a leading member of the new Torfaen County Borough Council, and remained as my very effective agent until I retired in 2015. John's wife Pat also became a great friend.

A new MP has to build up a profile in his constituency, and I was no exception despite having been a councillor in Torfaen for fourteen years.

I held advice surgeries up and down the valley, visited local schools and factories and maintained a close relationship with Torfaen Council, aided by my friend Brian Smith, leader of the council. Having lived all my life in Torfaen, it was easier for me than for MPs who had to get to know their constituencies for the first time.

I made my maiden speech in the House of Commons on Friday, 3 July 1987, in a debate on tourism. I naturally paid tribute to my predecessor Leo Abse, and to my valley. I referred to the commitment of the Welsh valleys to Democratic Socialism; to the achievements of the 1945–51 Labour governments; and to the Monmouthshire education system, which had allowed me as a miner's son to develop. I told the House that the welfare state and equal opportunities – both long supported in the valleys – had been eroded under the Tories and that 2,000 people in Torfaen were homeless. I attacked the poll tax (which I described as "the curiously-misnamed Community Charge"), and lamented the fact that 6,000 people were out of work in the Eastern Valley (2,000 of whom were under the age of 25). I accused the government of having "no conception of how ordinary people live", and argued that the "great" in Britain is defined by the way citizens are treated. I added that "if regions such as mine are ignored, they are ignored at the Government's peril", and that the people of Torfaen would be insulted if the situation continued.

John Butterfill, the MP for Bournemouth, spoke after me and congratulated me on the speech and how it continued in a tradition of oratory from the Welsh valleys. I learned later that Gordon Brown had stepped into the Chamber to listen. The *Free Press* remarked: "The speech was hailed as one of a number of first class maiden speeches with one MP saying Mr Murphy 'seemed to equal the mellifluous tones of Leo Abse'". The Minister for Tourism, John Lee MP, wound up the debate and described the speech as "eloquent and outstanding", adding: "I can pay him no higher tribute than to say he is as eloquent as his leader, and perhaps he has the added advantage of a degree of brevity."

The local press also received the speech well, running such headlines as: "My People Want Hope – Murphy"; "Don't ignore regions plea by new MP"; "Insult to South Wales"; and "Murphy pleads for the region". The essence of what I said was that the consensus over the economy and the welfare debate, built up over forty years, was being destroyed by the Thatcher government. It was a theme I was to return to time and time again in later speeches in parliament.

On 31 July 1987, the *South Wales Argus* profiled the two new Gwent MPs – the two Pauls (and how we were mistaken for each other in the thirty years to come). The interviewer was veteran journalist Martin Mason, who was very kind to the two of us. We told him that we both found the work of an MP very tiring but hugely enjoyable, and that we had both spoken on the Welsh Grand Committee. I admitted that as an MP I had far less power than I did in my old role as the chair of the council's finance committee, but I conceded that I had much more influence. Martin Mason thought we had pulled off our first coup by getting a shared office in Old Palace Yard – "Typically," he wrote, "the office door has pinned to it a notice announcing: 'You are now entering little Wales beyond England.'"

My first speeches in the House of Commons were on local government finance, the forthcoming poll tax and urban development corporations – subjects all reflecting my previous experience. My first oral question was to Ian Grist, the Junior Welsh Office Minister and MP for Cardiff North, on the ReChem hazardous waste incineration plant in Pontypool. I had researched the subject well, but read out the question. I was told I shouldn't do this – it had to be just a written note. Later, when I asked my first question as a Shadow Minister, I was encouraged to read my question – such is the strange way of parliament!

In April 1988, the shadow Welsh Secretary Alan Williams, MP for Swansea West, asked Neil Kinnock if I could be his parliamentary private secretary (PPS). Alan sent me a note with an attached letter from Neil, which said: "You might like to have this for your autobiography!" Neil had confirmed that he was very happy to see me as Alan's PPS, adding "as you know, I consider him to be a great asset". Alan told the Welsh press:

> It's mine and Neil Kinnock's way of saying this is a man who we consider can go far in the Labour Party. I need someone with a safe pair of political hands to work with me. My post takes me out of the House a lot, and I spend lots of time in Wales, so I need someone who can keep a check on parliamentary business. I was impressed with Paul's very detailed work on the Poll Tax Committee.

Alan Williams was a veteran Labour MP, and a former Minister of State in the 1974–9 Labour government. A Privy Counsellor, he was one of Wales's most senior MPs and was appointed shadow Welsh Secretary in July 1987. He was great to work with, and he could not have been more helpful to me. He shadowed Thatcher's new Welsh Secretary, Peter Walker, the MP for Worcester, a notorious "wet" in Thatcher's Cabinet.

Checking back over thirty years, I came across many instances when I attacked Walker on a number of Welsh issues, notably the poll tax. I think I over-did the opposition and anger, since Walker's views were, by Thatcher's standards, very liberal. But I was a young new MP, and Walker was the

Tory target. Such headlines as "Murphy attacks Walker" were frequent and I suppose my job was to oppose, but I am not sure I would have been so aggressive in later years!

Walker had two Junior Ministers: Ian Grist (another mild-mannered and one nation Tory); and Wyn Roberts, the Minister of State for Wales and MP for Conwy. Roberts was to become the longest-serving Minister in the Conservative governments of Thatcher and John Major – a Welsh Office Minister for 18 years! I always got on with him. Again, he was more of a consensual politician than most Conservative MPs and, eventually, I shadowed him for over six years.

The poll tax was a flagship policy of the Thatcher government. It was meant as a fairer local tax to replace the rating system, but it was deeply flawed and hugely unpopular – not least among many Tory MPs – and was to prove the reason for Thatcher's eventual downfall.

The Environment and Local Government Secretary Nicholas Ridley, an old-fashioned right-winger, was charged with introducing the new tax and steering its legislation through parliament. I was appointed to the standing committee on the tax, and it was there that I learned my legislative trade. So important was this legislation to the government that, unusually, Ridley as Secretary of State and his formidable deputy Michael Howard (later to be Home Secretary and leader of the Conservative Party) both sat on the standing committee. Such committees deal with the line-by-line scrutiny of a bill, and this was a huge and controversial one. The committee sat for three days a week, and often through the night, certainly a baptism of fire for all, but still great experience.

Thousands of amendments to the bill were tabled, but the government usually defeated the opposition ones. Untypically, I was successful in moving an amendment (with Julian Brazier, MP for Canterbury) exempting monks and nuns from the tax! I suggested, during the debate on the issue, that Michael Howard "should go into contemplative retreat in a religious community for one week to consider his response!"

As a result of having served on the committee, I was chosen to head Labour's Welsh campaign against the tax. At meeting after meeting up and down the country, I argued that the poll tax would have a disproportionate and adverse effect on Wales, and told the Welsh press:

Out of 37 districts in Wales, 25 will be worse off because of the poll tax. In Wales, for every 1% increase in expenditure by local authorities, there will be a 6% increase in tax. Households with a single adult would pay 10% more; with two adults 119% more; with three 229% more; and an extra 339% with four adults.

I was the only Welsh Labour MP on the standing committee, out of a total of 44 MPs, and I kept on stating that the rich would get richer and the poor would get poorer if the tax came into force. In the end, it was introduced and proved to be the disaster we had all predicted in Wales. After Walker left the Welsh Office, I continued (by then as a shadow Welsh Office Minister) to attack the government – now represented by David Hunt MP, the new Welsh Secretary. In his first appearance at the despatch box as Secretary of State, David Hunt called me "a self-appointed expert on the poll tax". The comment went down badly across the House, and writing in the *Western Mail* about the exchange, Kim Howells commented:

> This was a slur too far. It is no secret that had a certain shadow Minister relied less on their academic advisers and more on the likes of Mr Murphy, to draw up Labour's alternative to the poll tax, we might have had a perfectly viable one by now. His expertise on the subject was recognised by Neil Kinnock, who gave him his first front-bench appointment. A roar went up of "Ref, that's not fair".

I subsequently found David Hunt to be a reasonable and courteous opponent, whose feelings for Wales were more genuine than those expressed by some of his ministerial colleagues.

Early in my parliamentary career, before becoming a front-bencher, I was appointed a member of the standing committee of a private bill to consider Hampshire County Council's proposals for a by-pass around Lyndhurst in the New Forest. It was a very controversial subject – on the one hand there was the fact that traffic was (and is) extremely heavy during the summer and blocks up the town; and conversely, there was the argument that the New Forest, now a national park, was an area of outstanding natural beauty. The *Western Mail* reported on my enforced membership of the Private Bill Committee, which it regarded as a stint which all new MPs have to do; the bill procedure amounted to what was, in effect, a public inquiry, with barristers appearing for and against the proposals. The committee was chaired by Nigel Spearing, Labour MP for West Ham, and its deliberations took a number of months. In the end, we recommended that the by-pass should not go ahead. I was myself to chair a similar Private Bill Committee, which went on for only a few weeks, on horse riding in Epping Forest!

One of the side effects of my being on the Lyndhurst Committee was that I befriended an extremely pleasant and highly capable Conservative member, Gillian Shephard, MP for South West Norfolk. A former teacher and schools' inspector, and an Oxford graduate, Gillian agreed to be my pair in the House of Commons. We got on famously and remained pairs until that system ended. Leo Abse had advised me to find a pair who was of the same age and with the same majority, and Gillian and I almost met Leo's criteria!

When Gillian became a Minister at the Department of Social Security, mine was the first oral question addressed to her. I asked her if 16- and 17-year-old claimants should be interviewed and automatically assessed for severe hardship benefit. She replied that some claims would be handled "more effectively and sympathetically", and that improvements would be made in the training of staff who handled young people's claims. The two of us had agreed our position on both question and answer beforehand! That exchange, incidentally, was the first oral question in the House of Commons to be broadcast on television.

My early interventions and questions in the House were inevitably about Wales, local government finance and education. I also spoke on the subject of urban development corporations, since the Cwmbran Development Corporation was in my constituency.

The shadow Welsh front bench was in some turmoil, with the result that Roy Hughes MP, deputy to shadow Welsh Secretary Alan Williams, resigned "only too readily" as he put it. In November 1988, Neil Kinnock appointed me as shadow Welsh Office Minister, along with Alun Michael, MP for Cardiff South and Penarth. We worked for the new shadow Welsh Secretary Barry Jones, MP for Alyn and Deeside, and a former Minister under John Morris at the Welsh Office. The leader's office said the new appointments were "a reward for many of the younger MPs who had performed well on the back benches". Rhodri Morgan was made a Junior Energy spokesman, while Alan Williams became shadow Deputy Leader of the House; Paul Flynn was appointed shadow Social Security Minister. The *South Wales Argus* praised Paul and me: "Torfaen's Paul Murphy is another new Gwent MP who has obviously caught the eye of his leader (and neighbour)! He, too, has represented his constituency with energy and diligence, and has been rewarded". The newspaper also rightly pointed out, "to be blunt, there was not that much new blood in Labour's ranks last time around", and added that Labour in that period was "not exactly awash with scintillating, talented new boys and girls!"

Others from the 1987 intake who found themselves on the new front bench included Hilary Armstrong, Alistair Darling, Mo Mowlam and David Blunkett. I had been in the Commons for 18 months, and from that point on was to serve a total of 20 years on Labour's shadow or government ministerial team.

My new boss as shadow Welsh Secretary, Barry Jones, was (and is) a remarkable politician, He is the son of a former Labour Party agent, and Labour through and through. In 1983, he held his constituency when many in similar circumstances had been lost to the Tories; holding his seat in

1983 was testimony to his popularity and hard work. His time as a Minister in the 1970s had given him rare experience amongst those on the front bench, and his political antennae were unique.

My colleague Alun Michael had entered parliament with me in 1987 – we shared an office and many values. A North-Walian, Alun had been a journalist and a youth worker, and had been chair of his council's finance committee, as I had been of Torfaen's; he was an astute and hugely hard-working MP, who was eventually to become a Home Office and Agriculture Minister, Welsh Secretary and the inaugural First Minister of Wales. On the 1988 shadow Welsh front bench, Alun looked after the health brief, as well as economic issues and the Welsh language, while I had responsibility for local government, environment and education.

Barry led us with great energy, and we travelled the length and breadth of Wales. Altogether, we had a territorial instead of a UK brief, and this could sometimes hinder career prospects. However, we enjoyed the compensation of having a distinctive Welsh press and broadcasting media, and we gained enormous experience through our regular appearances on television and radio. We had a very special relationship with people in Welsh local government and education, and with our fellow Welsh MPs – parliament allowed for Welsh distinctiveness by having Welsh Questions, Welsh Day debates, and a Welsh Grand Committee. A Select Committee on Welsh Affairs now existed too – the first chair of which was my own predecessor, Leo Abse. I served on the committee for a short time when it was chaired by the Gower MP Gareth Wardell, again gathering valuable experience.

Our opponents in the Chamber were Welsh Secretary Peter Walker, with Ian Grist and Wyn Roberts: after Peter Walker, chronologically, David Hunt, John Redwood and William Hague were to follow as secretaries of state. Although the Conservatives did have Welsh MPs in junior Welsh roles – later examples being Nicholas Bennett (Pembrokeshire) Roger Evans (Monmouth) and Gwilym Jones (Cardiff North) – all the Welsh secretaries represented seats in England. This fact was especially noticeable in John Redwood's case; his seat was in the Home Counties, and he incurred infamy for sending back unused government funding that had been earmarked for Wales!

My first speech in the Chamber from the front bench was late at night in December 1988, in a debate on the rate support settlement for Wales. It was a lively occasion, since most government MPs had dined well and were very boisterous! It was, however, a fine introduction to the sharp end of a shadow front bencher's role!

I had to do my share of committee work, including a period serving on the Environment Bill (where I worked with Ann Taylor MP) and on local government finance (with David Blunkett MP). On one occasion, I was sitting in the Chamber next to David when his dog became agitated. David asked me to take the dog to the leader's office just down the corridor, which I did; some ten minutes later I received a message to go and fetch a very unhappy and strong dog who dragged me back into the Chamber . . . watched by all MPs, the Speaker and the people sitting in the visitors' gallery. David asked if all was well, and I replied: "Fine!"

In 1990, the *Wales on Sunday* newspaper compiled a Welsh "TV Star Chamber", in which I appeared: "Not perhaps an immediately obvious choice, given his slightly lugubrious appearance, but he has impressed with his quick thinking performance plus clear and concise speech in the Chamber". Another newspaper referred to the "dry sense of humour" I had shown when I replied to Welsh Office Minister Nicholas Bennett's speech: "If one removes the beginning and the end of the speech of the Honourable Member for Pembroke, and then extracts much of what he said in the middle, I would find little with which to disagree!"

During this time as shadow Welsh Office Minister, many controversial and important issues faced me. I took on Peter Walker's so-called valley initiative, which, though well-intentioned, was a repackaging of schemes already announced or which were already actually happening. I spoke on housing and education and, under Ann Taylor MP, scrutinised the Environment Protection Bill as it went through its Commons stages. Dominating my time was local government finance, and I spoke in the Commons on the rate support settlement for Wales, the Unified Business Rate and the valuation of domestic properties. The poll tax was still a huge issue, and we opposed it at every opportunity.

Two other pieces of legislation loomed large in 1992: the Severn Bridges Bill and the Cardiff Bay Barrage Bill. The former resulted from the government's decision to build a second Severn crossing in order to relieve the pressure on the first bridge that had opened in September 1966. The new one was to be built privately, with tolls on both, which continued until December 2018. Legislation was required, and I led from the opposition front bench. We generally supported the bill, but raised specific concerns, such as the level of tolls.

The Barrage Bill was more controversial. Nicholas Edwards – by this time Lord Crickhowell – had initiated the idea of developing Cardiff Bay. Today, Cardiff Bay is a lovely place, central to the city's economy and home to the Welsh Assembly. However, in 1992 it looked very different – Rhodri Morgan, MP for Cardiff West, and many valleys MPs were against the idea of creating a barrage, believing that it would cause flooding in parts of the city and have an adverse effect on bird life. Additionally, MPs from outside Cardiff were concerned at the concentration of spending in one place to the detriment of poorer parts of Wales.

However, as MP for Cardiff South and Penarth, Alun Michael backed the scheme and a memorable parliamentary battle ensued. Bills came and went and, on one famous occasion, the Commons sat through the night and the Bill was "talked out". I was told, as the relevant opposition spokesman, to sit on the front bench and say absolutely nothing, so divided was the Labour Party on the subject. I dutifully remained in my place overnight, sleeping for an hour at some point, and reward came in the form of a new office from the relevant whip, Ray Powell. From now, I was to be on my own in Abbey Gardens! I spoke on a number of occasions on amendments to the proposed legislation and, eventually, the bill passed.

In the constituency, a variety of issues occupied me during these years. One was a controversy briefly touched upon in the opening chapter of this book. The Gwent Health Authority wanted to close the Cefn Ila maternity unit at Panteg hospital, a move bitterly opposed by me and by the entire valley. Protest marches and demonstrations took place, and I was even threatened with eviction at a public meeting. But, despite early day motions in parliament and almost universal opposition, the unit was moved to the Royal Gwent Hospital in Newport.

We were luckier on the future of St Alban's, the Catholic comprehensive school in Pontypool. Gwent County Council wanted to close it, but there was a determined campaign against the proposal. Don Touhig (at that time a Gwent county councillor) was disciplined by the Labour group on the council for opposing the closure – he received a Papal knighthood for his stand a few months later – and in the end the school was spared. It was a different outcome for Trevethin comprehensive school, however, which occupied the premises of the old county grammar school for girls, and was experiencing a severe fall in pupil numbers. I did my best to save it, but the closure went ahead.

During this period, there was also mounting resentment over the growth of "quangocracy". In 1989, I questioned Welsh Office Minister Wyn Roberts about the jobs of those individuals running public bodies in Wales ("quangos"), and was told that Peter Walker had made such appointments on forty occasions. Colonel Geoffrey Inkin, a top Conservative in Wales, was chairman of both the Land Authority for Wales and the Cardiff Bay Development Corporation (and had previously been chairman of the Cwmbran Development Corporation, succeeding Lord Raglan, after the Tories took office at the 1979 General Election). Other Conservatives held a number of such jobs, and rarely were individuals with Labour allegiances appointed to these senior positions. As Welsh local government was mainly Labour, and more people in Wales voted socialist than for any other party, the issue became increasingly controversial as the years went by. It was one of the reasons why, after substantially rejecting devolution in the 1979 referendum, people in Wales changed their views on the subject when they were asked again in 1997 (it was the "democratic deficit" argument).

In Cwmbran, the development corporation wielded great power. Increasingly, there were calls to hand over the CDC's assets to the local authority, but only housing assets were actually transferred. The New Town's shopping centre (a regional one) was privatised, and the industrial assets went to the Welsh Development Agency – in other words, the liabilities went to the council!

My relations with the CDC were, however, generally good (although we sometimes disagreed on policy), but those with my local authorities were excellent. I had, of course, been a member of Torfaen Borough Council, and I knew virtually all the members and officers of the Gwent County Council. Additionally, my four community councils (Blaenavon, Pontypool, Cwmbran and Henllys) were always helpful. I believed strongly in a vibrant local government system, and my front bench role kept me in touch with Welsh local government in general.

Much of my case work was effectively local government business, and it was vital that the MP and the local authorities worked well together, especially before the advent of devolution.

One of the areas we collaborated on was economic development. The nature of employment in Torfaen was changing very quickly. When I became a councillor in 1973, people were employed in coal mining, steel, engineering, and at British Nylon Spinners. BNS (which became ICI Fibres), together with Lucas Girling (the brake manufacturer based at factories in Pontypool and Cwmbran), BSC Stainless Steel at Panteg, Parke-Davis Pharmaceutical at Mamhilad, ROF Glascoed and Daniel Doncaster at Blaenavon, between them employed tens of thousands of people; they were heavily unionised and wages were good.

By the time I retired in 2015, however, the pits were closed, and so were BSC Panteg, Parke-Davis and ICI Fibres. More and more people now worked in retail and service industries. New industrial estates sprang up, but the days of the big factories were gone, as often were good wages and conditions. I felt it was vital that I should be involved in the fortunes of my local employers, but it was very much a changing scene.

I had been an active trade unionist all my working life – I was, at various stages, a member of the Electrical, Electronic, Telecommunications and Plumbing Union (EETPU), the National Association of Co-operative Officials, USDAW and the lecturers' union NATFHE. But my longest membership of a trade union is with the TGWU (now Unite), and on entering the House I became one of its sponsored MPs. My father had been a TGWU shop steward at ICI Fibres, and I had been a member since 1978. I was an executive member of the TGWU parliamentary group, and was especially involved in the power and engineering, chemical, manufacturing and oil refining and public service groups of the union. These groups reflected employment patterns in Torfaen. I have always been a firm believer in the link between the Labour Party and the trade unions, as well as holding the view that trade union sponsorship kept MPs' feet firmly on the ground! Eventually, sponsorship effectively died out, which is something that I deeply regret.

In late 1988, Brynmor John, the able MP for Pontypridd and a former Minister, suddenly died. Dr Kim Howells was selected to succeed him as Labour candidate, and the ensuing by-election was held in early 1989. Kim was 43, and the researcher for the National Union of Mineworkers (NUM) in Wales. He had been a student activist in the 1960s – famously at the Hornsey College of Art – and he went on to the Cambridge College of Arts and Technology and Warwick University, where he gained a doctorate in Labour history. He had been heavily involved in the miners' strike of 1985, but was no friend of Arthur Scargill. Kim and I, on the other hand, were to become great friends, and I have enjoyed nearly 30 years of friendship with his lovely family – his wife Eirlys, and their three children, Cai, Scott and Seren.

Kim was an excellent MP, and soon joined Labour's opposition front bench as spokesman on Trade and Industry, Home Affairs, Foreign Affairs and International Development and Co-operation. The diversity of portfolios continued in government when he was Minister for Education, Culture Media and Sport, Higher Education and, finally, Foreign Affairs. He was a Minister of State and, on becoming chairman of the Intelligence and Security Committee, a Privy Counsellor. Kim was often controversial, a brilliant media performer, a fine speaker and a hugely effective Minister; he was not, however, given a seat in the House of Lords on his retirement from the Commons in 2010 – a loss in my view for parliament and for our country.

I remained good friends with my predecessor Leo Abse after his retirement in 1987. Leo and his wife Marjorie lived at Strand-on-the-Green in Chiswick, in a beautiful house overlooking the river Thames. In 1988, I bought a flat in Chiswick Village, in a large 1930s block, and was able to visit Leo frequently. I would often have lunch with him (he quite rightly thought Marjorie was "the best cook in London"), and we exchanged much gossip. By now, Leo had started writing again, and he was to produce six new books before he died at the age of 91 (the last of which was published posthumously). Among them were volumes psychoanalysing Germany, Daniel Defoe and Tony Blair. Indeed, when writing his book on Blair, Leo wanted to mention me in the foreword and would have liked me to be present at the launch, since I had just been made a Minister in the new

Labour government. I politely declined – Leo understood! Between us, Leo and I would represent the Eastern Valley in parliament for almost 60 years, and I owe him a great debt – he was in many ways one of my political heroes.

On the day of Thatcher's downfall in 1990, Leo took me to a wine tasting of Puligny Montrachet in a Wandsworth wine shop – it was a strange place to learn of such an historic event, but it strengthened the view that the Conservative Party is a ruthless political machine. I had watched Geoffrey Howe maul her in the Commons, witnessed her defiant "no, no, no" speech and, for a fleeting moment, even felt sorry for her. Thatcher had been knifed by the very people she had promoted. Many thought the world had changed, and in some ways it had. I reminded my party members that even though Thatcher had gone, the Tories were still there. And, in the next two years, the new Prime Minister John Major gave the impression of heading a new regime, almost a new and different government.

By 1992, most of the opinion pollsters were predicting a Labour victory. Neil Kinnock had done a brilliant job in transforming the party. The hard-left militants had been expelled and the party adopted sensible and election-winning policies. Kinnock had an able shadow Cabinet and an effective shadow Chancellor in John Smith, and MPs like Tony Blair and Gordon Brown were the coming men.

When Major called the election, there was everything to play for. As well as fighting my second election in Torfaen, I spent a great deal of time travelling around Wales in my capacity as a shadow Welsh Office Minister; but the country was not yet ready for a Labour government, even though we gained 42 seats, which was itself a considerable achievement.

In Torfaen, Labour did really well. My vote increased to 30,352, and I achieved a majority of 20,754. At the count, I said: "I share with those 30,000 who voted Labour in the Eastern Valley, the unique disappointment of facing another five years of Tory rule."

Locally in the election, we had attracted the second highest vote ever, but as the *Free Press* reported, "the Torfaen count had a strange feel about it". The constituency party had planned a celebration for that night, but it was abandoned in the light of the national result.

Neil Kinnock decided to resign. While I totally understood his feelings, I thought he was wrong to do so. We had gained a great number of seats and many of us felt the Tory majority would eventually peter out (as it did). I phoned him and also wrote, urging him to stay, but he was determined. In the forthcoming leadership election, I voted for Brian Gould, the young and dynamic MP for Dagenham. Gould lost out to John Smith who, despite my not supporting him, kept me in position as shadow Welsh Minister.

My new boss as shadow Welsh Secretary was Ann Clwyd, MP for the Cynon Valley, and I was to be joined in the team by Rhodri Morgan; Alun Michael, meanwhile, went to the Home Affairs team, under Tony Blair.

Rhodri and I had known each other since the early 1980s, and we had entered the Commons together in 1987, sharing an office for four years. We became good friends and, at his funeral in 2017, I was privileged to be asked to give one of the tributes. Rhodri was one of the most memorable politicians I have ever known, brilliant in so many ways, and intellectually a giant. He was able to talk about anything to anyone, and had absolutely no "side", despite a distinguished academic background of Oxford and Harvard. A Welsh speaker, he was a passionate advocate of devolution, and our lives were to become intertwined over the next twenty-odd years in so many ways.

Ann Clwyd had been the MP for Cynon Valley since 1984, a formidable politician and a former journalist who took a great interest in human rights, especially in the Middle East. She was easy to work with, and we journeyed throughout Wales together including once a visit to the National Eisteddfod in Aberystwyth. Ann remained as shadow Welsh Secretary only until the autumn of 1992 when she became shadow Culture Secretary; she was succeeded by Ron Davies, MP for Caerphilly since 1983, and the former Agriculture spokesman. Ron was passionately committed to devolution, delegated well and was good to work for.

Between 1992 and 1994, local government finance was still an important political issue. This period saw the end of the poll tax (it finally went in 1993) and the creation of its replacement, the council tax. I was heavily involved in the legislation to set up the new system and I often shadowed Michael Portillo, the new Local Government Minister.

In Wales, the Tories had decided to change the structure of local government. Welsh Secretary David Hunt published a consultation in 1991, and introduced a White Paper in 1993. The legislation to introduce these changes created 21 (eventually 22) new unitary authorities (county councils or county borough councils), which replaced the old system of 8 county councils and 37 district councils. John Redwood succeeded David Hunt in May 1993, and the new authorities came into force in 1996.

I led for the opposition in the committee stage of the bill, and I travelled all over Wales consulting with Labour local authorities. There were sometimes fierce disagreements between the Labour county councils and the Labour district councils, especially over how many councils there should be. We tabled amendments altering the government's proposed number – all of them failed, although Merthyr Tydfil and Blaenau Gwent did become separate local authorities, which had not originally been the intention. Torfaen remained the same as in the original proposals – the Eastern Valley of Gwent – but now took on the powers of the old county councils, mainly education and social services.

During the passage of the bill, I had objected to having two forms for the name "Torfaen", which I considered to be a Welsh name anyway. The Welsh Office would have none of it and insisted on the correct orthography in Welsh – and the hyphen in "Tor-faen" became the most expensive hyphen in history, since the dual use would now be compulsory throughout the valley!

The ReChem waste incineration plant had been a major issue in Torfaen for years. Originally built in the 1970s and supported by the then Pontypool urban district council, the plant would become the subject of major controversy. Claims were made about the impact upon people's health, especially in the New Inn community, and the very first oral question I asked in the Commons related to ReChem. It was not to be the last time I raised the subject, and a campaign developed to remove the facility from its urban site. The campaign intensified when the plant began to import toxic wastes from other countries – the impression was that the UK in general and Torfaen in particular provided the dumping ground for the world's unwanted toxins.

The biggest cause of unease was the importation of PCBs – polychlorinated biphenyls, highly poisonous substances, which, unless they are correctly incinerated, handled or stored, present a huge risk to human life. About 16 per cent of all toxic wastes coming into the UK at the time ended up in Pontypool – this included roughly 500 tonnes of PCBs each month. Supporters of the trade argued that the PCBs came from under-developed countries, although the waste material came in fact from Spain, Italy, Australia, Belgium, Canada, Ireland, Iceland, Germany, Holland, Norway, Portugal, Switzerland and Austria. It entered through 17 ports in the UK, and was part of an international trade in such material. In a Commons debate, I said that Wales was "fast becoming the dustbin of the world's worst poisons"; ReChem was a main beneficiary of this trade, and made considerable profits.

PCBs have to be incinerated at very high temperature. There were doubts expressed over the adequacy of the ReChem incinerator for this task, and there were a number of local incidents – an explosion in the incinerator, chemical spillages, unpleasant smells and deep black smoke emissions – which caused a great deal of concern. The company was fond of litigation, relations with Torfaen Council were poor, and the local authority had to spend many thousands of pounds on monitoring the plant.

From the start of my time in the Commons, I pursued the case for a public inquiry, putting down early day motions, asking written and oral questions, and using every parliamentary opportunity I could find. The Welsh Secretary Peter Walker and other Ministers flatly refused to have an inquiry or even to meet me or the council to discuss the issue.

In 1989, Canada became involved, and pledged not to export 3,600 tonnes of PCBs which were on their way to Pontypool – the Montreal newspaper *The Sunday Gazette* ran an article headlined: "Welsh town doesn't want our PCB waste". Alan Rogers and Llew Smith, when they were the local MEPs, took up the matter with the European Commission, and in March 1989 hundreds of us, including Roy Hughes MP, Paul Flynn MP and the local authorities' mayors and chairmen, marched on the plant. The TUC called for a ban on the import of toxic waste, and the shadow Welsh Secretary Barry Jones echoed this, pledging a ban.

The Select Committee on Welsh Affairs reported in 1990, and addressed toxic waste disposal in general and the ReChem plant in particular. It acknowledged the public concern, drew attention to the understaffing of Her Majesty's Inspectorate of Pollution and the serious problems of unpublicised emissions, and recommended the monitoring of PCB levels. In its response, the government also acknowledged the level of public concern and engaged Professor Lewis Roberts of the University of East Anglia to make an independent assessment of the situation and consider the question of an independent inquiry. Nothing much happened on the matter and, in July 1992, I was fortunate in winning a full day's debate in the Commons, on a subject of my choice – naturally, I submitted "Toxic Waste Disposal (Wales)" as the theme for the day, and the debate again brought to light the overwhelming concern of my constituents with regard to ReChem.

The issue rumbled on. After devolution, the new Assembly Government, while accepting many of my arguments, still declined a full public inquiry; it agreed, however, to greater public scrutiny from the relevant government agencies. Controversy continued around the plant, including concern over its involvement in dealing with BSE-infected carcasses, and it finally closed in late 2002. It has been a long and sorry story, and I hope that future governments and councils will take seriously the Welsh Affairs Committee's conclusion that such plants should never be built in urban or residential areas.

On 12 May 1994, John Smith, the popular leader of the Labour Party, died of a heart attack. He was 56 years of age. Only a few days before his death, I had been talking to him in the Commons Tea Room about current election campaigns and, as I wrote in my tribute to him in the local press, "he was his usual vibrant, witty and incisive self". He had been due to visit Aberystwyth and Swansea in the week that he passed away. On the morning of John's death, I paid tribute to him at the standing committee of the Local Government Bill – and all members of the committee, both government and opposition, were in a state of deep dismay at the news. John Major and deputy Labour leader Margaret Beckett led tributes to John in the Chamber.

The race to succeed John culminated in the election of Tony Blair as party leader ahead of John Prescott and Margaret Beckett. Gordon Brown had decided not to run in the contest. I had no doubt that the party had to continue to modernise itself, and to appeal to people who did not normally vote Labour. Times were changing – the old tribal loyalties of British politics were disappearing, and so the choice had to be between Gordon and Tony. Both were highly intelligent, politically astute, young and energetic; "New Labour" was their creation.

In the end, I decided to cast my vote for Tony, who thanked me, writing: "I greatly appreciate your confidence and support".

Tony retained me as shadow Welsh Minister until the reshuffle in October 1994, when, driving down the motorway to London, I saw on my car phone that Mo Mowlam had rung me. I stopped at a motorway service station and returned the call – she told me that Tony was to contact me that same day to ask if I would become her deputy on the shadow Northern Ireland team. I said I would love to, but that I would have to consult one person before accepting – my father!

In July of that year, Dad had been diagnosed with terminal lung cancer. He had always told me not to tell him if he received a terminal diagnosis, and so was not aware of his condition during the conversation we had. Dad was my most important political adviser and hero, and I deeply valued his wisdom; he said I should accept, and so at around eight thirty on the evening of 25 October 1994, I telephoned Tony Blair and he duly appointed me to the position.

I had known Mo since we entered the Commons together in 1987, and we were friends until her death in 2005. I know she had asked Kim Howells about my possible appointment as one of her Ministers of State, and it was always felt that the Northern Ireland team should contain a Catholic MP.

My shadow Ministerial colleagues were Adam Ingram, MP for East Kilbride, who was a fellow 1987 intake, as was Eric Illsley (who had previously shared an office with me and was MP for Barnsley Central); and the shadow Lords Minister was Gareth Williams, a fellow Welshman and outstanding barrister, who would eventually lead the House of Lords. We were close friends and met weekly to go through the business when we were both members of the Cabinet – often to take a "Welsh line" on issues! Gareth died tragically of a heart attack in 2003.

We were blessed with two excellent special advisers – Anna Healy (now in the Lords), and Nigel Warner. Nigel was one of the brightest and most able young advisers of his generation, and would go on to play a significant role in the negotiations leading up to the Good Friday Agreement. We have remained very good friends ever since.

The 30 years of the Troubles in Northern Ireland had visited destruction and despair on the people living there; 3,500 people had died as a direct result of the conflict, with tens of thousands injured mentally and physically. Sectarianism, with its accompanying violence, was appalling. Of course, religion played its part in causing all of this, but the central issue was identity shaped by history. A million Unionists, mainly Protestant, believed themselves British and saw themselves as besieged by a Catholic and hostile country to the south, while just under a million nationalists, mainly Catholic, felt trapped in a foreign and equally hostile state. For years, Northern Ireland was governed by Protestants, and the nationalist population's civil liberties were eroded. All of this led to the British government and army intervening, and the government and parliament of Stormont being abolished. Into the vacuum entered the Provisional IRA and its loyalist counterparts; violence intensified and the region was close to civil war.

By 1994, things had improved slightly. Mrs Thatcher negotiated the Anglo–Irish Agreement in 1985, and by 1993 Prime Minister John Major and Taoiseach Albert Reynolds had signed the Downing Street Declaration. Britain no longer had any "selfish, strategic or economic" interest in Northern Ireland, and the principle of requiring the consent of the people of Northern Ireland to decide the province's future was widely if not universally accepted. A united Ireland could only come about by peaceful means. In August 1994, the IRA announced a ceasefire, and the combined loyalist military command (representing the Ulster Volunteer Force (UVF), the Ulster Defence Association (UDA) and the Red Hand Commandos) followed suit in October. In February 1995, the so-called framework documents were published.

On 27 October 1994, I made my first speech on Northern Ireland in an adjournment debate opened by the Northern Ireland Secretary, Sir Patrick Mayhew. I commented on the excellent speeches made on all sides of the House in what were some very thoughtful and serious exchanges, and I welcomed the work done by the Prime Minister and the Conservative government. I was followed by the Minister of State, Michael Ancram, whom I was to succeed three years later. Ancram was the heir of the Marquis of Lothian and is now the premier Catholic peer; he was a first-class Minister and a great champion of peace in Northern Ireland. We were to work closely together many years later when we both served on parliament's Intelligence and Security Committee.

In my speech, I reiterated what Mo had said in her opening remarks. The Labour Party had shifted its position from one of open advocacy of a united Ireland to a stance which, in line with increasingly widespread feeling, emphasised the principle of the people's consent. For any peace settlement to be successful, both Unionists and nationalists had to agree. Violence could not be tolerated and, in that context particularly, we were all heartened by the work of the Social Democratic Labour Party (SDLP) leader and future Nobel Prize winner John Hume, who was separately in contact with the Sinn Féin leader Gerry Adams.

For years, the Tory government had been secretly talking to the IRA, but now civil servants were to have discussions with Sinn Féin about the future of Northern Ireland. In February, 1995, I myself spent 90 minutes with a delegation from Sinn Féin, which consisted of Francie Molloy of their national executive (and later a British MP), Gerry MacLochlainn, Sinn Féin's representative in Great Britain, and Danny Power, a Sinn Féin member.

We talked about policing, fair employment and economic regeneration. After the event, I said that "we regarded this as exploratory talks with people from the same groups as the government had spoken to some weeks earlier; we discussed a range of issues and mine was mainly a listening role". It was a small, historic moment, and taking part in these discussions had been the right thing to do.

Over the next few months I continued to question Northern Ireland Ministers and made a major speech on children in the province. I met with other leading players there, including Gusty Spence of the UVF, who had been responsible for the loyalist ceasefire. Naturally, I spoke to senior figures from the Northern Ireland parties as well as making regular visits to both Belfast and Dublin. The NIO looked after me well, and provided me with transport and hotels. Although I had visited the Republic of Ireland, I had never gone to the north until I was made a shadow Minister. The visits made a great impression on me, especially the fortified police stations and the sectarian symbols on the Falls Road and the Shankill Road.

I was seven months into the job when, in July 1995, I was reshuffled to the shadow Foreign Office team. I suspected that Peter Mandelson had something to do with what was considered a promotion – he had held sessions on media training for shadow Ministers, and I think he was quite impressed with my mock television interviews (I had gained a lot of experience of television and radio work when I was a Welsh Office spokesman for six years). All this coincided with the sacking of Ann Clwyd as Foreign Secretary: she had been absent without leave in Iraq.

I was very sorry to leave the Northern Ireland job – it had been fascinating and different. Gareth Williams wrote to me saying he was sorry to see me leave the team; so did Mo, who wrote: "Just a note to say I will miss you on the team something indeed. Hope we don't miss out on seeing each other – we must still eat together. This promotion will mean onwards-upwards into Government."

My new boss was Robin Cook, the shadow Foreign Secretary. I went to see him in his offices in Parliament Street, and he asked me what particular parts of the world I would like to cover. I replied: "Those parts for which you don't have to have injections to visit!" As it was, I was given the Middle East and Asia!

In personal and family terms, the previous year had been traumatic. With my father now increasingly ill, I had nursed him between November 1994 and his death in January 1995. They were difficult months, but I felt privileged to have been with him in his last days. Sometimes he was in very great pain, and I had to give him liquid morphine. He had smoked cigarettes since he was a child, but otherwise he had been a strong and healthy man; he had a great wit, formidable intelligence and considerable literary gifts. Dad would visit the Commons a couple of times a month, and became a well-known figure among Welsh Labour MPs.

He passed away in January 1995 at the Royal Gwent Hospital in Newport – peacefully, with my brother Neil and me at his bedside. He was 75 years of age – 20 years older than my mother when she died.

I received a great number of letters of condolence, including one from Tony Blair who wrote: "Despite his age, it must have come as a shock and somehow, even if we expect it, these things always go hard, touching our innermost lives."

Dad's funeral took place at Our Lady of the Angels Church, Cwmbran, on 27 January 1995, and was conducted by the parish priest, the Very Reverend Canon Francis O'Donnell. It was attended by hundreds of people, including family, personal friends, former workmates and trade unionists, Labour Party members, the mayor and many councillors. Two members of the shadow Cabinet – Mo Mowlam and Ron Davies – were there, as well as seven other MPs. At the funeral Mass we sang "Abide with Me", "Hail Queen of Heaven" and "Going Home". On the back of the order of service was printed my father's poem, Slagtips (see chapter 1), which was much admired and showed the sort of man my father was. Dad was buried with my mother at Panteg cemetery, where I hope to be laid to rest too when my time comes.

A couple of months earlier, in November 1994, a happier event took place. Don Touhig was selected as Labour candidate to replace Neil Kinnock as MP for Islwyn, with Neil becoming the UK European Commissioner in Brussels. The Islwyn by-election was held in January 1995, and I did as much as I could bearing in mind it all happened during my father's last days. After Dad had died, and before election day, Peter Hain stayed with me in my home in Cwmbran – an act of great kindness. Peter had been elected MP for Neath at a by-election in April 1991, and proved to be an excellent MP and friend. Over time, our political careers frequently took parallel courses.

In 1991 my brother Neil and sister-in-law Claire left the local area, moving first to live near Newark in Nottinghamshire, where Neil became national field sales manager with Crookes Healthcare Ltd, a subsidiary of the Boots company, before taking a senior job with Kodak (based at Hemel Hempstead) and living in Milton Keynes. By now, Neil and Claire had two children – Daniel (born in 1988) and Rachel (born in 1991) – a source of great joy to my father, and to become a major and very happy part of my own life.

My new shadow ministerial job meant that I worked with some very capable colleagues on the team – including Tony Lloyd, MP for Stretford, later Rochdale, and Joyce Quin, MP for Gateshead East, now a peer. Tony and Joyce went on to be Foreign Office Ministers.

Within a few days of acquiring my new role, I was asked to wind up a debate on China and Hong Kong in the House. The debate was opened by Foreign Secretary Douglas Hurd, and his shadow Robin Cook. It was only two years before the planned handover of Hong Kong to China, and I addressed some of the issues facing the people of Hong Kong, including democracy, human rights and the future of the Hong Kong Civil Service. I concluded: "We must all ensure that our efforts are aimed at bringing about stability and harmony after 1997. These must be the most important objectives of all honourable members and of those who govern Hong Kong". I was welcomed to the despatch box by Alastair Goodlad MP, Minister of State at the Foreign Office. Not long after the debate, I received a letter from Chris Patten, the Governor of Hong Kong:

> I hope this won't wreck your career, but I just wanted to write and thank you – as I have written to Robin Cook – for speaking in such constructive terms in the House . . . I particularly appreciate that you have had to become an expert on our affairs in very strict order; I hope that before too long you will be able to come and visit us here in Hong Kong. You would be welcome any time.

I was to take up Chris's offer some years later, and met him at Government House, where he was doing his best to maintain democracy and human rights before China's takeover.

The Middle East was a huge part of my brief. My first oral question to Douglas Hurd related to an aid package for Gaza and Jericho. I spent a great deal of my time meeting with ambassadors from the region and, in November 1995, gave a speech to the Arab Research Centre entitled "The Labour Party and the Middle East Issues". The session was attended by journalists, academics and diplomats, and mine was a detailed address which covered mainly the Arab–Israeli peace process, but also touched on North Africa, Iran and Iraq. Little of what I spoke about in 1995 has changed today – the problem of East Jerusalem, Gaza and the West Bank, and Palestinian refugees – and I emphasised that we could not tolerate violence in any form and that Saddam Hussein's passion for weapons of mass destruction was a major stumbling block. My address was followed by a lively discussion, all of which was published in booklet form along with the speech.

I had been on a delegation to the region only a week before – as I've already noted, it was where I became friendly with the future Liberal Democrat leader Charles Kennedy. One of my most poignant memories of that time is of our visit to a Palestinian refugee camp, including a school in the camp.

I had travelled to Israel with the Labour Friends of Israel in February 1992, my MP colleagues on that occasion being Bill O'Brien and John McFall. February was still very much winter in Israel, and we spent most of our time in Jerusalem in the snow! We met with leading members of the Knesset and paid an emotional visit to the Holocaust memorial, as well as meeting with Shimon Peres MK, who was at that time the chairman of the Israeli Labour Party. I would meet him again in subsequent years, and I always admired him as one of the giants of Israeli politics.

For me as a Christian, some special memories from that time are of the visits to Nazareth, to the Sea of Galilee and to the holy sites in Jerusalem. We also managed to meet with Hamas in East Jerusalem, a meeting counterbalanced by sessions with Israeli Intelligence! The visit was a huge learning experience for me, and also very relevant five years later when I went to Northern Ireland.

I also visited Saudi Arabia leading a cross-party delegation along with Jonathan Aitken for the Tories. Saudi Arabia was a mysterious country, well-advanced in many ways and obviously very rich, but I found attitudes to women very primitive. By that time, Tony Blair was Labour leader and I carried greetings from Tony to the Crown Prince (later the King). We also celebrated St Patrick's Day at the Irish Embassy, where there was certainly no ban on alcohol!

Mention of what might be seen as the lighter side of a parliamentary representative's life prompts me to suggest that one of the more enjoyable and useful duties of an MP is to take the opportunity to visit parliamentarians elsewhere in the world, as a member of the Commonwealth parliamentary association, the inter-parliamentary union, or the various country groups that flourish in parliament.

My first such trip was to France, as the secretary of the Franco–British Group, in January 1988. The trip included a flight to the Plateau d'Albion (the now-closed launch site of France's land-based nuclear missiles), where I actually touched a nuclear bomb! Dinner that evening was less dramatic, with the Senate president. Six years later, I visited the National Assembly again, and went on to Marseille to see the nearby headquarters of Airbus's helicopter manufacturing. In 1989, I travelled with the CPA to Australia on a three-week visit planned to include Sydney, Darwin, Adelaide and Canberra, led by Sir Michael Shaw, MP for Scarborough and Whitby (later Lord Shaw). It was a fascinating experience, not least when I sat in the Prime Minister's seat in Canberra's Cabinet Room.

We stopped off on our way in Singapore to meet the CPA branch there; and on the return journey, we visited Hong Kong (it was the first of two trips I made to that dependency). We were greeted by the governor, now Lord Wilson, and met members of the Hong Kong legislature and civil service.

Australia is a very interesting place for a British politician. It is a key ally of the UK, and every MP will have hundreds of constituents who have connections to Australia.

On this occasion, on an internal flight to Sydney we had to land at Melbourne for some hours. I took advantage of the unplanned stop to spend a little time with Stathis Gauntlett, my old friend who was by then a professor at the city's university. When I rejoined my British CPA colleagues, we flew on to Sydney, visiting Randwick Labour Club as well as the state parliament. South Australia had been the home of the first Labour government in the western hemisphere, and we met with the Labour premier of South Australia at that time, John Bannon, in the Parliament House in Adelaide.

I have never encountered such humidity as I did in Darwin, where the meeting with members of the Northern Territory Legislative Assembly was offset by a trip to "Crocodile Dundee" territory three hours' drive away in the Kakadu National Park.

In September 1996, I joined a CPA delegation to the Windward Islands – Dominica, St Lucia and St Vincent – this time led by Robert Atkins MP. I knew about the Windward Islands because my mother's brother, Bill Pring, had named his house "Windward" on account of the fact that it was from there that his banana company Geest imported most of its produce. They were tiny republics in the Commonwealth and, in the case of Dominica, for instance, had a smaller population than my constituency! I presented a gift to the island's President, Crispin Sorhaindo. St Lucia and St Vincent were equally interesting, and we witnessed great affection towards the UK wherever we went. A memory that has stayed with me is of the impeccable turnout of boys and girls as they made their way to study for their GCSEs in school. The subject of the banana industry came up in most discussions as a source of a significant proportion of the islands' GDP.

For a short time, I was a member of the Select Committee on Welsh Affairs. In 1988, we travelled to South Korea and Japan to look at how inward investment to Wales from these two countries had come about, and how it could be extended. Gower MP Gareth Wardell led the visit, and we met with the top bosses at firms such as Hyundai and Sony. The chairman at Sony revealed that Wales had been chosen for investment because of our grants regime, yes, but also because of his love of Welsh choral music and Welsh hospitality! Part of my time on the visit was overshadowed by severe food poisoning contracted in Seoul, and the Japanese bullet train certainly lived up to its name! One evening, when my colleagues were at a scheduled event, I was confined to my hotel bedroom overlooking the Imperial Palace in Tokyo . . . in bed watching *Dances with Wolves*!

In July 1989, along with Doug Henderson MP, Kim Howells and I attended the Biennial Assembly of the Atlantic Association of Young Political Leaders in Ottawa. From Ottawa, we flew to Washington – it was the first time I had visited North America. Despite the loss of my my suitcase somewhere between Amsterdam and Canada, the trip was very worthwhile, with just one discordant note when the Belgian delegates (one Flemish and one Walloon) quarrelled with each other.

In September 1990, the Shadow Welsh Office team – Barry Jones, Alun Michael and I – visited Germany to study the country's federal system as a guide to our continuing work on devolution for Wales. We went to Bonn and to Saarbrucken, the latter as a part of Germany that isn't dissimilar to Wales with the relative decline of the coal and steel industries.

In the same year, I made another visit to Germany with the parliamentary roads study group. The trip took in meetings in Bonn, Cologne and Dusseldorf, to look at road and transport investment in West Germany at federal, regional and municipal level. I was a member of this group and of the all-party motor industry group because of the large motor parts industry we had in Torfaen; I was usually accompanied by Roy Hughes, MP for Newport, who had worked in the car industry. Other visits during these years took me to France, the USA, Sweden and Finland – and in Finland I took in the world's northernmost car assembly plant, where I watched Girling brakes made in Cwmbran being fitted to the Saab cars.

During my years as an opposition MP, I was the treasurer of the Anglo–Austrian Society, a body which had its headquarters in Westminster, but which was more than parliamentary. Sir William Clark MP (later Lord Clark of Kempston) was the chairman, and I visited Austria with him and other members of the executive committee.

Apart from the visit to Israel already described, one other overseas trip that stands out is my visit to Taiwan in April 1996 with fellow MPs Menzies Campbell, Archie Kirkwood and John Reid. Leo Abse, my constituency predecessor, had been much involved in British–Taiwanese relations, and I was interested to see this very unusual country for myself. Taiwanese investors had put money into RighTel Electronics in Torfaen, and we were anxious to explore ways of increasing their investment in the UK.

Meanwhile, as my first decade in the Commons progressed, I was scheduled to visit Egypt, the Gulf, North Africa and India in my Foreign Affairs job. However, as at other points in my career, events conspired and another reshuffle was held in October, at a time when I had been at Foreign Affairs for only six months! I had enjoyed working with Robin Cook, who was to go on to become a formidable Foreign Secretary, but who would die too young in 2005 at the age of 59. I had studied Diplomatic History at Oxford, and was fascinated by Foreign Affairs. I often thought I would have enjoyed being a Minister in the Foreign Office, but it was not to be and now I had to turn my attention to Defence matters.

The reason for this reshuffle was that Derek Fatchett, MP for Leeds Central, wanted to move from Defence to Foreign Affairs. That was what he did, and he eventually became Deputy Foreign Secretary, but died in 1999 at the age of 53. To accommodate Derek's move, I made a straight swap and took on the role of shadow Minister for the Navy, Personnel Matters and the Reserve Forces. My new boss was the MP for South Shields, David Clark, a Labour historian who had been in the Commons since 1979 and would join the Cabinet after Labour's election to government in 1997. David was a kind man and easy to work with, and an excellent debater. My other colleagues on the new team were John Reid, MP for Motherwell North (who was to hold a whole host of senior Cabinet positions) as Shadow Army Minister, and John Spellar, MP for Warley (who eventually became Minister for the Armed Forces, and for Northern Ireland, amongst other jobs) who had responsibility for the RAF. Our spokesman in the House of Lords was Charles Williams, Lord Williams of Elvel, step-father of now Archbishop of Canterbury Justin Welby. Charles was a formidable cricketer and former soldier.

My first Defence question was to Michael Portillo, Secretary of State for Defence, on 24 October 1995. It was a question on European security, and I seem to recall being unfair and slightly impolite to Michael; and he was the complete opposite in reply. I was to ask a large number of questions on Defence issues over the next 19 months, as well as speaking for the opposition in the navy debate and on the Reserve Forces Bill.

In the summer of 1996, the *Daily Mail* ran the headline: "Labour call to beat the tormentors". It related to an issue that I had taken up on sexual harassment in the armed services, and I had asked for a special Ministry of Defence unit staffed by women officers and a helpline. This was one of a number of aspects of personnel subjects that I concentrated on. Obviously, I also continued my constituency work, and in November 1996 the Bishop of Monmouth, Rowan Williams (later to become Archbishop of Wales and of Canterbury), worked with me in addressing the proposed closure of the Cwmbran benefits agency offices.

My last question in my Defence role was on 11 March 1997, and concerned the army vehicle depot at Ashworth. The job took me to different military venues all over the country, including Aldershot, and I spent a very enjoyable day on an aircraft carrier in the Solent!

In early 1997, Mo Mowlam approached me about Northern Ireland, and said that she and Tony Blair were interested in my becoming a Northern Ireland Minister were Labour to win the forthcoming General Election. I was to liaise with Jonathan Powell, Tony's chief adviser, and I was to familiarise myself with leading politicians and civil servants in Northern Ireland. I visited Belfast and met with Sir Quentin Thomas, political director of the NIO, and with representatives of the political parties. I was also introduced to Sir John Chilcott, Permanent Secretary in the NIO. It was all very unusual and unorthodox – here I was, a shadow Defence Minister, talking to nationalists and Unionists about the peace process!

During the General Election campaign, I remained shadow Navy Minister and visited Plymouth, Falmouth and Exeter as well as canvassing in my own constituency. The election was held on 1 May 1997, and both mine and the national results were never in doubt. But the scale of the victory was beyond what we expected; there was a huge swing to Labour, and in Wales the Tories were annihilated. At Westminster, Labour had a majority of 179; with a turnout of 71.7 per cent in Torfaen, the majority of 24,536 was almost 70 per cent of the total votes cast for all candidates in the constituency. It was an outstanding result, nationally and locally, and like all potential Ministers I didn't venture far from a phone for the next few days!

My brother was now working for Gillette and, having spent some years in Warsaw and in Prague, he had moved to Singapore. The family had come to Wales for the General Election, and were returning to the Far East on the Sunday after Election Day. Tony Blair had named his Cabinet, but I heard nothing until my brother was walking through the departures lounge at Heathrow airport. That was when my mobile rang: it was No. 10 telling me to expect a call from the Prime Minister. I obviously had a job – I wouldn't have been called to be told I didn't have a job – and I returned to my flat in Chiswick, locked myself in and waited. A call came, but only to tell me that I would be contacted again on the Monday; and, as promised, the phone rang on Monday and Tony asked me to be Minister of State at the Northern Ireland Office. Shortly afterwards, Richard Lemon from Belfast phoned to inform me that he was my new private secretary. My whole life was to change again as I now entered this new phase.

Northern Ireland

1997–1999

TONY AND MO had decided that I should be the Political Development Minister for Northern Ireland. As direct rule from Westminster was in operation, I would also be Finance Minister and Minister responsible for European issues. I was plunged straight in at the deep end, and I faced enormous challenges; I had had no ministerial experience but, at almost 50 years of age, I had been a shadow Minister for nine years and, before that, had served as chair of my council's finance committee for a decade. In Northern Ireland, I was blessed with a great boss in Mo Mowlam, who was also a friend, and I had some fine and experienced team colleagues.

By this time, Mo was building up a formidable reputation as a communicator and motivator. She brought with her a fresh approach to Northern Ireland and, as a woman, reached out to many people who previously had no interest in politics. She had a fiery enthusiasm and a superior intellect, and took to the job very easily. By this time, of course, she had been diagnosed with the brain tumour that eventually killed her, and she wore a wig to cover the hair loss caused by radiotherapy treatment. She often found the hairpiece irritating, and (to the astonishment of those with whom she was in conversation) would sometimes take it off without warning, frequently at some point of impatience, frustration or celebration in proceedings.

Mo was very easy to work with, though rightly demanding, and I cannot recall ever having a disagreement with her. We would constantly meet socially, either at her residence at Hillsborough Castle or in a restaurant in Belfast or in London. I got on very well with her husband, Jon, a Labour-supporting banker, and both her step-children. Often on weekends, we would spend time together with her guests at Hillsborough – Neil Kinnock, actor Richard Wilson, Andrew Marr, Mike Cashman, the American ambassador, always somebody interesting – and we even played charades indoors and croquet outdoors!

Her mind was constantly active and she would often phone me in the middle of the night to discuss some issue or other, and would arrive at the office armed with a list of 20 or 30 problems and issues she would want to attend to during the day. She had a keen sense of humour and often used very colourful language – sometimes shocking the more staid politicians in Belfast. Younger than me, Mo was all in all an amazing character who became the darling of the Labour Party, and to a certain extent of the country. We maintained our friendship all her life, and I still miss her.

Alongside me, with responsibility for security and economic issues in Northern Ireland, was my fellow Minister of State Adam Ingram. Adam had served as a NALGO trade union official before becoming MP for East Kilbride in 1987, and we had been friends for a decade. Adam had worked as PPS to Neil Kinnock, and was a tough no-nonsense character, ideally suited for the role of Security Minister. He did his job very well indeed, and was to become Minister of State for the Armed Forces; he would in my view have been an excellent Northern Ireland Secretary.

Tony Worthington, MP for Clydebank and Milngavie, was an Englishman who had studied at Glasgow University, becoming a further education lecturer in Strathclyde before being elected an MP in 1981. He served as a parliamentary under-secretary at the NIO until the July 1998 re-shuffle. Tony was replaced by my friend John McFall, who took on the education and health briefs and remained a NIO Minister until 1999, when devolved ministers took over.

The NIO Minister in the House of Lords was Alf Dubs, who had been MP for Battersea until 1983. Alf had been a child refugee from Hitler's Czechoslovakia, and was in 2016 responsible for introducing legislation to help European child refugees. He dealt with environmental and local government matters, and was a first-class Minister, who also became a good friend. In the Lords, Alf spoke on all Northern Ireland matters and, as was the case with and for the same reason as John, he left the NIO in 1999.

The NIO team was helped by a number of special advisers, most notably Nigel Warner, who had first served under Mo in opposition. Nigel and I have remained very good friends over the years, and he played a hugely significant role in the talks leading up to the Good Friday Agreement.

As a Minister of State, I was entitled to a parliamentary private secretary. I chose Mike Gapes, MP (from 1992) for Ilford South. A former chair of the National Organisation of Labour Students, Mike had also been the international secretary of the Labour Party, and he was to become chair of the influential House of Commons Select Committee on Foreign Affairs.

The Northern Ireland departments were run by a technically separate civil service, the Northern Ireland Civil Service (NICS). The NIO civil servants were some of the finest in the so-called Home Civil Service, and were specifically chosen to deal with one of the country's most serious problems. They came from various other government departments, particularly the Home Office, and the Permanent Secretary Sir Joseph Pilling, a very bright and energetic Yorkshireman, had previously been director of the Prison Service. His was a steady hand, and he was to remain as Permanent Secretary until 2005.

Political director Sir Quentin Thomas had very deep experience of the Troubles and of Northern Ireland politics; he was succeeded in 1998 by Sir Bill Jeffrey, a clever and engaging Scotsman who was to finish his civil service career as the Permanent Secretary at the Ministry of Defence.

The Deputy Political Director was Sir Jonathan Stephens, later to become Permanent Secretary at the Department of Culture, Media and Sport, and to return to the NIO as director/permanent secretary; and the Head of the Finance Department was Sir John Semple, later to be the Head of the NICS itself.

My private secretary, Richard Lemon, was a very gifted and pleasant young civil servant, assisted by my diary secretary, the able and unflappable Norah Donnelly; between them, they looked after my every need.

I knew that the nature of my new post would mean significant changes in everyday life, but I hadn't quite anticipated to what extent. It wasn't just that I was new to the life of a Minister – I also had to adjust to the special circumstances of Northern Ireland. This meant having personal protection officers there – first Billy and Jimmy. Billy was a Protestant, Jimmy was a Catholic, both were armed members of the Royal Ulster Constabulary (RUC), and they went with me everywhere. I couldn't have asked for more loyal and supportive officers, and we became great friends. However, while their constant presence was reassuring, it was also a daily reminder of the potential dangers in my new job.

Naturally, much of my time was now spent in Belfast. I had one office in Stormont castle, a second as Finance Minister in Bangor, County Down, and a third in Castle Buildings where the talks were being held. I lived in Stormont House where, as with the other Ministers, I had a bedroom and bathroom. I also shared the building with MI5! One weekend every month, I had to remain in Northern Ireland as so-called duty minister, and then stayed in a maisonette in the grounds of Hillsborough Castle, which was the residence of the Secretary of State.

All of this provided the domestic background to the high drama of the political talks, which were jointly sponsored by the British and Irish governments. On the British side, the NIO and No. 10 were the major players. Tony Blair was hugely committed to the peace process, and without him there would have been no Good Friday Agreement. Tony visited and stayed in Belfast on countless occasions, and put all his energy and talents into the success of the process. His main advisers were his chief of staff Jonathan Powell, his chief press officer Alistair Campbell and his most senior private secretary Sir John Holmes.

Jonathan Powell was a 41-year-old former diplomat who had joined Tony as his chief of staff in 1995. He was a pivotal part of Tony's team and an expert on diplomacy, crucial to the talks' success, and I would speak to him on an almost daily basis. Alistair had been with the *Daily Mirror* (where I had come to know him through Neil Kinnock), and started to work for Tony in 1994 (in his autobiography, Tony rightly described Alistair as a "genius"); Alistair's *Diaries* are a great source for researchers into the Blair years, not least in their documenting of Northern Ireland, and he too played a vital role in the talks. John Holmes was a career diplomat in his mid-forties. He was brilliant at his job and in 1999 was unusually made a KBE for his work in Northern Ireland. He was to become British ambassador to Portugal and to France.

Our Irish counterparts were no less formidable. Bertie Ahern, Leader of Fianna Fáil, was Taoiseach of Ireland from 1997 to 2008. Ahern had been a highly effective Cabinet Minister in the Irish government and had acquired considerable negotiating skills as a Minister for Labour, and these skills he brought to the peace process. Described by George Mitchell as "a man of peace and a builder of bridges", Ahern worked closely with Tony Blair during the entire period of the talks; just as was the case with Blair, it was equally true that we would not have had an agreement without Bertie Ahern. I got on very well with him and, in his autobiography, he observed of me that I was "a very calm character, good at building consensus, and prepared to put in the hours in the North".

During my time as Minister of State, a number of Irish Foreign Ministers passed through, all of whom were responsible for dealing with the peace process. Dick Spring TD and I coincided for just a few months, since the coalition in Ireland between his Labour Party and Fine Gael lost the 1997 General Election; he was succeeded by Ray Burke, whom I liked and with whom I subsequently visited the USA. Unfortunately, Ray had to resign over corruption allegations in October 1997. He was succeeded by David Andrews TD, a barrister and a well-known and respected politician who was to remain Foreign Minister until 2000, when he was in turn replaced by the future Taoiseach Brian Cowen.

My exact Irish counterpart was Liz O'Donnell, a 41-year-old Irish Progressive Democratic politician, and TD for Dublin South. She was the Minister of State at the Department of Foreign Affairs, and as well as dealing with Northern Ireland she had responsibility for overseas development. Liz was a great colleague, very easy to work with, who left politics in 2007.

Naturally, the Northern Ireland politicians were at the centre of the drama and all of them were soon part of my life; most became good friends, and although they differed enormously and often dramatically, I never doubted their sincerity or commitment to the overall objectives of peace and stability in Northern Ireland. Naturally, they all had their own views on how to achieve these two objectives, and it was to take many years to find reconciliation.

On the Unionist side, David Trimble, Reg Empey, Ian Paisley, Peter Robinson, John Taylor and Ken McGuinness all played their part – as did David Ervine and others among their loyalist counterparts. They were ably advised by Professor Paul Bew of Queen's University, Belfast. From a nationalist point of view, John Hume, Seamus Mallon and Mark Durkan had spent their time bringing peace and prosperity to Northern Ireland, while the Republicans Gerry Adams, Martin McGuinness and Gerry Kelly brought Sinn Féin into government and led the Republican movement out of the so-called armed struggle. The Alliance Party under Lord John Alderdice played a central role in the talks, as the non-sectarian party in Northern Ireland, while the unique Women's Coalition under Monica McWilliams, Bronagh Hinds and Baroness May Blood often lowered the temperature and acted as intermediaries on many occasions.

The players in the drama were not confined to these islands. The USA had a huge role, especially under President Bill Clinton and later George W. Bush. Congress was to play its part too, with the likes of Senator Ted Kennedy and many others, and Irish America in general. The European Union saw Northern Ireland as a major problem to be dealt with in its own jurisdiction, and the UK's and Ireland's joint membership of this club meant that we were able to contemplate change that had been impossible to achieve in the past.

These were the main actors in the talks process, which now had imposed upon it a complex and unique structure in Castle Buildings, Belfast.

The overall chairman at the talks was Senator George Mitchell, who was a former federal judge in the USA before becoming Senator for Maine. From 1989 to 1995, he was Democrat Senate Majority Leader. George's formal involvement in Northern Ireland began when he led the commission establishing the principles of non-violence – the Mitchell Principles – that applied throughout the negotiations. For the work he did in Northern Ireland, he was awarded the Presidential Medal of Freedom and the Liberty Medal; he was also made an Honorary Knight Grand Cross of the British Empire. In his own words: "I believe there's no such thing as a conflict that can't be ended . . . No matter how ancient the conflict, no matter how hateful, no matter how hurtful, peace can prevail."

I came to know George very well, and had a huge admiration for his qualities and skills. He was another one of those players in Northern Ireland without whom there would not have been a settlement. He was kind enough to say the following about me in his book on Northern Ireland, *Making Peace*: "Paul Murphy was resilient and pragmatic. An affable bachelor with an easy-going manner, he came to be well-liked by both unionists and nationalists."

George was assisted by two vice-chairmen – the first was General John de Chastelain, the former head of the Canadian Armed Forces and Canada's Ambassador to the USA, who had also chaired the IIC on decommissioning. A kindly and generous man, John was of Scottish descent, and had been educated in Scotland before his family emigrated to Canada in 1954.

The second vice-chairman was Harri Holkeri, former Prime Minister of Finland and president of the United Nations General Assembly. Widely respected by all sides, he died aged 74 in 2011.

This board of referees had substantial offices and staff at Castle Buildings, paid for jointly by the British and Irish governments. Good progress had been made in Northern Ireland after John Major had introduced the so-called Framework Agreement in 1994, and the IRA and loyalist paramilitaries both announced their ceasefire in the same year. After the publication of the Mitchell Principles in 1996, the talks formally started. In the same year, the IRA bombed Canary Wharf in London, and then Manchester's Arndale Shopping Centre; despite these setbacks, and also in 1996, proximity talks began. This meant that the parties would not actually meet face to face, but would be in the same building (or at least, not far away from each other), and a Northern Ireland Forum was elected. Representatives of the parties elected to this body were appointed to be formal negotiators at Castle Buildings – providing the structure of the talks process, which was eventually successful in producing the Good Friday Agreement.

The peace talks were suspended for the British General Election, which was to be held on 1 May 1997. The Irish General Election also took place just over a month later, on 6 June.

The talks began again in June, while the IRA were at the same time given five weeks to resume their ceasefire, which was the pre-condition for Sinn Féin's entry to the talks. In the large, rather ugly office buildings that were Castle Buildings in Belfast, George and his vice-chairmen had their own offices along with the two governments and all the participating political parties. Activity was constant, generally over a five-day week and sometimes at weekends. It was very much a full-time process, and enabled meetings to take place at every level – government to government, government to parties, all to George Mitchell and his team. I have travelled to many places in an advisory capacity on conflict resolution, and I have always emphasised that any peace process must be full-time.

George had responsibility for Strand 2 of the talks, dealing with north–south relations, and for all plenary sessions. I chaired the talks on Strand 1, internal matters for Northern Ireland, including setting up an assembly and executive, and other issues such as human rights, equality and languages. I jointly chaired Strand 3 with Liz O'Donnell, which looked at east–west relations. Single big issues which stood on their own – such as policing, decommissioning, military issues, and the release of prisoners – were the responsibility of the Secretary of State and the Security Minister Adam Ingram, who also dealt with parades.

On top of all of this, of course, as Finance Minister I had to oversee a multi-billion pound budget and my first speech in the Commons as Minister of State was on finance.

The purpose of the order I was introducing to the House was to agree the total spending for Northern Ireland (minus law and order spending) amounting to £7,000 million. It was effectively the budget for the people of Northern Ireland, and in concluding I observed:

[The debate] is about the other Northern Ireland, the real Northern Ireland. It is not about the horrors we have witnessed or the sometimes frustrating talks process. It is about jobs, schools and hospitals; it is about the quality of life for 1.5 million people in Northern Ireland, whose needs and aspirations are the same as those of anyone else in the United Kingdom.

A few days later, on 30 June, I spoke on the order keeping direct rule in Northern Ireland, but clarified for the House that we sincerely hoped this would be only a temporary order.

We were now entering the season of parades and marches. The most significant and dangerous one was at Drumcree on Sunday, 6 July; it provided an uneasy backdrop to the talks. Three days later, I replied to a question on the relationship between Sinn Féin and the IRA, and commented that the two organisations were "inextricably linked", that Sinn Féin would have to renounce violence and accept the Mitchell Principles, and that there would have to be a proper IRA ceasefire.

This was not enough to satisfy the DUP under the leadership of Ian Paisley MP, or the tiny United Kingdom Unionist Party (UKUP) led by Robert McCartney MP, and they left the talks on 16 July. Three days later, an IRA ceasefire was announced. The reason the DUP and UKUP left the talks at that time was because they felt there was insufficient progress by the IRA with regard to the decommissioning of arms. This issue was to bedevil the peace process for years to come. The IRA had a much bigger arsenal than their loyalist counterparts, and many within the organisation considered decommissioning as surrender to the British. Unionists, however, believed that decommissioning was an essential part of the process, and George Mitchell wanted it to coincide with progress in the talks; a huge responsibility therefore lay on the shoulders of John de Chastelain and his commission.

On 29 August, Mo accepted that the IRA ceasefire was genuine and agreed that Sinn Féin should be allowed into the talks. I had been present at the plenary session when Ian Paisley walked out of Castle Buildings, and that was was a significant setback. Now, Sinn Féin, accepting the Mitchell Principles, were to walk in! I vividly remember when Mo and I, looking out of her office window, watched Sinn Féin, led by Gerry Adams and Martin McGuinness, arrive. We were to meet them later that day, and it was the first of many such encounters to follow. On one occasion, the four of us had fish and chips together, with Martin saying he never imagined a day would come when he was eating fish and chips with two Ministers of the British Crown!

Not long afterwards, I chaired a meeting of the parties on Strand 1 issues and, due to the atmosphere with the Ulster Unionist Party (UUP) not talking directly to Sinn Féin, all communication between the two parties in the meeting had to be through me as intermediary. In this first meeting, Gerry Adams began his contribution in Irish, causing much consternation among the Unionist ranks. I intervened in Welsh (though I can't speak Welsh, I know some useful words and phrases), declaring that we should have some *chwarae teg* – which means "give and take" or "fair play" – and this changed the atmosphere (not least because my pronunciation of *teg* sounded like "Taig", which is a pejorative term for Catholics, of which I was one!).

The Unionists hadn't returned to the talks immediately after Sinn Féin had entered. On 5 September, the UUP and the two small loyalist parties – the Progressive Unionist Party (PUP) and the Ulster Democratic Party (UDP) – met and agreed that they would take part; they entered two days later. The DUP, however, still stayed away. On 24 September, procedures were agreed, with the issue of decommissioning side-stepped by the launch of the IIDC.

On 7 October, discussions and negotiations began in earnest, with Mo leaving much of the detailed work to me. It was a hard slog, but necessary. The idea was that every party would express whichever views they wanted to, so long as they didn't break the Mitchell Principles. The talks went on for hours, days and weeks – talks with parties, with governments and with civic society. This constant dialogue meant that people got to know each other well and, very slowly, different types of relationship were formed. It may have taken a long time for Sinn Féin and the Unionists to engage, but engage they eventually did.

The involvement of the USA – President, Congress, and "Irish America" – was vital to the process, especially on the nationalist and republican side. President Clinton played a huge role, as did Hillary Clinton at a later point. The conversion of Irish-American politicians and businessmen to the concept of a political agreement between all sides in Northern Ireland meant a great deal. Unionists were now welcome to the USA in a way they never had been before, and even hard-line supporters of Sinn Féin backed the talks process. The towering presence of George Mitchell was a major influence in encouraging this developing new sensibility, and funding and charitable organisations that helped in the process were completely on board.

In late September 1997, I visited Washington to meet with senior politicians and others who were to play a big part over the forthcoming months. It was the first of many visits to the USA which I would make over the years. On this occasion, I was to make contact with members of both Houses of Congress, and with senior advisers to the President. I had fruitful meetings in the famous West Wing with James Steinberg, Assistant to the President for National Security Affairs, and with officials at the State Department. In Congress, I spoke with Republican Senators John McCain (Arizona) and Connie Marsh (Florida), and with Democrat Senators Chris Dodd (Connecticut) and Patrick Leahy (Vermont), while I later met with Democrat Congressman Richard Neal (Massachusetts) and Republican Peter King (New York), and other members of the ad hoc Congressional Committee for Irish Affairs. The ambassador Sir John Kerr arranged extremely useful press lunches, and I took part in television interviews with CNN.

I also visited New York, where I met Bill Flynn, the president and chief executive of Mutual America, a huge insurance company, and his deputy and eventual successor Tom Moran. These were serious people, and I got to know them extremely well; they played a significant role in the process, and in gathering support for it in the USA. I really cannot overstate their influence, and British politics owes a great deal to them. I lunched with

Cardinal O'Connor, the Cardinal Archbishop of New York, and attended a vast Irish-American dinner at the Waldorf Astoria along with the Irish Foreign Minister Ray Burke, who was sadly soon to leave office (I liked Ray and I thought he brought great energy and commitment with him).

I issued a press release prior to what was to prove a very successful visit, stating:

> For the first time since the unrest began in Northern Ireland, we are at a point where most of the parties will be at the table. I shall be asking for the continued support of the US Government for what we are achieving in Northern Ireland. I know that President Clinton takes a personal interest in what is happening here, and that is something we value highly.

On 23 October, I appeared on the BBC's *Question Time* being broadcast from Belfast. The headline in the *South Wales Argus* read, "MP Murphy makes history in the TV Studio – the first Government Minister to share a television studio platform with Sinn Féin President, Gerry Adams". Joining Adams and me were John Hume of the SDLP, Conservative MP Andrew Hunter, and former Moderator of the Presbyterian Church in Ireland, Dr John Dunlop. No local Unionist would appear on this show, and Mo judged it better for me, rather than her as Secretary of State, to take part. During the programme, a protestor leapt out of the audience and stopped just feet away from Adams, accusing him of terrorism. My own protection officer was on edge that night, to say the least! On a far less dramatic level, I made a statement in the Commons six days later on the Spending Settlement for Northern Ireland, and later answered questions on the European Union.

A much more significant event in my life occurred on 11 December 1997, when Sinn Féin leaders went to No. 10 Downing Street to meet with Tony, Mo and me. Along with the Ministers on the government side were John Holmes, Alistair Campbell, Quentin Thomas and Jonathan Powell; Sinn Féin fielded Adams, Martin McGuinness, Martin Ferris, Lucilita Bhreatnach, Richard McAuley, Siobhán O'Hanlon and Michelle Gildernew.

I have never seen so many journalists and cameras in Downing Street. When Sinn Féin arrived, it was as if a huge lightning storm was taking place. It was undeniably an historic moment: notwithstanding Unionist criticism of Tony, it was the right thing to do. I sat next to Tony, who was blunt and firm but polite. Only seven years previously, I had been in the tea room of the House of Commons when news came that the IRA had tried to blow up Downing Street with a mortar attack. This latest meeting was evidence of the progress made in Northern Ireland since then.

Progress though was shattered by the murder on 27 December of the loyalist, Billy Wright, killed in the Maze prison by Irish National Liberation Army members. Over the next few months, murders were to take place time and again.

On 9 January, against this background of disturbances and killings, Mo went into the Maze prison to meet with loyalist paramilitaries in the hope of persuading them of the merit of backing the peace process. I had advised against the risky visit, but Mo was right. Her gamble paid off, and she secured the backing she wanted – although sectarian killings continued.

Meanwhile, the talks were transferred to Lancaster House in London, where the loyalist UDP was temporarily barred from the talks for breaching the Mitchell Principles. Later, at the end of February in Dublin, Sinn Féin were similarly barred, but also returned to the fold in March. In early February, I had visited Paris and Bonn to update our European allies on the progress of the talks and, on 5 March, I called on the parties to seize the day! They listened to George Mitchell (who now set a deadline of Easter for a final agreement before he returned home), rather than listening to me.

Holy Week 1998, was to be one of the most important weeks of my life. George was absolutely right to insist on bringing the talks to an end. I travelled to Belfast on Sunday, 5 April, and had a brief meeting with George about what was ahead – it wouldn't be easy, and I gave success a fifty-fifty chance.

The week has been very well documented by Alistair Campbell, Jonathan Powell, George Mitchell himself, and many others. Suffice it to say that drafts flew back and forth, tempers flared, countless meetings were held by the two prime ministers, who were constantly engaged and, miraculously, we all stayed in Castle Buildings.

My job was to concentrate on Strand 1, relating to the Northern Ireland institutions and related issues such as languages, but, all the time, I had to try to encourage people to keep talking and not to leave. The big negotiation took place on Maundy Thursday and Good Friday. No one went to bed, and we carried on talking throughout the night. Two particular episodes come to mind. The first is Mo telling me to deal with Ian Paisley and his supporters, who were at that point marching on Stormont through the snow (they stopped!). The second is welcoming John Hume and Reg Empey into my office at about three in the morning to sign up to the agreement on how the assembly and the executive would operate.

I recall taking the decision that the assembly's members would be known as Members of the Legislative Assembly (MLAs), as was the case in certain Commonwealth countries, and advising on a final number of 108.

I remember also my visits to Tony's office, and listening on one occasion as he spoke on the phone with Bill Clinton, who was urging all participants to agree on the deal.

By the morning of Good Friday, 10 April, we were all exhausted – Nigel Warner and I had perhaps managed an hour's sleep on sofas in my office – but we had to continue. The rest of the day proved no less dramatic than had the entire week, with everyone finally waiting for David Trimble's Unionists to come on board.

At precisely 5.36pm, George Mitchell announced that agreement had been reached. It was a very moving and emotional moment. I was sitting next to Tony and Mo as the parties and governments, one by one, formally agreed the deal. There were many in tears. This was the beginning of the end of the conflict, and the culmination of years of negotiations.

I went over with Tony and Mo to meet the hundreds of journalists gathered outside Castle Buildings, and my own comments centred on the work done by all of the parties and on the fact that the agreement was, appropriately, made on Good Friday. Certainly, for my part, I have always used the phrase "Good Friday Agreement".

People were very kind to me over the role that I played. Bertie Ahern paid "tribute to the sheer determination and skills of Tony Blair, Mo Mowlam and her deputy, Paul Murphy", and George Mitchell said later "it is very clear that Tony Blair, with Mo Mowlam and Paul Murphy, clinched the deal." George wrote to me to say, "it was really great to work with you", and speaking at the meeting in Castle Buildings noted that I had done "a truly outstanding job". Mo considered me to be better than her in the art of compromise.

I was most touched by their kind comments. I received dozens of letters over the days that followed and, at the end of this remarkable week, I travelled to Singapore to spend a little time with my brother and his family.

The Good Friday Agreement was wide-ranging, covering institutions, human rights, the release of so-called political prisoners, the police, military issues and decommissioning, north–south and east–west relations, the two constitutions, and a host of other matters. It was a political compromise, expressed in the formal language of an international agreement between two sovereign states. The cover of the agreement in its published format, portraying a family looking towards sunrise, was chosen by me.

It was now time to start implementing the agreement. I took the Northern Ireland Elections and Referendum Bill through the Commons in late April, and the referendum held in the north and south took place on 22 May. During the weeks leading up to the referendum, I travelled the length and breadth of Northern Ireland talking to local and regional newspapers, and presenting the case for a "Yes" vote. The *Belfast Telegraph*, *The Newsletter* and the *Irish News*, between them representing both communities, backed the agreement, as did a majority of the people in both parts of the island of Ireland. Following the declaration of the result, Mo and I addressed the world's media – it was the biggest media event I have ever seen and, uniquely, the journalists and cameramen burst into spontaneous applause. I was almost in tears. The whole meaning of what had taken place seemed to hit me in just a few seconds.

Now we had to elect a new Northern Ireland Assembly, and the campaigning quickly gathered pace. The DUP, of course, campaigned against the agreement, while all the other parties argued for it. I kept out of this election – it was up to the people in Northern Ireland to decide for themselves who they wanted to govern them.

In late June, joined by Liz O'Donnell, I spoke to the parliamentary assembly of the Council of Europe about the agreement, and about the situation in Northern Ireland. Previously, in May, I had briefed the secretary general of the Organisation for Security and Cooperation in Europe (OSCE) in Brussels, together with the new Irish Foreign Minister David Andrews.

There was huge international interest in what we had done and part of my job was to explain the details of the agreement to other countries and to international bodies. Much was made of how the agreement could be used as a blueprint for addressing other conflicts around the world.

Not everyone in Northern Ireland supported the process, and as I was speaking at the Council of Europe a small bomb planted by dissidents exploded. There were no fatalities or serious injuries, but it was a sign there was still much more work to be done.

The day after my address to the council was election day, 25 June, after which the UUP and the SDLP became the two largest parties in the Assembly. The following month, I had to steer the Northern Ireland Bill through its Commons stages and, although the opposition supported us, the DUP MPs and a few others made sure that many amendments were debated; behind the scenes, I held myriad discussions on issues such as human rights and equality. The bill essentially set up the new Northern Ireland institutions of government – the Assembly and the executive – and was, necessarily, very detailed. The House of Lords debated the bill after the summer recess, and it returned to the Commons for its final stages in mid-November.

Tired, but pleased, I went on holiday to France in August with my friends Phyllis Roberts, Bernice Price and Father Bill Redmond. We travelled by car to the Lot valley, and stayed not far from the mediaeval city of Cahors.

On the Feast of the Assumption, 15 August, we drove to the great Christian pilgrimage site of Rocamadour to attend Mass in the Chapel of Our Lady. On our way there in the car, we heard a radio news bulletin about an explosion in the town of Omagh in the west of Northern Ireland, which didn't at the time appear to be very serious.

At our later return to our lodging, our hosts Barbara and Andy Szilagyi told us that the explosion was very much worse than we had first thought. I turned on the television to see my new ministerial colleague, John McFall MP, giving an interview.

The bombing was the worst ever experienced in Northern Ireland; 29 had been killed, and many others were seriously injured. A few days later, I had to cut my holiday short and return to the UK, flying to Belfast on an RAF plane. It was a lonely and awful journey. I went to Omagh, where I witnessed the terrible devastation, and spoke to the families of those who had been killed or critically injured. Words cannot adequately describe my feelings, and I can well understand Tony Blair breaking down when he visited the injured in hospital. As terrible as it all was, it didn't lessen the determination of the people of Northern Ireland to carry on with the peace process. If anything, it increased it.

In early autumn, I travelled to Viareggio in Italy to receive a peace prize on behalf of Mo – a heady occasion. On the journey, I had the memorable experience of meeting the granddaughter of the composer Puccini, who lived in Lucca, and who showed me around her grandfather's house. I then went to Rome where, accompanied by Mark Pellew, our ambassador to the Holy See, I was to meet Pope John Paul II. In the Welsh press, I described the event as "the meeting I will treasure all of my life", and so it was. I had never met a pope before, and it was a special occasion for me as a Papal Knight (I had been made a Knight of the Order of St Gregory, on the recommendation of Archbishop Ward of Cardiff, in March 1997); I had the great privilege of attending a private Mass with the pope at his summer residence in Castel Gandolfo, outside Rome. When I met him afterwards, the pope gave me a rosary and wished the peace process well. I then held meetings with officials at the Vatican's Secretary of State's department (the Vatican's equivalent of the Foreign Office).

During September, Gerry Adams and David Trimble met for the first time, paramilitary prisoners were released, and demolition began on the towers on the border.

At the beginning of October, Mo and I attended the Labour Party conference – the famous occasion when Mo received a standing ovation in the middle of Tony's speech. Later in the month, the Prime Minister asked me if I was interested in becoming the Leader of Welsh Labour – I was flattered, but declined, explaining that I was very much a House of Commons man and I didn't see my future in the Welsh Assembly. Tony wrote back and said that he fully understood and respected my position.

At the beginning of November, in my capacity as European Minister for Northern Ireland, I took the entire newly-elected Northern Ireland Assembly to Brussels. The event was an historic first for the European Union – a visit to Brussels by an elected parliament practically in its entirety (88 out of 108 members). I joined David Trimble and Seamus Mallon (by this time First Minister and Deputy First Minister designate) to meet with the President of the European Parliament (José María Gil-Robles) and party leaders, and President Santer and Commissioners Kinnock, Brittan, Flynn, Wulf-Mathies and Fischler. Many of our discussions concerned European funding for Northern Ireland. Later our ambassador to the EU, Sir Stephen Wall, commented: "Members of the Assembly sat down together at meals in Brussels who have never sat together or talked to each other before." It was a memorable and useful visit. From there, David, Seamus and I travelled on to Bonn for further and equally successful meetings.

On 23 November, I formally learned from the Prime Minister that he "had it in mind" to recommend my name to the Queen that "she may be graciously pleased to approve that you be sworn of Her Majesty's most honourable Privy Council", on the occasion of the 1999 New Year's Honours. I was thrilled and, as my fiftieth birthday was two days later, it was a unique birthday present. The trouble was that I was sworn to secrecy and couldn't tell anyone about it at my birthday party!

At the beginning of December, I travelled to the USA again to relay details of the agreement to our friends in Congress and more generally. In Boston, the John F. Kennedy Profile in Courage Award was presented to George Mitchell and to the party leaders who participated in the final negotiations. We were all shown around the J. F. Kennedy Library and Museum by Senator Ted Kennedy, a great friend of Ireland north and south.

The following day in Washington, the National Democratic Institute for International Affairs presented the W. Averell Harriman Democracy Award to the same people. I spoke at the event, as did the new Irish Foreign Minister David Andrews, and the whole visit was hugely enjoyable. We met briefly with President Clinton: without his commitment and all of the other American involvement, it is hard to see how success could have been achieved.

The New Year's Honours list was announced at the end of December. Adam Ingram and I were to be made Privy Counsellors, and awards were given to George Mitchell, John de Chastelain, Harri Holkeri and Reg Empey. What a difference a year had made! The next year, 1999, was not to be so ultimately successful or productive. Serious problems over decommissioning and north–south institutions were to hinder progress. On Good Friday, 1998, George Mitchell had said that the agreement signalled the beginning of much more negotiation; it was to take another decade before the Executive was to function properly. Much of my time was now spent on trying to implement the agreement, and I seemed still to be constantly in talks.

On 10 February, I went to Buckingham Palace to swear the oath of allegiance as a Privy Counsellor, along with Adam Ingram and Menzies Campbell. The Queen was, as always, very courteous and she expressed real interest in the Northern Ireland peace process.

The remaining six months of my time as Minister of State in Northern Ireland were dominated by attempts to set up the executive. The Assembly was elected and was meeting, but there was no governance. I remained the Finance Minister, and in June announced the budget in the House of Commons as well as in the Assembly, and answered questions, but it wasn't the same as if the MLAs had formed their own government or had their own Finance Minister.

The UUP and Sinn Féin were deadlocked on the issue of decommissioning, and all our efforts were put into talks to try to break the impasse. All-night sittings in Hillsborough Castle with Tony, Bertie and all of the parties became commonplace, as did secret meetings in No. 10 Downing Street.

I took the order, setting up north–south bodies, through the Commons on 8 March; I gave a progress update on 26 May, and introduced a new Northern Ireland Bill on 13 June.

But the sticking point was still the decommissioning of IRA weapons. For the Republicans, this was tantamount to surrender; for the Unionists, it was a prerequisite for Sinn Féin entering government. David Trimble and Gerry Adams were talking, but that wasn't enough.

In the meantime, huge speculation was mounting over a possible Cabinet reshuffle. The Unionists were asking for Mo's removal, while there was much talk of Peter Mandelson's return to the Cabinet, possibly to replace Mo as Northern Ireland Secretary. All the newspapers thought I was to be promoted – either to Wales in place of Alun Michael, who was to become First Secretary of Wales, or to replace Mo.

The Daily Telegraph said I was "the front runner to succeed Mo Mowlam"; the *News of the World* agreed. The *Sunday Express* and *The Observer* speculated I would go to Wales, while *The Times* hedged its bets and simply said that I was "regarded as a certainty for promotion to the Cabinet" – although its 23 July leader said I should go to Ulster. *The Guardian* mused how "Paul

Murphy, number two to Mo Mowlam in Belfast and widely credited with attending to much of the detail of agreements so far, is still strongly favoured for the job by many".

Michael Brown in *The Independent* said that I was "a dark horse whose pager could yet ring" – he wrote of how I was Mo's "trusty Minister of State" who had "impressed Tony Blair with his grasp of the minutiae of negotiating with the disparate political parties in Ulster". *The Daily Telegraph* said: "[Paul Murphy is] clearly heading for the Cabinet on the basis of his skills in keeping the Peace Process going, [and] he is also being strongly tipped to take over in Wales". Jo Hibbs, who wrote the article, went on to say that I was "the only Minister of State with a Welsh constituency and is streets ahead of junior Government rivals". Hibbs even speculated that John Morris MP, the Attorney General, might be asked to go back to his old job as Welsh Secretary!

On 27 July, I responded to what would be my last written Northern Ireland Question as Minister of State – a question concerning fish! The following day, Tony Blair phoned me at the Northern Ireland Office in Millbank, and asked me to become the Secretary of State for Wales. I was fifty-one years old, and now a Member of the British Cabinet. It was a daunting thought.

The newspapers were very kind. *The Times* ran an article headlined "Murphy wins the lesser prize", written by James Landale and Mark Inglefield; they suggested I might have felt "the slightest twinge of disappointment" because I had not replaced Mo in Northern Ireland, but they said "Mr Murphy will be content with the position: he is in the Cabinet, he is well-regarded by Mr Blair, and he could well use the position as a springboard to higher office". The leading article in the same newspaper suggested I should have remained in Northern Ireland to continue dealing with the peace process and Christopher Walker, again writing in *The Times*, said that my going and Mo's staying in Northern Ireland was a "double disaster" for the Unionists.

Donald Macintyre wrote in *The Independent* that "the new Welsh Secretary, Paul Murphy, who had proved beyond doubt in Northern Ireland that he has 'bottom' – that elusive quality so acclaimed by the older generation of politicians – was one of the very few who was clearly ready to join the Cabinet".

Mo was to stay in Northern Ireland until November, when she became the Cabinet Office Minister in the Cabinet. She was replaced, as we all thought she would be, by Peter Mandelson. In August, she wrote me a lovely letter, saying "I miss you already – I hope you have enjoyed working together as much as I have. I think we made a good team and you got a lot done."

I did enjoy working with Mo enormously. I have no doubt she played a pivotal role in the peace process. It was, looking back, a great pity she didn't take the job of Secretary of State for Health, which she had apparently been offered. But her own health was not good, and I don't think she really found pleasure in her time at the Cabinet Office in the same way that she relished her position in Northern Ireland. We remained close, right up to her death.

I was now off to the Wales Office, and taking another step into the unknown as I entered the Cabinet.

In Cabinet

1999–2002

I T DIDN'T REALLY HIT ME until the following day that I was actually a Member of the British Cabinet. I was over the moon, but there was a tinge of sadness that my mother and father were not alive to see their son sit at the top table.

The press was pretty good. The *Western Mail* predicted my appointment the day before it was announced: the paper's main headline read, "Murphy ready to take over as Welsh Secretary", with a spokeswoman for the Northern Ireland Office saying that I had returned to London and that my diary was "believed to be clear of any engagements in Ulster for the rest of the week". The following day, the same newspaper proclaimed: "Murphy's the new man for Wales as Blair reshuffles". It went on, "Ulster's loss was widely seen as Wales's gain". I had a sincere welcome from Alun Michael as well as Dafydd Wigley, and from Richard Livsey, who noted that "the need to obtain sufficient match-funding to draw down the £1.2 billion worth of Objective 1 funding from Europe will provide him with a severe test of his negotiating ability". My shadow, Nigel Evans, said: "Finally, we have someone who should take the job seriously instead of concentrating on his own career."

Nick Speed wrote a sympathetic article: "Coming out from Mo Mowlam's Shadow". The article outlined the main responsibilities of the new Welsh Secretary, which were not what they had been before devolution. My new duties were to represent the Cabinet in Wales and Wales in the Cabinet, as well as being responsible for primary legislation relating to Wales; to negotiate the Block Grant for Wales; to counsel the Assembly on the government's legislative programme; and "to ensure that the arrangements for co-operation between the Assembly and the UK Government are working effectively". It was a political and diplomatic job, not an administrative one. The old Welsh Office functions were now devolved to Cardiff. With regard to my previous anti-devolution views, Nick Speed observed, "when it comes to giving Wales a greater say in its own affairs, this devout Catholic is seen as having had something of a conversion on the road to Derry".

The main headline in *Catholic People*, the newspaper of the Catholic Archdiocese of Cardiff, read: "From Welsh Catholic to Cabinet", while the Protestant Northern Ireland newspaper wrote about my "switch to Wales" at a time when Unionists had wanted Mo to be switched! Rhodri Morgan told the *Daily Mirror*, "his appointment is well-deserved: the most memorable thing which makes him stand out is that he is not driven by ambition and doesn't have an ego!"

The next thing I had to do was to visit Cardiff and meet up with Alun at the Assembly. I believed that my friendship with Alun could overcome many "teething problems" as far as the Cardiff–Westminster relationship was concerned, but I acknowledged that differences were "the inevitable consequence of devolution", and realised immediately that the issue of finance, and particularly Objective 1 funding, was going to dominate my next year in office.

I received many letters of congratulation, among them one from the Prince of Wales, and others sent by organisations and individual constituents from Torfaen. I was particularly pleased with those letters that came from the Foreign Minister and Deputy Foreign Minister in Ireland – David Andrews and Liz O'Donnell – as well as from politicians and people from all sides in Northern Ireland. These really meant a lot to me, because I had felt so strongly that I wanted to be part of making peace there.

A very senior NIO official could not have moved me more than when he wrote: "whatever the future holds for us, Northern Ireland is a better place because you helped make it so".

Before I left for France on my annual holiday, I had to collect my Seals of Office from the Queen at Buckingham Palace. I tied myself in a knot trying to open the red box (which contained the Royal Seal), and Her Majesty was duly amused! At the end of the holiday, with Stuart, Pam, Phyllis and Bernice, I drove back to Northern Ireland to pick up my personal possessions. It was the first time I had actually driven in Northern Ireland, and I decided it would be the last!

Back in Wales, I started meeting all the Assembly members, speaking to many of them at a Labour AMs' away day in the Rhondda in early September. I then attended my first Cabinet meeting – a "political cabinet" held in Chequers on 16 September. I naively asked the Cabinet Secretary if I could sit anywhere and I was quickly and literally put in my place – which was not next to the Prime Minister. I was to Tony's left, sandwiched between Andrew Smith and Alan Milburn. Over the years, I gradually shifted along the table, and by 2005 ended up next to the Deputy Prime Minister John Prescott, just one seat away from Tony Blair!

The day before this meeting, the Pontypool weekly *Free Press* published an interview with me entitled "The miner's son from Abersychan", and it struck me how very fortunate I was to be in the Cabinet; I have never forgotten where I came from and how I owed my job, essentially, to the people of Torfaen.

Two weeks later, I was in Bournemouth for the Labour Party conference. I had been attending these events off and on since 1978, but this time I was one of the top team and had to address the full gathering, which I did on the Wednesday.

My speech was crafted by my new special adviser Professor Hywel Francis, who had given up his job as the Professor of Continuing Education at Swansea University. He was, and is, a distinguished Welsh Labour historian, co-author (with Dai Smith) of a famous history of the South Wales miners. Indeed, his father Dai Francis had been the leader of the South Wales NUM.

Hywel was to become the MP for Aberavon in 2001, and was eventually chair of both the Welsh Affairs Committee in the House of Commons and of the Joint Human Rights Committee of both Houses. He and his wife Mair have remained close friends of mine over the years.

The *Western Mail* headline about my speech read: "Murphy gives Wales a new rallying cry". It was my exhortation for "Assembly and Westminster together", and I told the delegates that Labour was pledged "to make our new democratic achievement a settled question, unlike our opponents who live in a make-believe world of claiming new powers without a people's mandate". I concluded: "Together we will achieve so much: a strong, prosperous Wales within a strong United Kingdom; proud to be Welsh, proud to be British together".

My message of "settled devolution" was contrasted with Ron Davies's view that devolution was a "process". Davies was probably right, looking now at developments over the last 20 years. But the referendum result had been extremely close, and at the time I believed that we had to settle down and deal with the issues that affected people's lives, like health and education. I was attacked by the Liberal Democrats and Plaid Cymru, but that came as no surprise. I was unable to commit to match-funding for Objective 1 finance for Wales – the great debate over this was yet to come.

On 6 October, I attended the memorial Requiem Mass for the former Cardinal Archbishop of Westminster, Basil Hume, in Westminster Cathedral. It was a solemn and sad event, also attended by the British and Irish Prime Ministers. Shortly before his untimely death from cancer, Cardinal Hume received the Order of Merit from the Queen – it was a symbol of the way in which British Catholics were now seen to be very much part of the community.

On 25 October, the House resumed and two days later I answered my first questions as a Cabinet Minister from the despatch box. The questions concentrated on my liaison role with Alun Michael and, inevitably, on European funding.

The *Western Mail* said that I made "a relaxed and trouble-free first appearance in the House of Commons as Secretary of State for Wales". The previous day, I had made another debut, this time before the Select Committee on Welsh Affairs. The session, chaired by Martyn Jones, MP for Clwyd South, debated "The role of the Secretary of State for Wales", and many of the exchanges centred on the new relationship between Westminster and Cardiff.

One of the questions put to me by Owen Paterson, MP for North Shropshire, was about my new department's name. I had had many weeks of discussion about this with Alun Michael. The Assembly understandably did not want to retain the old Welsh Office title, preferring the Office of the Secretary of State for Wales (OSSW). I wasn't too keen on this because we now had the Scotland Office and the Northern Ireland Office. We compromised on the Wales Office followed underneath by OSSW!

Another question Owen asked me was about the staffing and the cost of the Wales Office. The annual running costs were around £2 million and there were 32 staff at that time. Alison Jackson was the very competent head of the office, while my principal private secretary was Simon Morris. Simon was to be with me for the two spells I had as Secretary of State. He was appointed on the day before Ron Davies resigned, which was a traumatic event, and he then worked for Alun Michael. Simon was a brilliant civil servant who had come up through the ranks – politically astute, he had very sound judgement and great common sense. He and his wife, Carol, are still good friends of mine. Simon's deputy was Cherie Jones from Bridgend, and my press officer was Pat Wilson, the longest serving government press officer. I had an excellent team that was to serve me well over the years.

David Hanson, MP for Delyn, was the parliamentary Under-Secretary of State. He was a very bright, hard-working and sensible deputy, who deservedly became Tony Blair's parliamentary private secretary and, later on, Minister of State at the Northern Ireland Office, the Home Office and the Ministry of Justice. My own PPS was Gareth Thomas, MP for Clwyd West, a barrister and Welsh speaker, who was an assiduous aide.

My special adviser Hywel Francis was accompanied by Adrian McMenamin, a superb spin doctor originally from Northern Ireland. On

25. WITH PRINCE CHARLES

26. WITH MO MOWLAM, 1998

27. WITH BERTIE AHERN *(above)*

28. WITH THE QUEEN AND PRINCE PHILIP *(opposite, top)*

29. WITH TONY BLAIR AND GEORGE W. BUSH *(opposite, bottom)*

30. WITH GEORGE W.
BUSH, TONY BLAIR,
BERTIE AHERN,
BRIAN COWEN
AND MICHAEL
MCDOWELL

31. WITH GEORGE W. BUSH AND TONY BLAIR AT HILLSBOROUGH CASTLE *(above)*

32. WITH TED KENNEDY *(opposite, top)*

33. WITH DAVID TRIMBLE, JOHN HUME AND SEAMUS MALLON *(opposite, bottom)*

34. WITH AUNTY BETTY AND MY COUSINS MARGARET AND MARSDEN PAGET, ON MY 50th BIRTHDAY *(above)*

35. WITH NEIL, CLAIRE, DANIEL AND RACHEL IN WARSAW, PHOTOGRAPHED BY ME *(opposite, top)*

36. WITH STUART, PAM, PHYLLIS AND BERNICE, 1999 *(opposite, bottom)*

40.   THE CABINET, 2002 *(above)*

41.   FORMER WELSH SECRETARIES *(opposite)*

45. WITH POPE JOHN PAUL II

46. WITH NICK THOMAS-SYMONDS

leaving government for another job, Adrian was replaced by Dr Andrew Bold, a former political and research officer for the Welsh Labour Party. Towards the end of my first stint as Welsh Secretary, Owen Smith joined me as special adviser; the son of Dai Smith, the highly regarded professor of Welsh History, Owen had worked for the BBC as a producer on the *Today* programme and *Newsnight*, before joining BBC Wales. Owen came with me to Northern Ireland, where he did a great job, before entering parliament himself as MP for Pontypridd. He was to attain national prominence when he stood against Jeremy Corbyn for the Labour Party leadership.

A great deal of my time was now spent in Wales. I had an office in the Assembly (with a small staff there), and I was expected to go to visit all parts of Wales and to meet with all sorts of organisations: in November for instance I addressed the Institute of Directors, the Merthyr and Rhymney Constituency Labour Party and the Annual Awards Day of my old school, West Mon!

I was also very pleased to be named as one of the winners of the annual *Spectator* Parliamentarian of the Year Awards, held over lunch at the Savoy Hotel in London. John Major received the main award, while I was named "Minister to Watch" and presented with my prize by the *Spectator* editor Boris Johnson, who kindly referred to my time in Northern Ireland.

The judges noted that "it was said that the secret of Mo Mowlam's success as Secretary of State for Northern Ireland was her willingness to throw her arms around people on all sides of the conflict and hug them. Perhaps the reason things have not totally collapsed over there is that there was always someone to comfort those whom Mo had hugged! This year's winner has been widely admired for the way he has gone to those Unionists, reeling from her embraces, and persuaded them to look on the bright side."

The previous month, I spoke to the Welsh Assembly for the first time in my capacity as Welsh Secretary. I had an official desk in the Assembly Chamber and, although I was entitled to sit in the Chamber at any time, I did so only when I was to make the annual speech outlining the government's programme. Eventually and rightly, the desk was removed!

I focused on the three bills that would affect Wales the most – the Countryside Bill, the Learning and Skills Bill, and the Local Government Bill. Plaid Cymru AM Rhodri Glyn Thomas tried to intervene, but was told by the Presiding Officer Lord Elis-Thomas to sit down!

I also warned that constantly threatening no confidence motions against the First Secretary and giving insufficient thought to the Objective 1 European Scheme was debilitating, and this was the beginning of the storm that was to hit the Assembly in the New Year.

I had no doubt that the outcome we could achieve to the continuing row over match-funding for £1.2 billion of Objective 1 money would be crucial to the sustainability of the minority Labour government in Wales, led by Alun Michael. The issue was raised constantly in Cardiff and Westminster; it came up in Welsh Questions on 19 January and now dominated Welsh politics.

In March 1999, the EU Commission had granted Objective 1 status to West Wales and the South Wales valleys. The £1.2 billion grant was the most significant type of European funding – awarded only on very strict conditions and to the most deprived areas in Europe. It was due to be drawn down after 1 January 2000, but it had to be matched by an equivalent amount from the UK government. This was the so-called "additionality argument" – the extra money had to be genuinely on top of normal funding.

Tony Blair said he would not let Wales down, but Gordon Brown, the Chancellor of the Exchequer, wanted any settlement to be part of the comprehensive spending review, to be concluded later in the year.

This was not good enough for the opposition in the Assembly. They wanted blood, and they were to table a no confidence motion in the First Secretary Alun Michael. I spoke out against what I saw as the opportunism of Plaid Cymru and the Welsh Conservatives, telling the press: "There will only be one nominee for the job of First Secretary – Alun Michael. We are not going to let the decision be overturned by a rag-bag alliance of Tories and nationalists". The *South Wales Argus* headline on 18 January read: "Murphy rides to the rescue".

Events were to unfold very quickly and very dramatically. I camped in my office in Cardiff Bay, spoke to all Assembly Ministers and others, and even tried to persuade Mike German and his Liberal Democrats to come on side. Tony Blair asked Charles Kennedy to intervene, but it was all to no avail. On 11 February, Alun Michael resigned as First Secretary before a vote of no confidence could be called; Tony Blair phoned me and said that we should try to get Rhodri Morgan confirmed as Labour leader before the six o'clock news. The Welsh executive of the Labour Party met, and this was duly achieved.

It was a sad and terrible business. Alun didn't deserve the treatment he received. One of the problems was that the Welsh Labour Party was still reacting to the Welsh leadership battle between Alun and Rhodri after Ron Davies's resignation. The Assembly elections had produced a minority Labour government, and instability was now the order of the day. The time had come for a coalition, and Rhodri skilfully negotiated a pact with the Liberal Democrats, which Tony Blair and I backed.

The Objective 1 row was finally settled in July, when Gordon Brown agreed to provide the extra match-funding for Wales. The *Western Mail* reported:

Welsh Secretary, Paul Murphy, who had been locked in negotiations over the settlement ever since taking up his post a year ago, trusted that the review meant 'no worthwhile scheme' under Objective 1 would be denied funding.

"This is the first time ever that a settlement has gone beyond Barnett. It is unprecedented. The money is completely extra: it is above and beyond the block grant," I observed. Tony Blair and I wrote separate articles for the *Daily Mirror* welcoming the money, and Rhodri and I toured Wales spreading the good news!

The *Daily Post* editorial said: "the Wales Secretary has achieved an unprecedented transfer of EU funds to Wales", which was a good end to what had been a long and sometimes tragic story.

In the meantime, I had to deal with the report of the inquiry into the North Wales child abuse scandal, chaired by retired High Court Judge Sir Ronald Waterhouse QC. The inquiry had taken three years and cost £13 million. It investigated the physical and sexual abuse of children in care homes in Clwyd and Gwynedd, including the now infamous Bryn Estyn children's home in Wrexham. The tribunal sat for 203 days: it took evidence from 250 witnesses, and heard from over 650 people. The amount of information was so overwhelming that the publication of the report had to be delayed; the report itself ran to more than 500,000 words, and contained 700 allegations of abuse involving 170 individuals. Over 80 people were named as child abusers; it was the biggest investigation of its kind ever undertaken in the UK.

The report *Lost in Care – the Waterhouse Report* concluded that there was regular abuse of children in residential establishments in Clwyd between 1974 and 1990. It did not conclude that there was a conspiracy involving "prominent persons", but said there had been a paedophile ring in the Wrexham and Chester area. It fell to me as the relevant Cabinet Minister, to handle this report, which made grim and awful reading – identifying as it did widespread failures across the board. The report contained 72 recommendations for changes, constituting a massive overhaul of the way in which children in care are dealt with by public bodies; it also led to the eventual establishment of the position of Children's Commissioner for Wales.

On 15 February 2000, I made a major statement to the House of Commons on the report, saying that, "it is a tragedy that such treatment should have been meted out to children in care". I added:

to those whose lives have been shattered, to the families of those who have died, and to all decent thinking people, we all say sorry. But sorry is not enough and we are determined that this report will lead to a society where young people can be cared for safely and where they can truly enjoy their childhood.

I told the House that "these were appalling misdeeds, wickedness and total abuse of trust", and, as *The Guardian* said at the time, "The system was devoid of leadership, management or planning. No part of it escapes censure – social services, councillors, police, or the Welsh Office."

In a note to the Prime Minister for the Cabinet meeting, on17 February, one of the points made was that "Murphy handled it well". It had been one of the most disagreeable things I have ever had to do in politics.

At the beginning of March, I opened the traditional St David's Day debate in the Commons by announcing that an independent Children's Commissioner for Wales was to be appointed as the first example of the National Assembly requesting changes to legislation at Westminster. According to Nick Speed, writing in the *Western Mail*: "To cheers from all sides of the House the Torfaen MP said the Government would bring forward an amendment to the Care Standards Bill, to establish a commissioner with statutory power."

In March 2000, Rhodri Morgan and I visited the site of the former Thomas and Evans "Corona Pop" factory to look at the new Avanti Television project that had been named "The Pop Factory", specialising in rock music. It was a remarkable example of transformation from one sort of industry to another; *Wales on Sunday* followed up on the visit with a piece about the relationship between myself and Rhodri, titled "It's the hottest new double act in town!", in which we were compared to the comedians Ryan and Ronnie; and Martin Shipton, the veteran political commentator, said it was our "joint task to rebuild Labour's fortunes in Wales for the General Election". Rhodri and I were the not-so-secret weapon of the Wales Labour Party. Martin went on to say that I was "the linkman between Welsh Labour in Wales and the seat of UK power in Westminster. But instead of being some remote Governor General figure Murphy wants to be in among the action, emphasising his strong and authentic Welsh roots." The rest of the article was a joint interview with Rhodri and me. We emphasised our long and close friendship and what message we would convey to the Welsh electorate at the 2001 election.

Our First Minister–Secretary of State partnership lasted for over four years, and throughout both occasions when I was Welsh Secretary. I believe the fact that we worked together so closely meant that we really did overcome the frequent problems and difficulties that were to arise between the governments. We spoke almost every day and saw each other once a week, usually on a Monday morning in Rhodri's office. The personal aspect of politics is too often overlooked; I've always considered my profession to be one which is ultimately about people and personal relationships, whether in Belfast or Cardiff, and I never believed in or used personal attacks or abuse in debates – there was nothing to be gained from it.

Rhodri and I worked together again at the hundredth anniversary conference of Welsh Labour, held in Llandudno in late March. The *Western Mail* headline read: "Murphy to put Labour on election alert", and I told delegates that the fight in Wales would be between Labour and the Tories, and that the people of Wales could not afford a Conservative government to wreck what Labour had achieved in its first term. I also wrote an article for the *Daily Mirror*, saying that Labour is the real party of Wales, outlining Labour's achievement and warning Welsh voters against Plaid Cymru.

At the beginning of April, Rhodri and I were able to combine work and relaxation when we visited Dublin to discuss economic regeneration, but also to watch the Wales–Ireland rugby match as Lansdowne Road! We met the Irish President Mary McAleese, as well as Bertie Ahern and other Irish Ministers. It was to be the first of many international rugby matches Rhodri and I watched together – he was the expert and I was the novice, and I marvelled at how he kept his patience in explaining every few minutes what was happening on the field.

A few months later, on 11 June, I went as a Member of the Cabinet to a service of celebration and thanksgiving for the life of Queen Elizabeth The Queen Mother, who was reaching her hundredth birthday.

The job of Secretary of State for Wales post-devolution was very different from when the Welsh Office ran everything in Wales. The role was slowly defining itself – regular meetings with Rhodri and his Ministers, attending Cabinet and Cabinet committees, answering questions in the House and taking debates, and generally maintaining good relations between Cardiff and Westminster. Other major activities included attending First Ministerial committees around the country (bringing together members from the UK government and the three devolved administrations), visiting Welsh universities, dealing with issues such as the future of the steel industry, and meeting with bodies like the Welsh TUC, CBI and the Royal College of Nursing.

I was hugely helped in all this by my parliamentary Under-Secretary of State – David Hanson MP, until the 2001 General Election, after which he became PPS to the Prime Minister; and thereafter Don Touhig MP. Both were brilliant at their jobs, answering questions, meeting Welsh Ministers, and travelling all over Wales. They also attended Cabinet committees.

Having been made a Privy Counsellor in the 1999 New Year's Honours, I was required from time to time to attend Privy Council meetings – usually at Buckingham Palace, occasionally at Windsor Castle. By tradition, the Queen and her counsellors would meet for about 20 minutes, passing various orders-in-council.

On 11 October 2000, I acted as president of the council in Margaret Beckett's absence on a visit to Mexico. I had a private audience with the Queen before chairing the council. The first item of business was the appointment of Rhodri as a Privy Counsellor, and I was particularly moved that I was to present him to the Queen on this occasion. I always valued and enjoyed meeting the Queen, and when we met in Windsor to lunch with her and the Duke of Edinburgh, she was able to recall many years of government activity, and her experience was vital to understanding so many issues. She also had a fine sense of humour!

Some weeks later, I spoke at a gathering of European lawyers in Cardiff, and I welcomed Labour's pact with the Liberal Democrats, adding that it would bring stability to the Assembly and "would allow a clear programme of policies to go through", and that:

> the success of devolution will be judged by the people in terms of how many more jobs come to Wales, how many more people our hospitals treat, and how many of our children get the skills and qualifications they need to compete in today's labour market.

I next flew to Spain to see devolution at work, visiting Valencia, Madrid and Barcelona. It was a useful and often fascinating trip – perhaps the highlight of the experience was a long meeting in Barcelona with Catalonia's President Pujol. Spain's system of asymmetrical devolution was similar to ours in the UK, with widely different systems of government in the Basque country, Catalonia, Valencia, Galicia and elsewhere. Hardly had I been back in Wales when, after only a few days, I returned to Spain to attend a British-Spanish Tertulias in Santiago de Compostela, which brought together for discussion politicians, business people, academics, soldiers and many others. I thoroughly enjoyed this meeting and the place – despite the constant rain we had to endure!

Towards the end of 2000, there was a great row over the naming of Millennium Cities – two towns in England and one in Scotland were to be given this designation, but none in Wales. I reacted furiously at a Cabinet meeting, and was subsequently promised that at the time of the Golden Jubilee in 2002 all the home nations would have a new city. After much deliberation, I recommended that the choice for Wales should be Newport

– it was our third-largest town, with a university and a cathedral. I understood the disappointment of other potential cities – especially Wrexham – but a decision had to be made.

January 2001 began with the parliamentary introduction of the bill to approve a Children's Commissioner for Wales, a major innovation arising from a recommendation in the Waterhouse report. The post was the first of its kind in the UK, and I introduced the bill at second reading on 16 January 2001. It was also the first Wales-only bill to come before parliament since the establishment of the Welsh Assembly. The first commissioner to be appointed in Wales was Mr Peter Clarke, and the legislation paved the way for Children's Commissioners in the other parts of the UK.

February 2001 took me to Brussels to meet the European Commissioners and Welsh MEPs. Then, on the 26th, I attended the Rite of Welcome in Westminster Cathedral for the new Cardinal Archbishop of Westminster, Cardinal Cormac Murphy-O'Connor, who had succeeded the late Basil Hume. Cormac was a wonderful man. He came from a Cork family, although he had been born in Reading, and had a fine sense of humour and was tremendous company. I was to attend his funeral sixteen years later.

In the same month, the steel company Corus announced enormous job losses in Wales, over 2,600 in total, at Llanwern, Shotton and Gorseinon – and at Ebbw Vale, where the steel plant closed altogether, causing the loss of nearly 600 jobs in the community. I had been working very closely with Rhodri and with the Department of Trade and Industry secretary Steve Byers, and had had numerous meetings with Corus chairman Sir Brian Moffat, soon to be labelled "the most hated man in Wales". Tony Blair asked Moffat to reconsider his plans, but to no avail. These were dark days for Wales.

I had done everything that I could, working especially with the general secretary of the Steelworkers' Union ISTC, Michael Leahy from Pontypool – I had sat on the council with Michael's father Cyril. Michael was a moderate and highly effective trade union leader, who had followed my colleague Lord Keith Brookman as general secretary, and he wrote to me later in the year saying:

[I am] writing to you my deep gratitude and that of my colleagues in the ISTC for your unfailing support and assistance during the discussions with Corus since December. We were not able to save the jobs in Wales and England in the steel industry which Corus will destroy through its narrow and short-term approach but with your help we were able to make clear the issues to the public and the need for manufacturing companies generally to be encouraged to take a strategic view of their responsibilities to their employees and

to the nation at large. Thank you in particular for your role in securing the modified ISERBS benefits for working people in the steel
industry who are being made redundant. This will greatly assist the
regeneration of Welsh communities.

As if the plight of the steel industry weren't enough, Wales was then hit by
the biggest outbreak of foot and mouth disease it had ever experienced – an
outbreak that caused a major crisis in British agriculture and tourism, forc-
ing the cull of over six million cows and sheep. The worst affected county
in Wales was Anglesey, but the problems faced throughout the counties
were severe. As Welsh Secretary, I sometimes attended the COBRA security committee meetings on a daily basis, and I was heavily involved in
coordinating efforts between the UK government and the Welsh Assembly
Government. Rhodri and I met regularly, together with the Rural Affairs
Minister for Wales, Carwyn Jones. I vividly remember the three of us travelling to Anglesey on a small plane to meet with farmers and local government leaders, and stopping off en route in mid-Wales. It was a terrible time
for all concerned, which ended with the epidemic being contained, but both
Welsh agriculture and the tourist industry took a long time to recover.

The issue featured heavily in the St David's Day Debate on 5 March, as
did the death the previous month of Cledwyn Hughes, Baron Mostyn, MP
for Anglesey from 1951 to 1979 and a former Welsh Secretary. I called him
"a great Welshman because of his passion for Wales: in that, few were equal
and none his master"; I was privileged to read a lesson at his memorial service in St Margaret's, Westminster, later in October.

One major political consequence of the foot and mouth outbreak was
the postponement of the General Election until 7 June 2001. As Welsh
Secretary, I led the election campaign in Wales, which meant I had to tour
the Welsh marginal constituencies, basing myself at Labour's HQ in Cardiff
at Transport House, and appearing on radio and television. The role that
I played was fascinating but, given the amount of time that I had to spend
away from my own constituency, I had good reason to be grateful that my
seat was a traditionally safe Labour one.

One notorious episode during the campaign took place in Rhyl on
16 May. I had just returned from the Cabinet launch of the Labour manifesto,
and had driven straight to North Wales to preside at a rally in Rhyl town
hall with Labour's deputy leader (the Deputy Prime Minister) John Prescott as
main speaker. What complicated matters was that the hall was picketed by
people supporting various countryside issues, and one protestor threw an egg
at John from point-blank range. John immediately reacted with a punch, and
it became the incident that led the news for the new few days.

I was in the hall when I was told what had happened, where I then had to try to calm an understandably irate Deputy Prime Minister. Then the phone calls started – Alistair Campbell and Tony Blair among others – and we were locked in the hall for many hours before the police allowed us to leave. The incident actually enlivened a rather dull campaign, and the following day one voter actually suggested to me that John should have hit his assailant harder!

I was in Ynys Môn that day, with Labour's excellent candidate Albert Owen. Albert was from Anglesey, and had spent his early career in the Merchant Navy before working with the Citizens' Advice Bureau and at a welfare rights centre in Holyhead. After graduating in Politics at the University of York, he became Labour's candidate: he won the seat in that 2001 contest and has held it ever since. We are close friends, and Albert is one of the most effective Labour MPs in the Commons, well-liked by his colleagues and hugely admired by his constituents.

The 2001 election was a great triumph for the Labour Party, and for Tony Blair also. In Wales, there was no overall change other than Labour's losing Carmarthen East and Dinefwr to Plaid Cymru, and Albert returning the compliment by winning Ynys Môn. In Wales as a whole, Labour took 48.6 per cent of the vote, and 34 of the 40 seats; there were still no Tory MPs in the country, and I was extremely pleased with Labour's performance, in which I had played some small part.

In my own constituency, my majority was just over 16,000, and I took 61 per cent of the vote – less spectacular than the 1997 result, but it was just fine!

Later that year, in October, with changed rules in the House of Commons, I was able to appoint a researcher. I already had Irene as my secretary and Pam as my case-worker, but I now went about the business of advertising for a parliamentary researcher. With quite a few applications to choose from, in the end I appointed 21-year-old Anthony Hunt from Stevenage. Anthony had graduated in Law at Cardiff University, and was working for the Labour group at the National Assembly. He came to me with good qualifications, some excellent relevant experience, and a real enthusiasm, and he was to stay with me until I retired from the Commons in 2015.

Anthony has become a very good friend, together with his wife Lizzie and his sons Evan and Owen. The family first lived in Cardiff, before moving to Pontypool, where Anthony won a seat on Torfaen County Borough Council – in time, he became the executive member for finance (my old job on the council!), then deputy leader, and finally leader. He was also Labour's parliamentary candidate in Ludlow at the 2010 General Election.

When I was Welsh Secretary for the second time, Anthony was one of my special advisers, and an excellent one too; he is one of the new generation of Labour leaders in Wales.

During this period, I was elected to an Honorary Fellowship at Oriel, my old Oxford college, and was deeply moved by this honour.

There was also an event in my own constituency. As I've already noted, my home village of Abersychan is unusual in having been the home or birthplace of no fewer than seven Members of Parliament and, on 11 September 2001, Roy Jenkins and I unveiled a plaque on the old Lock-Up in the village to recognise five of them. Roy, as always, was fascinated by the statistical rarity of the situation!

The date 9/11 is now, of course, remembered around the world for a very different reason. Immediately after the unveiling in Abersychan, I had to leave in my role as Secretary of State to fulfil a commitment in North Wales. When I arrived at my destination, I learned more of the atrocity that had taken place in New York that morning. Whatever had been the original purpose of my visit, it was forgotten as I returned to London for a special Cabinet meeting and session of the Commons the next day.

Towards the end of the year, I travelled to the First World War battlefields of Flanders, and stayed in Ypres with Stuart Cameron and his family. It was to be an annual pilgrimage in the years ahead.

The beginning of 2002 saw a by-election in the Ogmore constituency, caused by the sudden death of Sir Ray Powell. Labour Party chair Charles Clarke MP and I were charged with arranging the selection of a new candidate, and such a safe seat attracted many applicants (including my friend Richard Lewis, who was a native of the constituency), and the local party chose Huw Irranca-Davies as its candidate.

After a vigorous by-election campaign, and a great eve of poll rally with Dennis Skinner MP, we retained the seat on 14 February with 52 per cent of the vote.

A couple of weeks later, I led the first Welsh Day debate in the Commons since the General Election, and teased my shadow Nigel Evans MP about his predictions of ten Tory victories in Wales, which I described as "Mystic Nigel's Tips for the Top"! The debate ranged over the economy, public services, foot and mouth, and the steel industry.

A few days after this debate, on St David's Day itself, I returned to my former workplace in Ebbw Vale College to meet Prince Charles. We both wanted to visit the town, which had now seen the last of its steel jobs disappear, and it felt quite strange to come back to my old college after the many years that I'd spent teaching there – but this time in the company of the Prince of Wales!

Steel was not going away as an issue, though. On 5 March, I was selected by the government to reply in a debate initiated by Adam Price (then a Plaid Cymru MP, but now the party's leader, sitting in the Welsh Assembly) regarding the decision of Tony Blair to support the bid by steel company Mittal to purchase a steel plant in Romania. Lakshmi Mittal had donated £125,000 to the Labour Party, and the accusation was that this new steel plant would have a detrimental effect on the British – and specifically the Welsh – steel industry, and that Mittal's donation had influenced Blair's decision.

I had drawn the short straw as Welsh Secretary. Plaid Cymru had tabled the motion, backed by the Tories, and the Secretary of State for Transport, Local Government and the Regions Steve Byers was let off the task of responding! So it fell to me to defend the government, and particularly the Prime Minister. I was repeatedly interrupted by David Cameron, Michael Fallon and Boris Johnson (all of them at that time backbenchers), among many others – even Diane Abbott intervened, but not to help me! Don Touhig wound up the debate with an excellent speech, knocking down the arguments of both Plaid Cymru and the Conservatives.

Don was a first class Minister with a good political brain, and it was great that since the General Election, we were now working together in the Wales Office.

The Welsh Labour Party Conference was held in late March 2002 in Llandudno, and my theme for that year was improvement in public services – particularly schools and hospitals. David Blunkett also addressed conference, calling for more local power for the people. Tony Blair didn't attend, but he sent a message congratulating the party on its "fantastic performance" in the General Election, and noting that "these tremendous results demonstrate the health of the party in Wales; your hard work and campaigning skills; and strong leadership from Rhodri Morgan and Paul Murphy."

I flew to Spain some weeks later, visiting the traditional coal and steel region of Asturias, and then Segovia where I addressed an international conference on regional government in Europe. I was very amused at the conference when I was addressed as "Your Magnificence"!

On 2 May, the Commons debated the report of the Welsh Affairs Committee, *Wales in the World*. The committee was chaired by Martyn Jones, MP for Clwyd South, who had entered parliament with me in 1987. His report made good and interesting reading, and it also showed how parliament was adapting itself to the new political landscape. The committee had taken care to involve the National Assembly, which now had responsibility for economic development, and in the debate I took the opportunity to pay tribute to Rosemary Butler and Brian Smith, who represented Wales at the EU's Committee of the Regions.

I also told the House how the Assembly was taking part in European affairs – between April 2001 and March 2002, there had been seven EU Council meetings attended by Ministers from Cardiff dealing with such varied topics as culture, the environment, agriculture, education and youth issues. The debate in the House ranged from tourism to inward investment, evidence of the extent to which Wales was becoming a modern European country in its own right.

As if to emphasise this, President of the European Commission Romano Prodi, the former Prime Minister of Italy, visited Wales in May with European Transport Commissioner Neil Kinnock. There are two events that I recall very clearly: going up in a helicopter and enjoying the view across the South Wales valleys; and visiting the Swansea Italian community in the Mumbles, and eating delicious ice-cream.

June saw the Queen's Golden Jubilee celebrations, beginning with a very moving thanksgiving service in St Paul's Cathedral. I welcomed Her Majesty to North Wales on 11 June when she visited Beaumaris Castle and Anglesey, before attending the Jubilee service for Wales in Bangor Cathedral. It was a fine and joyous occasion.

Owen Smith had moved from the BBC to become my special adviser in April. His experience in the media, his intellectual acumen and his sound political judgement made him a brilliant aide, and his skills were to prove hugely valuable in the years ahead. However, his time with me at the Wales Office ended unexpectedly when I was offered a different Cabinet position just a few weeks after his appointment.

I took part in what turned out to be my last Welsh Questions as Secretary of State on 17 July; in September, I spoke to the Labour Party conference; on 10 October, I delivered the Keir Hardie lecture in Merthyr Tydfil; and, on 21 October, I answered my last written question.

My time as Welsh Secretary had been enjoyable, sometimes exciting and always challenging. Three years in Tony Blair's Cabinet was an experience in itself, but it also meant that I had lived through and taken part in the early years of devolution in Wales.

I had always been a critic of Welsh devolution, but these years saw me change my mind. The commitment of the Ministers in Cardiff convinced me that the constitutional leap in the dark had been successful. It would take time before the people of Wales became more aware and more fond of the Assembly, but this did happen. I hope it could be said that I had some influence in this transformation of popular opinion.

Ulster again
2002–2005

JUST BEFORE THE CABINET was due to meet on Thursday morning, 24 October 2002, I was asked to see Tony Blair. I had thought he would want me to report on some talks that I'd been having on the current firemen's dispute. Instead, after a brief meeting with the Prime Minister, I emerged as the new Secretary of State for Northern Ireland. It was a shock, and I felt stunned as the Cabinet meeting dragged on.

The Education Secretary Estelle Morris had decided that she wanted to leave her job in the Cabinet, which in turn led to a reshuffle. The Northern Ireland Secretary John Reid became the chair of the Labour Party, and I was to replace John.

The first and immediate effect of the Prime Minister's decision was that I would now be under personal protection at all times by the Special Branch. I was given this protection in Northern Ireland when I was Minister of State, so I knew it would now have a huge impact on my everyday life. A team of detectives led by an able and affable Scotsman was to guard me and I was to travel in an armoured Jaguar with a back-up Range Rover following. The team of six police officers rotated; three armed officers plus two drivers were always with me. For the next three years, I was not allowed to venture out without them – they would accompany me to church, the supermarket, the theatre, the concert hall, the restaurant and the pub! They were all decent and helpful men, who became firm friends and who shared a joke; but they were there for a very serious purpose and I never forgot it.

I flew straight to Belfast for a walk-about in the Bloomfield shopping centre in Bangor, County Down. As one newspaper put it, "the new Northern Ireland Secretary was trailed by a sizeable media pack which strained to get photographs, quotes or video footage of every conversation he had with shoppers".

The Irish Times reported that I got off to a "polite start" on my return to Belfast, and that at the end of my visit to the local Marks & Spencer store I received "a gift of some potato bread and soda farls which is traditional in these parts as politeness".

I had intended to attend a conference in Spain that weekend, but I ended up in Hillsborough Castle instead. This stately home had been the official residence of former governors of Northern Ireland, and it was now home to serving Northern Ireland secretaries, and to the Queen when she visited Ulster. It was a beautiful home, with dozens of rooms and a friendly and helpful staff headed by the butler, David; one of David's staff, Olwen, took care of my domestic needs. They were both to receive MBEs. I had a private apartment and an enormous bed, made especially for the 1992–7 Secretary of State Paddy Mayhew, who was very tall. The castle was to be my Northern Ireland home for three years, and I came to love it and the wonderful gardens surrounding it. It even had its resident ghost, seen by my brother and sister-in-law during one Christmas visit.

I travelled to Northern Ireland in a small aeroplane affectionately known as the Clipper, which flew to and from wherever I happened to be – Wales, London, wherever. It took me to Dublin for meetings, and occasionally to Strasbourg and other European destinations. It was a great asset, shared with other Ministers and civil servants; but, of course, it was really all about security.

Reaction to my appointment was generally very favourable, mainly due to the fact that I had been Political Development Minister just three years previously. Although I had to be briefed in detail on the current situation, I still had a pretty good knowledge of politics in Northern Ireland. I had made many friends, and I knew most of the key figures in Belfast and Dublin, as well as in Washington and Brussels.

Newspapers were supportive. The *Belfast Telegraph* said that I "was able to hit the ground running", and that I had "earned a reputation for even handedness". The nationalist *Irish News* offered me best wishes, saying I had "one of the hottest seats in the British Cabinet", and that the new Secretary of State would "have to use all his undoubted skills to rebuild strained relationships and create a climate in which progress becomes possible". The *Financial Times* thought I was "the obvious and perhaps the only possible choice to succeed Dr Reid", while the *Daily Mirror* said that "Trimble backed Murphy for the post".

Local politicians were kind about my appointment, and the Taoiseach Bertie Ahern wished me well in my new post. I had many letters of congratulation from Ulster and from Britain, sent by a wide cross-section of people, ranging from church leaders and civil servants to constituents in

Torfaen. The thanks I received for my work as Welsh Secretary were also a great source of comfort. From Ireland itself, one of the warmest messages of welcome came from the President, Mary McAleese, whom I had known when she was a Professor of Law during my time as Minister of State.

I had a great ministerial team to work with. Security Minister Jane Kennedy, Ian Pearson, Lord Des Browne and Baroness Angela Smith were all first-rate ministers and became good friends – and all would be promoted, rightly, to other positions. We were a special unit because we were unwilling "direct-rule" ministers, and were all thrown together far from our homes and constituencies. Des was to become Secretary of State for Defence, and Angela a senior minister and later an excellent shadow leader of the House of Lords.

Owen Smith had, fortunately for me and the peace process, decided to come with me to Belfast. He worked brilliantly with the parties and with the civil servants. Joe Pilling was still the wise and very able Permanent Secretary, assisted by Jonathan Phillips, a top civil servant who had come to the NIO from the DTI. He had a formidable intellect and a very engaging personality, and he shared with me a love of classical music. He was to be my right-hand man for the next three years in Belfast, and he eventually became Permanent Secretary and was later knighted for his work in Northern Ireland. No one deserved an honour more.

My chief press officer was Robert Hannigan, an Oxford classicist and former teacher, who had come late to the civil service. He headed one of the largest and most sensitive press operations in the British government, and he did it extremely well. With an engaging personality and a wife who came from Ireland, Robert brought much to the table. After some years, he was to replace Jonathan Phillips as political director, and after very senior positions at the NIO and the Foreign Office he became director of GCHQ.

David Brooks was my principal private secretary: he had been an NIO civil servant all his life, and no one knew more about the place than he did. A keen cricketer, he lived in England but came from Welsh stock and, along with his eventual successor Alan Whysall, David made my life manageable, and often agreeable! Without the two of them, I would have been lost.

On my arrival, my first official function was to attend the annual presentation of the Maguire Trophy to the winning Irish Gaelic football team in Parliament Buildings, Stormont. On that night, I met up with Gerry Adams and other political leaders from the nationalist side, and over the next few days I was to meet all of the leaders in my office in Belfast.

The task facing me was truly formidable. The Assembly, and the executive, was now suspended as a result of a complete loss of trust arising from the so-called Columbia Spy-ring, the IRA break-in at Castlereagh police station, and the police raid on the Sinn Féin offices at Stormont. The police found sensitive political material on computers, as well as the addresses of police officers and the details of the GOC's car. Public opinion among Unionists was now firmly against the Good Friday Agreement, and the British government had no option but to suspend the institutions. This happened just days before my appointment, and it was a bitter blow for all those who had worked hard to bring peace to Northern Ireland.

Tony Blair went to Belfast and told the people of Northern Ireland that Sinn Féin – and the IRA – could not be half-in half-out of the process; Gerry Adams responded with a helpful speech two days after my appointment.

My first Commons appearance in my new role was in response to a Conservative motion moved by my shadow Quentin Davies, MP for Grantham and Stamford. Quentin was a very clever man, very pro-Europe, and he had immersed himself in Northern Ireland politics. He was to cross the floor of the House in 2007 and become a Labour MP, a Minister and eventually a Labour peer. But on this occasion he was criticising us for allowing Sinn Féin to use Commons facilities when the party's MPs refused to take their seats. It was an opportunity to reflect on the wider picture, and in response to Quentin I said: "I came back to the NIO after an interval and with a determination to see the process brought to a conclusion. My first step will be to listen carefully to what all the parties have to say about the way forward." Robin Cook wound up the debate. A month later, at Northern Ireland Questions, the issue of decommissioning, the suspension of the Assembly, and the role of the IRA dominated proceedings. I did a great deal of media work, trying to focus politicians' minds on the need for a fresh start, and in an article for the *Financial Times* I warned of the enormous difficulties we would face in restoring the peace process. This coincided with the arrest of a young man who had worked for David Trimble as a diary secretary, and who was supposedly part of an IRA spy-ring in Stormont.

I made two visits to Ulster before Christmas to meet my counterpart, the Irish Foreign Minister Brian Cowen TD. Brian was an experienced and very able Minister who would eventually become Taoiseach. We developed a firm friendship, and I was sorry to see him leave politics at the time of the great financial crisis in Ireland. He was assisted as Foreign Minister by Dermot Gallagher, a wily and clever diplomat who became head of the Irish Foreign Service.

At the beginning of December, I travelled to the USA to renew my contacts there, and explain to them the seriousness of the position we were now faced with. By Christmas it was time for a break, and Neil and his family joined me in Hillsborough Castle for the first time.

The New Year began with an appearance on the BBC's *Question Time* programme from Belfast; and the day before, at Northern Ireland Questions in the Commons, the themes were the same.

Jonathan Powell, Tony Blair's chief of staff and a vital and pivotal figure in the peace process, worked on the idea of a joint declaration by the two governments. To further explore the idea, Bertie Ahern came to No. 10 on 23 January for lunch cooked by Jamie Oliver!

In February, intensive talks began, to try to break the deadlock – with meetings in Dublin and in Cork, with the Prime Minister in Hillsborough Castle, and finally a decision for the two governments to issue a joint declaration. The elections to the Assembly were postponed until the end of May, after the two prime ministers had met again in Hillsborough, where decommissioning continued to be the issue.

Two notable figures did their best in all of these meetings. They were Reg Empey of the UUP, and Mark Durkan of the SDLP, both deeply committed to a resolution of the problem, as was the excellent chief constable Hugh Orde (who really made his mark, both in Ireland and in the USA).

As a pleasant interlude to all this, I attended the consecration in Canterbury Cathedral of Rowan Williams as Archbishop of Canterbury. He had been my local bishop (of Monmouth), then concurrently Archbishop of Wales, and now of Canterbury. A Welsh academic of great gifts and deeply spiritual, Rowan was a radical who inspired many people within and without the Christian tradition. He became Master of Magdalene College, Cambridge after retirement, and was very helpful some years later when I was looking at Oxbridge admissions from Wales.

With Monica McWilliams, Mark Durkan, David Trimble and David Ford (who had been leader of the Alliance Party since October 2001), I travelled to the USA for the St Patrick's Day celebrations and, along with Bertie Ahern, we met President George W. Bush in the Oval Office of the White House. It was quite an occasion, and we were able to update the President and other American politicians on our attempts to re-establish the institutions of government in Northern Ireland.

Iraq was now dominating everything. The media had identified me as a "cautious Blairite" over the issue – and, of course, after the critical Cabinet meeting, Robin Cook resigned. None of us wanted war, but on 29 March, I wrote an article for the Catholic periodical *The Tablet*, headlined "Why I voted for the War".

I was writing from a Catholic point of view, and argued the case against the regime in Iraq, particularly its terrible human rights record. The other argument I used was the threat to global security and the moral right to intervene militarily in certain circumstances such as Iraq – and how we should have intervened in Rwanda, and how we had successfully done so in Kosovo.

With hindsight – a wonderful thing – we should have done many things differently. In particular, we (with the Americans) handled post-conflict Iraq very badly, and stored up trouble for ourselves.

On 7th and 8th April, President Bush came to Hillsborough Castle at Tony Blair's invitation. The purpose of the visit was twofold: to deal with Iraq, and to talk to the Northern Ireland political leaders. The whole event was awesome. Thousands of secret service and other personnel descended on the small village of Hillsborough, which was literally cut off from the rest of Northern Ireland. Bush was accompanied by Colin Powell and Condoleezza Rice, and Tony came with Jack Straw, David Manning (later our Ambassador to the USA and an Oriel contemporary of mine), and me! It was all very surreal. I liked Colin Powell very much. We had met before in his Secretary of State's office in Washington. George W. Bush, meanwhile, was very good at meeting the Northern Ireland parties, and much of the two government leaders' time was spent discussing Iraq.

In April, I reported to the House that paramilitary activities in Northern Ireland, including punishment beatings, had to end. I had been waiting for a more constructive statement from the IRA than the one produced earlier in the month, and President Bush's very able envoy to Northern Ireland Richard Haass and I had stayed in Hillsborough all weekend waiting for it. Nothing came. David Trimble was now in a very difficult situation, and things were looking bleak.

On 6 May, Tony Blair and I visited Farmleigh in Dublin to meet the Irish government. It was the Prime Minister's birthday, and the whole Irish Cabinet sang "Happy Birthday" and gave him a present – something that would have been unimaginable just a few years earlier. Brian Cowen and I were charged with initiating still further talks, but the atmosphere was rapidly changing – Jeffrey Donaldson, for example, tried unsuccessfully to oust David Trimble as UUP Leader.

On my return from Dublin to London on 6 May, I made a statement to the Commons shortly before eleven that evening indicating that the IRA's April statement was "neither clear nor unambiguous". Six days later, we passed legislation postponing the Assembly elections until the autumn, and the MLAs continued to be paid.

In June, Des Browne was replaced at the NIO by John Spellar MP, who became the Security Minister. Both men were in their own ways outstanding Ministers, and brought their individual styles to the positions that they held. Des would go on to become Defence Secretary.

In September, an Independent Monitoring Commission was set up to try to restore confidence, particularly within the Unionist community. The following month at Hillsborough, General de Chastelain's attempts to persuade David Trimble of the success of IRA decommissioning failed to impress the UUP leader, and when the Assembly elections were held on 26 November, they resulted in big wins for the Democratic Unionist Party (DUP) and Sinn Féin. During this period, in October, John Spellar's wife had suddenly died. In the Commons, the future Conservative Minister for the Cabinet Office David Lidington (later the de facto deputy prime minister under Theresa May) became my shadow. I could not have wished for a more courteous and pleasant opposite number, who very soon got to grips with the complex situation in Ulster.

Over the previous months, I had travelled a lot; I went to the USA in May, and again in July when I led a British delegation organised by the British–American parliamentary assembly, of which I was government vice-chair. As well as the usual official engagements, it was fascinating to visit Monticello, the home of Thomas Jefferson, and to talk to everyday Americans about Tony Blair and Iraq. I told the Cabinet about an encounter with a shop assistant in Macy's in New York who spoke of her high regard for the British Prime Minister.

I returned to North America in October, visiting Canada and the USA. At the Canadian parliament, I spent a memorable hour in the company of Prime Minister Jean Chrétien, whom I had met when he visited Northern Ireland during my time as Minister of State.

In September, I lunched in the Commons with Cardinal Cormac Murphy-O'Connor, and briefed him on developments as head of the Catholic Church in England and Wales. A few weeks later, I made an official visit to the Vatican, again to bring the relevant bishops up to date. Unfortunately, Pope John Paul II was too ill to be present, but I did brief the Cardinal Secretary of State, Cardinal Sodano. I also visited the Irish College in Rome, and attended Mass with priests of the diocese of Down and Connor who were in Rome at the time. Kathryn Colvin, our ambassador to the Holy See, organised a dinner with Cardinal Kasper and Irish bishops and archbishops.

During this period, Alastair Campbell left No. 10 Downing Street. He had been crucial to the peace process, and his *Irish Diaries* are testament to his involvement over the years. We would miss his wisdom. At the same time, Lord Gareth Williams, leader of the House of Lords, died suddenly of a heart attack, aged 62. Gareth had been a great friend of mine, especially in the Cabinet, and it was a terrible loss to the government and to the Lords, where he was hugely admired by all sides. His funeral was held at Great

Tew, in the Cotswolds, in the middle of the Labour Party conference; the Prime Minister and the entire Cabinet flew in a special RAF plane to attend the service, which was conducted by Richard Harris, Bishop of Oxford (and now, himself, in the Lords).

After conference, I returned to Belfast where I preached at the city's Anglican cathedral. The Protestant *Newsletter* published an article on my Christian faith and beliefs, headed: "Murphy spells out core belief". The Dean of Belfast, Dr Houston McKelvey, was very kind in his introduction when he said, "I firmly believe [Mr Murphy] has shown Christian patience, tact and immense sensitivity in fulfilling his responsibilities here in Northern Ireland. I appreciate that he has done so in a most low key manner."

The churches in Northern Ireland played a vital role in reconciliation and peace-making, and I was always eager to meet with all denominations and, on a number of occasions, to preach. I was happy to do so in St Patrick's Cathedral in Dublin as well as in Catholic churches in Northern Ireland; I also attended Presbyterian services in Belfast, where I received the warmest of welcomes, as I did when I addressed the UUP Conference in October.

In the same month, I met with Xanana Gusmao, the President of East Timor, who compared the two "half-islands" of his country with Northern Ireland. He was one of many international visitors who came to see how we were working towards peace, even though we were at that point struggling to implement the Good Friday Agreement.

President Bush returned to the UK in November, and I was privileged to attend the State Banquet in his honour at Buckingham Palace on 19 November. When the Queen introduced me to the President, he replied that we had met on a number of occasions and that he had stayed at "my place".

The political landscape in Northern Ireland had changed dramatically. I now had to deal with the DUP and, on 1 December, I met with Ian Paisley. The *News Letter* had on its front page a photograph of the two of us and the heading "Face to Face". Paisley was in no hurry to talk to anybody, and he said, "I can sit in the driving seat with a poker and give Tony Blair a poke in the ribs, but I don't need to come up with any solutions."

His deputy, Peter Robinson MP, said his party were "not wreckers"; I refused Gerry Adams's request that I reconvene the Assembly because I knew no executive would emerge at this stage. None of this was encouraging as we entered 2004.

The two biggest parties in the Assembly were now Sinn Féin and the DUP – some would say they represented the "two extremes" in Northern Ireland, which meant that on the face of it a resolution and settlement were unlikely. But it wasn't that clear cut. It was, in many ways, a great pity that the UUP and the SDLP, the two parties who were effectively instrumental in producing the Good Friday Agreement, were now in the second division. David Trimble and John Hume, Reg Empey and Seamus Mallon, John Taylor and Mark Durkan – each of them along with others had been major players and producers of the success, but the world had changed and the two prime ministers now instructed me to begin proximity talks.

In early February, the DUP gave Tony Blair and me a PowerPoint presentation at No. 10 Downing Street. It was professional stuff, and indicated that they would share power with Sinn Féin if criminality in the IRA ceased. Unfortunately, towards the end of the month, Robert Tohill, a Republican, was abducted by the IRA, which definitely did not help move things forward. In March, Tony came to Hillsborough, where some progress was made and we embarked on shuttle diplomacy.

In the meantime, one of my close parliamentary friends Roy Hughes, MP for Newport (subsequently Newport East) and later Lord Islwyn, died. I gave the eulogy at his funeral in St Mary's Church, Abergavenny, on 5 January 2004, when I spoke of his dedication to his constituents, his valley roots and his Welsh identity. Roy and I had been friends since I entered the Commons in 1987, and my father, brother and I often attended rugby internationals with Roy in Paris and in Dublin. I was very fond of him, his wife Marion, and his three daughters.

As well as trying to move on with the peace process and the running of Northern Ireland, I enjoyed visiting Irish universities – Cork, Galway, Limerick, University College Dublin, Trinity College Dublin – and found that they all had lively debating societies. My family and friends would spend time with me at Hillsborough, and I regularly attended Mass in Lisburn.

Another important visit took place in May. I went to South Africa to observe their truth and reconciliation programme, and to consider the potential adoption of a similar model in Northern Ireland. I spent four days there, and the experience was both revealing and emotional. I met with several South African Cabinet Ministers, and many others including former members of the Truth and Reconciliation Commission itself, members of conflict resolution bodies and religious leaders. I was particularly privileged to discuss the truth and reconciliation process with the former South African president F. W. de Klerk, and with his later successor Cyril Ramaphosa. I went to the parliament in Cape Town, and visited Johannesburg and Pretoria. In all, I met with over 30 people, many deeply affected by apartheid, and many deeply scarred both physically and psychologically.

Any similar process to the truth and reconciliation programme in Northern Ireland would have to be tailored, but we did nevertheless learn lessons from our friends in South Africa. Agreement across the board was prerequisite for any process to work, and the very business of storytelling – particularly by victims and their families – is extremely useful. Dealing with the past in Northern Ireland is probably one of the most contentious and difficult issues to address.

Naturally, I had to keep the Commons fully informed – attending Northern Ireland Questions, introducing the Justice (Northern Ireland) Bill which reformed the criminal justice system, and making statements on the security and political situations in Ulster.

I attended the St Patrick's Day celebrations in Washington, where I met the President and leading Irish American members of Congress; I also accepted on behalf of Tony Blair a peace prize awarded by the American Ireland Fund, and I visited Los Angeles to meet with politicians and other influential Irish Americans. Inevitably, my itinerary included New York where, among other things, I was interviewed by Adrian Flannelly, whose radio show attracted a million Irish American listeners! I returned to the USA in July, when I combined the primary purpose of my visit with my duties for the British–American parliamentary group. My co-vice-chair was Michael Howard, former leader of the Conservative Party, whom I had known and liked since entering parliament. Alan Williams MP was the group's secretary, and he had arranged for us to attend the special meeting of the two Houses of Congress to honour Tony Blair, particularly on account of his friendship with the USA over Iraq. It was a fascinating occasion to say the least.

I initiated some possible ways of looking at the past and, after I had left Northern Ireland, the Eames Bradley commission came up with a number of very interesting suggestions and recommendations. But the challenge of promoting reconciliation remains today a matter of huge controversy and very difficult to resolve.

Shortly before going to South Africa, I announced that I had requested a report on various controversial murders during the troubles. Following agreement between the parties at Weston Park in 2001, Judge Peter Cory, a retired Canadian Supreme Court Judge, was asked to report on deaths involving accusations of collusion between the authorities and paramilitaries. They were the deaths of Patrick Finucane and Rosemary Nelson, two prominent solicitors who had represented many Republican clients; Robert Hamill, a Catholic who had been beaten to death in 1997; and Billy Wright, leader of the Loyalist Volunteer Force (LVF), who had been shot dead in the Maze Prison. As a result of Cory's reports, I decided that there would be inquiries into three of the cases, but deferred an inquiry into the Finucane allegations until after criminal proceedings had been completed. An inquiry into this last case was subsequently held, and reported in 2011 that there was evidence of State collusion. The other inquiries found that there was some evidence of collusion in the death of Rosemary Nelson (whose funeral I had attended); none was found in the case of Billy Wright, but that inquiry did identify lapses in prison security.

The inquiries were to cost a lot of money, although the sum involved was nothing like the cost of the Bloody Sunday inquiry. But I considered the expense necessary, again in the attempt to deal with the troubled past of Northern Ireland.

Away from the inquiries, I attended the worldwide conference of all Anglican primates at Armagh on 11 May. It was hosted by the Anglican primate of Ireland, Archbishop Robin Eames. Robin, now deservedly in the House of Lords, was a great champion of the peace process, and it was always a pleasure to meet with him in Armagh where the two cathedrals, Catholic and Church of Ireland, face one another.

I frequently combined my meetings with visits to the Catholic Archbishop (later Cardinal), Sean Brady, who was also deeply committed to the peace process – I would often say that together we "bombarded heaven" with our joint prayers for reconciliation.

June saw all-party talks in Lancaster House in London, with an indication from Ian Paisley that he could do a deal if the conditions he set down were met.

I attended the Somme commemoration on 1 July, always a moving occasion – I had agreed to the purchase of woodland and field adjacent to the Ulster Tower Memorial. Allowing the field to be turned over for use as farmland would have been a tragedy since it was where one of the deadliest encounters of the Ulster regiment had taken place during the First World War. For the purchase of the land, I received the gratitude – and the tie – of the Somme Association, which had itself done much to improve community relations at home. As well as the ceremony held each year at the Ulster Memorial, the Somme Association also commemorated Catholic Irish regiments that had lost men in 1916.

On 25 July, my great friend Brian Smith, leader of Torfaen Borough Council, died of a brain tumour. I had visited him a few days before his death, and I was deeply upset at his early passing – he was only 63. I had been friends with Brian and his wife Jean for over 40 years, and his loss was felt by so many people. I was privileged to give the tribute at his funeral at St Gabriel's Parish Church in Cwmbran on 30 July. Brian had devoted his life to the Labour Party and to the valley, active as leader of the council and with a special interest in housing. He and I had represented the same ward on the council, and speaking to the congregation I said:

I will miss his companionship, his wit, and perhaps more than anything else, his laughter. He had a capacity to make people happier – he and I canvassed at countless elections together, and no one could match his style or his humour.

Brian had been a deeply committed European, and represented local government in Britain on the EU's Committee of the Regions. He had changed so many people's lives for the better, and the day of his funeral was a bad and sad day for his family, friends and constituents.

I spent the summer of 2004 on holiday in Italy and Austria with Phyllis and Bernice, and with my priest friend Bill Redmond. It was a wonderful break that took in Switzerland, Lake Garda, St Wolfgang and Salzburg.

Returning to the day job, I hosted a dinner in Hillsborough Castle on 1 September in the presence of the Prince of Wales, who frequently visited Northern Ireland attending the annual Royal garden party, or for other occasions. I had much to do with Prince Charles when I was Welsh Secretary, and it was good to be able to discuss various issues with him; he took a keen interest in the peace process, and in housing and conservation.

Later in the month, attempts were made again to restore the institutions. This time, all the parties and the two governments met at Leeds Castle in Kent, where Gerry Adams and Martin McGuinness presented me and the Prime Minister with a listening device apparently discovered in a Sinn Féin office; and Tony Blair and the DUP held talks in my bedroom (which had a large four-poster bed in it!); and although not much was settled, at least we managed to maintain the shuttle diplomacy.

That year's Labour Party conference was held in late September, in Brighton. I was due to speak after the Prime Minister's address, but never made it. At the end of Tony's rousing oration, I stood to applaud and promptly collapsed. I remember Margaret Beckett and Paul Boateng picking me up, before I was rushed to the Brighton Royal Infirmary, where I was monitored for a heart attack. To my relief, it transpired that I had suffered a case of food poisoning (I had eaten seafood the night before).

It certainly made the news. My collapse was flashed across live television screens, and Kim Howells intervened in a good old-fashioned Welsh way with over-zealous press photographers! Owen Smith, Anthony Hunt, Don and Jen, as well as my police protection officer, all came with me to the hospital.

I received a bottle of champagne from Prince Charles, a telephone call from Hillary Clinton, and letters and messages from many well-wishers – including Brian Cowen, Tony Blair, Gordon Brown, Mo Mowlam and the Taoiseach Bertie Ahern.

It was a very public event, and the Northern Ireland media headlines ran riot: "Gruelling talks take toll on NI Secretary", "Health Fear as Murphy Collapses", and later, happily, "Secretary of State on the Mend". The 2004 Labour conference was certainly an eventful one!

October and November proved a little less dramatic. I visited Madrid and, back at home, spoke to local Labour parties in Barnsley and Caerphilly. Work continued in Ireland to make some progress with the DUP and Sinn Féin. Then, during Christmas vacation at Hillsborough Castle, something else threatened to torpedo the talks.

On 20 December, the headquarters of the Northern Bank in Belfast was broken into and over £26 million stolen. It was the biggest bank robbery in Irish history and, according to the chief constable, was carried out by the Provisional IRA. In January 2005, I told *The Irish Times* that the British government would not abandon the "ultimate goal" of an inclusive political settlement, despite the "deeply damaging impact of the robbery".

It undoubtedly set the process back, but we continued to address illegal paramilitary activity across the board. During that January, I met with six brigadiers from the loyalist paramilitaries, and impressed upon them the need to abandon old-fashioned methods of coercion. To allay American concerns over the peace process, I visited Boston and New York between 5–8 January. The Foreign Office described my visit as "punishing", with 14 media interviews and five other engagements in one day alone.

I met with Congressman Richie Neal in Boston, while in New York Bill Flynn set up a meeting with 40 Irish Americans. The meeting coincided with Hugh Orde's accusation that the IRA was responsible for the Belfast bank robbery, which inevitably overshadowed everything else. I also met with Cardinal Egan, the Cardinal Archbishop of New York. Some of the guests at the meeting were highly sceptical of the IRA's involvement, but others did believe they were to blame, and in any event I had to work hard to keep the show on the road.

On a lighter note, I regularly travelled by train along the East Coast of the USA. Departing from Grand Central Station on this occasion, I was accompanied by a very friendly Italian-American New York transport police sergeant, who shouted "Make way for the President of Ireland" . . . there was nothing I could say to persuade him that I was *not* a head of state!

Things deteriorated in February. In Belfast, Robert McCartney, a Republican, was murdered – probably by an IRA operative – and McCartney's sister and fiancée together led a campaign to expose the IRA, culminating in a meeting with President Bush on 17 March. In February also, the IRA withdrew their "offer" of decommissioning.

On 10 March, I gave the Cabinet what is documented as "substantial briefing" on the situation in Northern Ireland, stating my belief that peace would prevail, but only if the IRA ceased all activity. The document concluded: "There was quite a substantial discussion on that, which was very supportive of the Secretary of State and Prime Minister's position."

A few days later, I travelled to Washington for the St Patrick's Day celebrations. I started my visit to the US, however, in New York, where I lunched with George Mitchell, Bill Flynn and Tom Moran. Later, I was guest of honour at Co-operation Ireland's annual dinner, following others – John Hume, George Mitchell and President McAleese – who had previously been granted this honour. I went on to Philadelphia where I addressed a joint meeting of the Welsh and Irish Societies, reminding those present that my Welsh great-grandparents had emigrated to Philadelphia (although they stayed there for just one year!), and that my Irish great uncles went to Boston.

In Washington, the feeling towards Sinn Féin was distinctly cool because of the bank robbery and the McCartney murder. Senator Kennedy refused to meet Adams, and Senator McCain adopted a very tough tone at the American Ireland Fund gala dinner. I went on to meetings with the President, with Hillary Clinton, and with the National Security Advisor Steve Hadley. Friends of Sinn Féin, Congressmen Pete King, Richie Neal and Jim Walsh, were all troubled by the recent events in Northern Ireland. At the Irish Embassy reception, Bertie Ahern spoke warmly of Tony Blair and me, and George Bush wrote to thank me for my "personal efforts to advance the cause of peace and reconciliation".

It had been a most unusual visit to Washington, and a very different mood had been evident among sympathetic politicians. It was also to be my last visit as Northern Ireland Secretary.

The mood change in Irish America undoubtedly had an influence on the Sinn Féin leadership and, in April, Adams called on the IRA to choose politics above fighting.

On 2 April 2005, Pope John Paul II died and I was invited to attend his funeral, representing the people of Northern Ireland, at St Peter's on 8 April. I travelled to Rome with Tony Blair and his family, and Jack Straw as Foreign Secretary represented the British government. Liberal Democrat leader Charles Kennedy also travelled on the Prime Minister's plane, while Conservative leader Michael Howard made his way to Rome separately.

We stayed with the British Ambassador in Rome, Sir Ivor Roberts, who was an old friend and someone who had previously done much to help the peace process as ambassador in Dublin. Ivor was a passionate Welshman. His father had met his Italian wife when he served in the army during the war in Italy, and the Italian job was his dream come true!

This, however, was a very solemn occasion, and I was deeply honoured to have been present. Prince Charles led the British contingent, and

Ministers sat next to the Americans, including Ted Kennedy and his wife. The Mass, lasting three hours, was attended by countless heads of state and government.

One direct consequence of the funeral was that the marriage of Prince Charles and Camilla Parker Bowles had to be postponed by one day. It was moved to 9 April, and again I had the honour of representing the people of Northern Ireland at that ceremony. The marriage took place at the Guildhall in Windsor, and was naturally of global interest. The following reception was at Windsor Castle, after the service of prayer and dedication in St George's Chapel, during which I was seated next to the Windsor Registrar who had married the couple.

A General Election was called for 5 May 2005, and I spent the election campaign travelling around key marginal seats in Wales and England.

On the Friday morning after Election Day, I received a telephone call at home from Tony Blair. He commended my work in Northern Ireland, but now told me that he wanted me to leave the Cabinet. This came as a huge shock. Tony assured me that it had nothing to do with my capabilities, but that it was a case of his needing room for new Cabinet members. He then offered me the role of chair of parliament's Intelligence and Security Committee: I hesitated at first, but rang him back a few hours later to accept.

That evening, I was phoned by Gordon Brown, Alistair Darling, George Mitchell, and by Peter Hain who was to succeed me as Secretary of State.

I received messages and letters from a great many people, including Bertie Ahern, David Trimble, the top civil servants in Belfast and Cardiff, and from Cherie Blair and Jonathan Powell. In his account of the peace process, Jonathan wrote: "Paul's inexhaustible patience and deep understanding of Northern Ireland had helped salve the wounds opened by all the preceding failed negotiations."

I was especially touched by letters I received from the two Archbishops of Armagh, from our ambassador in Washington Sir David Manning, from Hugh Orde, and from my most recent Conservative predecessor as Northern Ireland Secretary, Paddy Mayhew. Indeed, in a Lords debate on Northern Ireland, it appeared that my departure had created quite a stir – even Norman Tebbit deplored the decision to replace me.

The newspapers were kind, as was Bertie Ahern again, who added a very warm public tribute to his earlier personal message:

Paul's qualities of political wisdom, tolerance and unfailing courtesy were widely admired and appreciated by all those in the process who had the privilege of working with him. He made an immense contribution to the political process.

By this time, I had been a Minister for nearly eight years and a Cabinet Minister for six of them, so it had been a good stint. I think I fell off the edge in the reshuffle, and I wasn't the type to make a fuss. I quite naturally believed that it was to be the end of my Cabinet career . . . but not so.

I missed the people who had been part of my life at the NIO – the local politicians, who always treated me decently; my brilliant ministerial team; my PPS Gareth Thomas; the exceptionally able civil servants; my two advisers Owen and Adam; my personal protection officers in Northern Ireland and in Britain; and the people of Northern Ireland itself, for whom I had an enormous affection and respect.

The 2005 General Election result was still very good for Labour, especially bearing in mind how unpopular the Iraq War had been. Labour returned with a majority of 66.

At home in Torfaen, the Iraq issue seemed to have had no obvious impact on my vote, and I was given a considerable mandate, returning as the valley's MP with a very healthy majority of 14,791.

Spies and Wales again 2005-2010

MY NEW JOB OF CHAIRING the parliamentary Intelligence and Security Committee (ISC) seemed fascinating. I had had extensive dealings with the intelligence agencies as a Northern Ireland Minister, and I was familiar with some of the leading figures in MI5 and MI6. Later, serving as Secretary of State for Northern Ireland, I had to approve warrants for police interception on almost a daily basis, and I was routinely presented with intelligence assessments. This new job, though, involved overseeing the agencies, which was very different.

Before 1994, there had been no parliamentary oversight of the three agencies MI5, MI6 and GCHQ, but the Intelligence Services Act of that year set up the ISC to examine their "policy, administration and expenditure". Gradually, oversight extended to the Joint Intelligence Committee (JIC), the Intelligence and Security Secretariat and the Defence Intelligence Staff of the Ministry of Defence. The chair and members of the ISC were appointed by the Prime Minister, in consultation with the leaders of the two main opposition parties. The committee reported directly to the Prime Minister and, through its annual report, to parliament. Members of the committee have to sign the 1989 Official Secrets Act and operate within "the ring of secrecy".

Evidence is taken in secret from the heads of the agencies and the relevant Cabinet Ministers – the Foreign, Home and Defence Secretaries. Members have access to classified material, usually read in the committee's offices. In recent years, changes have been made affecting the committee's role and powers, making it more effective and accountable to parliament and, hopefully, gaining more public confidence.

In 2005, the committee was based in the Cabinet Office in Whitehall, and had a small and dedicated staff. During most of my time on the committee, the clerk was an extremely able and conscientious young woman who oversaw many changes for the better, including improved accommodation and wider powers.

In addition to the chair, there were eight other members, including one from the House of Lords. Generally, the members were experienced and, sometimes, former Ministers – always senior parliamentarians. In my time as chair, my colleagues included former deputy leader of the Liberal Democrats Alan Beith MP, former Conservative Minister Michael Mates MP, former deputy leader of the Conservative Party Michael Ancram MP, former Conservative chief whip James Arbuthnot MP, and Sir Richard Ottaway, MP for Croydon. My Labour colleagues were veteran MP and former Minster George Howarth, Dari Taylor MP, and Ben Champion MP. Representing the Lords was Baroness Ramsay of Cartvale, a Labour peer and a former senior official at MI6, eventually succeeded by another former Labour Minister, Lord Foulkes.

The Prime Minister formally appointed me to the position on 11 July 2005, a week after the terrible tube bombings in London. The committee was to report on the bombings in the following year. I told the press:

> It is a great honour to be given this most important job. I look forward to working productively with my parliamentary colleagues at a time when issues of national security are important to everyone. Last Thursday's [bombings] saddened and disgusted us all. My thoughts go out to all of those who were killed or injured and their families.

The job was almost full-time and unpaid – it took up most of my time, and was often rewarding, although sometimes frustrating. The committee worked very hard but, of course, because of the nature of the material involved, all of its sessions were private – unlike other parliamentary select committees. Questioning of witnesses was intense and very detailed, and the committee always reached a consensus. The only vote ever taken – and not in my time – was whether the committee should travel to a particular destination by plane or by train!

My first overseas visit with the committee could not have been made by train. It was to Thailand, Australia and the USA. The UK's most important intelligence partnership was as one of the so-called Five Eyes – the USA, Canada, Australia, New Zealand and the UK – and so it was vital that the committee kept abreast of our allies, both the intelligence agencies and our parliamentary/congressional counterparts.

In Australia, the committee met the UK's high commissioner Helen Liddell, a former Labour Cabinet Minister and a good friend (and now in the Lords). In the USA, as always, the committee met with the CIA, NSA,

FBI and with members of the two congressional committees on intelligence – both of which had far greater powers than we did! Later in the year, the committee visited Sweden to meet with the intelligence agencies there and with Swedish parliamentarians. Another of the committee's roles was to receive visiting Ministers, parliamentarians and senior officials from other countries, including, in my time as chair, those from France, Spain, Poland, Canada and Singapore.

Also, with Pat Carey TD, I became co-chair of the British–Irish inter-parliamentary body, an organisation essentially bringing together MPs and TDs from Ireland and the UK, but also now from Scotland, Wales, Northern Ireland, the Isle of Man and the Channel Islands. The organisation had been in existence since the 1990s and had done a great job reconciling differences between Ireland and the UK. It was now effectively the parliamentary aspect of Strand 3 of the Good Friday Agreement. I really was pleased in my new position because it kept me in the loop with developments, especially developments in Northern Ireland.

Apart from my role with the ISC, I now had to settle into the life of a government backbencher. Of the 18 years I had spent in the Commons, 17 had been on the front bench. The new situation was a strange experience. I had not asked a parliamentary question for a decade, nor taken part in debates other than those concerning my Ministerial responsibilities. In early June, I spoke during the debate on the Queen's Speech, dealing with the economy, prompting the Chancellor of the Exchequer, Gordon Brown, to write to me: "Thank you for your speech in the economic debate in the Queen's Speech. It was very well received, rightly. I look forward to working with you in the future."

The year continued with the death of Jim Callaghan, whom I had known and admired, and I attended the joint memorial service for him and his wife Audrey in Westminster Abbey on 28 July. It was a magnificent affair, and followed Jim's own wish:

> I would like any memorial service for me to be cheerful and joyful. The last hymn could be that splendid American one: "Mine eyes have seen the glory of the coming of the Lord. Halleluiah!" The congregation all singing. The great organ chords crashing out. The Marines on trumpets. That would be a splendid finish!

And it was!

A few weeks later, on 19 August 2005, Mo Mowlam died. After Mo retired from the Commons in 2001, she published her autobiography *Momentum* and made numerous television appearances – she was still a hugely popular figure, and from time to time I would have dinner with her and her husband Jon. But her health eventually deteriorated and she died in a hospice in Canterbury; I was invited to write her entry in the *Dictionary of National Biography*, in which I concluded:

> Mowlam's name will always be associated with Northern Ireland and the Good Friday Agreement – rightly so, since the impetus she gave to a flagging peace process was very real. She was seen as someone who was genuinely different from previous Northern Ireland Secretaries. She was, inevitably, overshadowed by Tony Blair and she could antagonise people, especially Unionists. But her achievements were genuine, her bravery unquestioned, and her popularity in the country among people of all political persuasions, unrivalled.

I still miss her.

In October, Don Touhig and I visited Gordon and Sarah Brown, and I addressed his constituency Labour Party on Northern Ireland. I also attended a lecture that Gordon gave at St Mary's Catholic Cathedral in Edinburgh, a very pleasant occasion. I was put up for the night in one of the children's bedrooms, surrounded by toys!

Naturally, I maintained a keen interest in Northern Ireland. In February, I met with Mitchell Reiss, President Bush's special envoy to Northern Ireland, and I continued to take part in debates on the peace process in the Commons. I was not too fond of the so-called "on the runs" proposal, which ended up being shelved, and I fully backed the all-party St Andrew's Agreement, dealing with Northern Ireland issues. In April, I co-chaired the British–Irish inter-parliamentary body plenary session in Killarney, where the DUP took up their seats in full for the first time.

Most of my time, however, was necessarily devoted to the ISC and to security issues. In May 2006, the ISC published its report on the London terrorist attacks of 7 July 2005. The committee needed almost a year to complete its work, having taken evidence from the Foreign and Home Secretaries, as well as from the heads of the three agencies. We examined a huge number of documents and listened to new intercepted intelligence.

The committee acknowledged that many plots had been thwarted by the agencies, but concluded that had more resources been available, the 7/7 outrage might have been prevented. We made various recommendations on threat levels and alert state systems, observing that lessons should be learned, including the need for better coordination between the services. The government welcomed the committee's conclusions, but some years later it emerged that greater powers for the committee would have made a fuller investigation possible. In 2009, then chair of the ISC Kim Howells presented a report to parliament on recent developments in the wake of the ending of a major trial concerning the so called Crevice Investigation. The 7/7 Inquiry itself had been intensive and sometimes distressing, especially when evidence was taken from the victims' families.

When I was a young man, the agencies were often seen as being too intrusive, particularly by those on the left. Nowadays, the public takes a different view. Over the July bombings, for instance, the criticism was not that the agencies were doing too much, but that they didn't do enough to apprehend the plotters.

The following month, June 2006, saw publication of the committee's annual report, in which recommendations were made to government on such matters as dealing with any dissenters among those working for the agencies, on funding, on regionalisation, and on the Butler Review which had looked into the intelligence on weapons of mass destruction that led to the government's decision to invade Iraq.

At the end of June, I visited the University of California, Los Angeles, to give a lecture and presentation entitled "Legislatures and Terrorism: American and British Views". It was a joint presentation with Democrat Congresswoman Jane Harman (California), the Ranking Democrat on the House Permanent Select Committee on Intelligence. My visit was short but fascinating, and demonstrated the great importance of British–American collaboration on intelligence issues.

With the forthcoming 90th anniversary of the Battle of the Somme in 2006, Stuart Cameron organised a hugely impressive commemoration on 1 July in Cwmbran, which featured the famous buglers who play The Last Post each day in Ypres. The Battle of the Somme was important for Northern Ireland (as previously noted), but it also had a significant impact on Wales. The event in Cwmbran was both timely and very well attended.

In September, I visited Boston and New York with Jonathan Phillips to discuss the Northern Ireland peace process, and I quickly followed this with an ISC visit to South Africa. This was an unusual occasion, since it brought together intelligence oversight committees from all over the world, but especially from African countries, some of which had still-recent histories as dictatorships. I spoke on the role of the ISC in the UK, and of course addressed the 7/7 bombings in London.

The following month, I represented the UK parliament at a similar conference in Romania, another former dictatorship. The conference was held in the huge and vulgar palace built by the Communist dictator Nicolae Ceausescu, who had ruled the country from 1965 to 1989. Again, it was interesting to see how many new Eastern European countries were developing scrutiny committees for intelligence agencies in their own parliaments.

In mid-November, I visited Sri Lanka at the request of President Mahinda Rajapaksa. Sri Lanka (formerly Ceylon) was a very beautiful country, with an educated and friendly population. Originally Portuguese and then British, but independent since 1945, Sri Lanka could have become another Singapore had it not been ravaged by civil war between the majority Sinhalese and the minority Tamil people. The so-called Tamil Tigers (LTTE), based in the north of the island, became very effective and deadly combatants; over 30,000 people had perished in the conflict.

Between 1998 and 2006, the two sides tried to reach a settlement facilitated by Norwegian mediators. Tony Blair met President Rajapaksa at Chequers on 31 August 2006 to discuss various possible strategies for achieving peace. President Rajapaksa was particularly interested to know if the British experience in Northern Ireland could help his domestic situation, but he wanted any British presence to be low-key for fear of giving more publicity to the LTTE. The Tamil diaspora in the UK was also very active. Tony said he would send experienced Northern Ireland "expats" to Sri Lanka in the following few months, and I was then asked by No. 10 to go there, accompanied by Chris McCabe, a hugely experienced civil servant from the NIO.

We set out for the capital Colombo on 13 November, and stayed in Sri Lanka for four days. We had a packed schedule. We were welcomed by Britain's high commissioner Dominick Chilcott, who had arranged the programme with the Sri Lankan government. We met with politicians from all parties, and with the co-chairs of the international group – Japan, the EU, Norway, the USA, Germany and India – trying to promote peace. Other meetings were held with academics, the private sector, the Ceylon Chamber of Commerce, and with the Peace Secretariat.

On 14 November, we dined with President Rajapaksa and members of his Cabinet, and I gained the clear impression that Rajapaksa was genuine about trying to find a way to end the conflict, but that the armed forces probably wanted a military solution rather than a diplomatic one. We flew to Trincomalee naval base where discussions were held with the governor of the north and the west, which were the areas most affected by the conflict.

The journey to meet with the Tamil Tigers based at Kilinochchi in the far north of Sri Lanka was a dramatic one. We travelled to the boundary between the two territories, having been flown over the jungle in a Sri Lankan army helicopter and seeing baby elephants playing on the way! We were then handed over to the Tigers, who drove us in a truck along a heavily-mined main road, finally to meet up with the LTTE leadership (but not Prabhakaran, the top man). Martin McGuinness had previously visited Kilinochchi and, like Martin, we were shown great hospitality and treated very well. There was huge publicity surrounding our presence. Most of the people we talked to during our visit perished in the war that came some years later. The Tamil territory was like a mini-state, with schools, hospitals and other public services. I genuinely believed our experience in Northern Ireland could help them achieve peace.

Back in Westminster, I spoke in the Commons on 2 May, to outline the issues and describe what we had observed. The Sri Lankan government, however, eventually abandoned the ceasefire that had been agreed before my visit, and a civil war broke out, in which at least 10,000 more Tamils were killed and a quarter of a million people displaced. Some years later, in 2010, I led a CPA all-party delegation to Sri Lanka and was able to see for myself the devastation that the conflict had caused (more of which in my closing chapter).

Meanwhile, 2007 saw me spend most of my time on ISC matters. In July, the committee published its report on rendition, the worst type being so-called extraordinary rendition – the extra-judicial transfer of persons from one jurisdiction or state to another for the purpose of detention and interrogation outside the normal legal system, and where there is a real risk of torture or cruel, inhuman or degrading treatment. We found that the UK agencies were not complicit in any such operations, but we concluded that they were slow "to detect the emerging pattern of 'rendition to detention', that occurred during 2002". The agencies, however, did not in our opinion collude with the USA in illegal or improper renditions – although a highly suspect operation at one point under consideration had been shelved. We also concluded that the USA "showed a lack of regard" for UK concerns, and that this could have "serious implications for the working of the relationship between the USA and the UK intelligence agencies".

Rendition was a thoroughly murky and unpleasant business, and we were right to report on it. Further revelations emerged in later years. Indeed, a report by the ISC in June 2018 found that the UK tolerated inexcusable treatment of detainees by the US during the war on terror following the 9/11 attacks. Because of the time taken investigating the issue of rendition, it was January 2008 before the committee produced its annual report for 2006–7. I reported that the ISC had sat through 49 formal sessions, and 19 other meetings, from July 2006. We welcomed the proposed reform of the committee, outlined in Gordon Brown's Green Paper *The Government of Britain*, specifically supporting its proposals on improved accountability to parliament.

In March, 2007, we visited Washington DC again and held the usual meetings with the CIA, and with our Congressional counterparts, together with the FBI, the Defense Intelligence Agency and the State Department. Later on, in June, the committee attended an international symposium on intelligence oversight held in the Netherlands.

In the Commons, I continued to speak on Welsh and Northern Ireland affairs. In the Welsh Day debate (usually held on St David's Day), I spoke out against a proposal to transform the former police training college site in Cwmbran, owned by the Ministry of Justice, into a high-security prison. There had been uproar because the site was in the middle of high density housing. The government, through my friend the Prisons Minister David Hanson MP, listened and the idea was abandoned.

In May, I welcomed the final setting up of the Northern Ireland Assembly, and spoke in other debates on further education and on reform of the ISC.

After leaving the NIO, I was regularly invited to other areas of conflict around the world to talk about the Good Friday Agreement. In November, I visited Palestine with Kamlesh Karia from the International Department of the Labour Party, to talk to Fatah. Almost fifty Fatah members attended, and it was a great opportunity to compare notes. I met the British Consul General, Richard Makepeace, in East Jerusalem. Being in the city again, some years after my first visit there in 1992, was another wonderful opportunity to visit the city's main sights including the Church of the Holy Sepulchre.

The only mishap occurred during a journey back to Jerusalem one night. The taxi driver took a wrong turn, and we were stopped by the Israeli army – who ignored my parliamentary pass, but were suitably impressed by my visiting card and let us through the road-block!

The previous month, with Anthony Hunt, I attended the Anna Lindh conference in Stockholm, where again I spoke about my Northern Ireland experience. This visit had been organised in conjunction with the Socialist International, and it proved to be very rewarding. The only problem I encountered was when an evidently mentally disturbed man became aggressive in the Old City and the police had to be called – they, of course, spoke perfect English. One of the officers had even received some training in the New York police department!

In June 2007, Tony Blair had resigned as Prime Minister and as leader of the Labour Party, and was succeeded by the Chancellor of the Exchequer, Gordon Brown. The legendary clashes between the two men were not good for the country or for the party, and at a PLP meeting I urged them to work together, because as a team they were formidable, and in my view unbeatable. When Tony decided to go, Gordon was the only credible successor. I admired them both, and the newspapers and commentators could never pin me down as either a Blairite or a Brownite!

During his leadership campaign, Gordon came to Cardiff and had a private meeting with me, indicating that it was unlikely that I would serve in his Cabinet. I replied on 27 June, saying that I understood his position, and outlining some changes I felt he ought to make to the ISC's role and powers. These included making more parliamentary time available to debate ISC reports; allowing the ISC chair to introduce their reports himself at the beginning of debates; holding some committee sessions in public, probably with the heads of the agencies attending as witnesses; giving the committee power to compel witnesses to attend; and making use of an investigator. All these and other ideas were eventually agreed; I also suggested I might be of some use in acting as a type of special envoy on peace-making initiatives.

As it turned out, 2008 would present a very different role for me as Welsh politics was again to dominate my life.

The 2007 Assembly election in Wales gave Labour just 26 seats – five short of an overall majority, even though Labour was the biggest party. Labour could form a coalition with the Liberal Democrats, or with Plaid Cymru; or it could go into opposition, with the other three parties in coalition government. The Liberal Democrat membership in Wales could not agree on a coalition with Labour, or with a so-called Rainbow Coalition, and First Minister Rhodri Morgan decided to go into government with Plaid Cymru. This needed support from a special Labour Party conference, which Rhodri secured, despite opposition from Neil Kinnock, Don Touhig, me and some other Welsh politicians.

I wrote an article for the *New Statesman* in July, in which I said that I would now accept the party's decision, but that Labour should strengthen its commitment to devolution while continuing its firm opposition to independence. This, then, was the background to the events that were to unfold in January 2008.

On New Year's Day, 2008, *The Times* ran an article headlined "Brown summons young courtiers in his Cabinet of all the talents". In it, the political editor Philip Webster wrote: "There could be a role for Paul Murphy, the former Northern Ireland Secretary, regarded as another solid operator"... but I thought no more about Cabinet until the afternoon of 24 January.

On that day, Peter Hain, the Secretary of State for Wales and Work and Pensions, resigned from the Cabinet. This came after he was told that the police would be investigating why he had not declared £103,000 in contributions to his campaign to become Labour's deputy leader. He told the media that he was "quitting to clear [his] name", and he blamed his administrative staff for the problems he faced. I never had any doubt that he was innocent of any wrong-doing, and he was later exonerated.

However, the Prime Minister had to appoint replacements for Peter in the Cabinet. James Purnell was made Work and Pensions Secretary and, surprisingly, Gordon Brown appointed me as Welsh Secretary. This meant that I was, effectively, the first person to hold the office twice.

On that Thursday, I had chaired a meeting of the ISC in the morning. The phone call from the Prime Minister came at about four o'clock in the afternoon. Don Touhig had heard that I might become Welsh Secretary, and he called at my office to tell me about the speculation. It was while we were talking that No. 10 contacted me, and Gordon told me that I was essentially to be a "caretaker" Secretary of State – he had promised Peter Hain that he could return at some point if his name was cleared, and in time he did.

Peter and I had been swapping jobs and offices since 2002. He succeeded me that year as Welsh Secretary when I went to Northern Ireland, and he became Northern Ireland Secretary in 2005 after I left government. Now I was taking over from him again, and he was to replace me as Welsh Secretary in 2009! Between us, we held the Welsh job for eight years and the Northern Ireland job for five; we also kept on exchanging the same office when either of us was on the backbenches. After we had both left the Commons, the office was next occupied by Ed Miliband; advantageously situated in Portcullis House, it boasts exceptional views of the Elizabeth Tower and its environs!

The press and Welsh politicians were kind to me over my appointment. Rhodri Morgan said that he had an "instinctive relationship of trust" with me, and that he was "absolutely certain that Paul, as Secretary of State for Wales, is good for the Labour movement and Wales". Letters I received from Plaid Cymru and the Conservatives were welcoming, but the Liberal Democrats felt I wasn't suitably pro-devolution!

BBC news anchorman Huw Edwards referred to my veteran status, and to the fact that I was coming out of retirement! After Jack Straw (who was two years older than me), I was the oldest member of the Cabinet at the age of 60. On the day that I was appointed, I had met Michael White of *The Guardian*, and he subsequently wrote:

When I left you this morning, I had a twinge as I walked off. I had failed to ask 'Are You Available?' You could only have given a bland answer, as another ex-cabinet member had just done. But I should have asked.

Bruce Anderson, in *The Independent*, said that Gordon had "finally made a good decision" over my appointment, and continued:

> For eight years Paul Murphy was that exceptionally rare commodity in the Blair Government; a Minister with a safe pair of hands. As Minister of State in the NIO under Mo Mowlam, he did the work when she showed off. Later, he was a thoroughly competent Northern Ireland Secretary. He was the sort of chap you want in a department where a lot can go wrong; which only hits the headlines when the news is bad. That suited Paul Murphy: he had no interest in leadership. This must explain why Tony Blair sacked him. Otherwise it was an incomprehensible decision . . . he disposed of a good man who had done well in a hard job. No member of the 2005 Blair government had done less to deserve the sack.

Gordon did bring me back into government, if only for 18 months. He restored the position of Welsh Secretary as a standalone job – it had frankly been daft to combine it with other Cabinet positions, as it had been with Peter Hain – but Gordon was still troubled that the London media would think I would not have enough to do. So, bizarrely, he also made me Minister for Digital Inclusion, covering different government departments.

More appropriately, Gordon asked me to take overall responsibility for devolution issues, including the Joint Ministerial Committee. I also dealt with the British-Irish Council, and chaired two Cabinet committees – a new cross-departmental committee on IT and information security, and the committee on local government and the regions.

In all this, I was to be assisted by the parliamentary under-secretary at the Wales Office: for a short time it was Huw Irranca-Davies, MP for Ogmore. He soon left to become a Department for Environment, Food and Rural Affairs Minister, and was succeeded in the Wales Office by the Caerphilly MP Wayne David. Both Huw and Wayne were highly capable. Wayne had led the European Parliament Labour group, and I had known him since his university days; he brought much experience and good sense to the department.

My special advisers were the veteran Dr Andrew Bold and, later, my own parliamentary researcher Anthony Hunt. I found them to be invaluable, and it was great that Anthony was given this opportunity of working in government – he took to the job like a duck to water!

My parliamentary private secretary was Nick Ainger, the very active MP for Carmarthen West and South Pembrokeshire, and a good friend. My principal private secretary was to be Simon Morris, who had asked to take on his old job again. I was thrilled at this and, of course, he was to prove as effective and capable as he had been in my previous period as Welsh Secretary. We had some very good colleagues in our department – John Williams, for example, our real expert on financial issues. The team was small but dedicated, and its members had to use all their skills in dealing with two governments, two civil services and two parliaments. Our common commitment to Wales and its people was our guiding principle.

I attended my first Cabinet meeting as Welsh Secretary (second time around) on 29 January. The way that Gordon presided over his Cabinet was very different from Tony's approach. Naturally, he controlled the agenda and who could speak, but Gordon was not fond of the armchair meetings so favoured by Tony. I thought I might return to my old position around the Cabinet table, but not a bit of it. My five previous years in the Cabinet didn't count, and I was at the bottom of the ladder again! I took my first Welsh Questions on 27 February and, the next day, had the debate in the House on Welsh Affairs. I don't think I had ever taken so many interventions, including some from the shadow Secretary of State Cheryl Gillan. Cheryl had been brought up in Cardiff and had a genuine feel for Wales, and I always found her to be courteous and very pleasant. She would become Welsh Secretary herself in 2010.

Much of my time was naturally spent in Wales and in meetings with Welsh Government Ministers. Just as had been the case when I was Welsh Secretary first time around, I generally met with Rhodri in his office in Cardiff Bay every Monday morning. More often than not, these meetings forestalled disagreements between the two governments, and they were also very positive, partly because Rhodri and I knew each other so well.

Things had changed since I was Welsh Secretary six years before. Whitehall was beginning to understand devolution better, and we now had a very pro-devolution British Prime Minister. The fact that both the Westminster and the Assembly Government were at that time Labour inevitably helped too.

Overseeing the Joint Ministerial Committee was an interesting and important part of my job. The committee brought together politicians from across the various administrations in the UK, and also looked at the devolution settlement generally. Reflecting on the responsibility I had been given for this new monitoring role, the *Western Mail* suggested that I was "the Welsh Minister drafted in to bring harmony" to the evolving devolved institutions, and that I had been asked by Gordon "to breathe new life into the JMC".

The committee was set up in 1999, but had not met since 2002. Now, preparing for its first session for some years, I discussed the proposed agenda with Rhodri and met Ian Paisley and Martin McGuinness in Belfast. The trickiest encounter, though, was with Scotland's First Minister Alex Salmond.

In mid-April I travelled to Edinburgh for a series of meetings with Salmond. It was not an easy situation because of the poor relations between the Scottish National Party (SNP) government and the Labour Scotland Office. I had to tread very carefully. The Scottish editor of *The Daily Telegraph*, Alan Cochrane, headed his article on my meetings with "Murphy knows how to handle this hot potato". Cochrane referred to me as the "ever-emollient-looking-and-sounding-but-actually-tough-as-old-boots Paul Murphy". Salmond had wanted to use the JMC to attack the Treasury over its proposal (which he claimed would have cost £400 million) to replace council tax with a local income tax – but this wasn't really the business of the JMC, which was intended to deal with more general issues affecting all of the UK.

At the beginning of March, the Human Fertilisation and Embryology Bill became a huge issue for Catholic MPs, including me. The bill allowed the creation of animal-human embryos (produced by injecting animal cells or DNA into human embryos or human cells into animal eggs) to be used in medical research and then discarded. Although there was much good in the bill – in trying to eradicate some terrible diseases – there were also huge ethical issues.

Traditionally, issues of this kind (and others such as hanging and abortion) were the subject of so-called free votes in parliament. The Tories were allowing their MPs a free vote on the bill, but the government was not. I had spoken to Gordon's advisers, and suggested that we could have free votes on the more controversial parts of the bill. But Geoff Hoon, the government chief whip, was adamant that the entire bill should be whipped. I received hundreds of letters, mostly in favour of a free vote, and more than 100 academics wrote to *The Times* to express the same view.

I liaised with Peter Smith, the Catholic Archbishop of Cardiff, and Cardinal Cormac Murphy-O'Connor, Head of the Catholic Church in England and Wales, to try to find a way through the mess – for that is what it was. However, Cardinal O'Brien, the Catholic Archbishop of Edinburgh, raised the stakes in a sermon on Good Friday, directly attacking the government over the issue. Three Catholic members of the Cabinet – Ruth Kelly (Transport Secretary), Des Browne (Defence Secretary) and I – were now in the spotlight. All three of us, along with a good number of junior ministers and whips, were likely to have to resign if forced to vote for what we, in all conscience, thought was wrong.

On Easter Day 2008, returning from Mass, I stopped in a car park in Corfe Mullen in Dorset – I was staying with my brother for the Easter holidays. There I had a long telephone conversation with the Prime Minister, a surreal experience, sitting in a car in the pouring rain talking to Gordon about my possible resignation.

By the following week, a compromise was reached and we had a free vote on parts of the bill. The government won easily, as I had predicted.

April saw the tenth anniversary of the signing of the Good Friday Agreement, and I travelled to Belfast to attend events marking the occasion. Along with George Mitchell, Bertie Ahern, John Hume, Gerry Adams, Monica McWilliams, Reg Empey and Davy Adams, I reflected on the previous decade and how Northern Ireland had changed for the better. My comment to the media, describing the events leading up to the agreement, was "By gosh, it was hard!"

The JMC later met in London under the chairmanship of the Justice Secretary, Jack Straw. It proved to be a useful meeting, paving the way for more of its kind.

In May, Yvonne, my friend Stuart's mother, celebrated her 90th birthday. She was, as they say, as bright as a button and still took holidays in France and made visits to Ypres and the Somme. She was to live another eight years, and was lively to the end.

On 6 July, I attended the Formula 1 Grand Prix at Silverstone – not an invitation I would have automatically accepted, but my nephew Daniel was a great fan of motor racing and we went along. I was really surprised at how much I enjoyed the day, which ended in my presenting the winner's trophy to Lewis Hamilton under the gaze of literally hundreds of millions of viewers all arond the world!

The July 2008 edition of *The House* magazine had me on its front cover, with the headline: "Murphy's Law: Welsh Secretary on come-backs, religion and peace talks". It was a headline that rather spoke for itself.

During the next month my predecessor, Leo Abse, died at the age of 91. He had come to dinner in the House on 19 April, and it was clear his time was limited. I gave a eulogy at his funeral in St Gabriel's Church, Cwmbran, on 29 August, an unusual joint Anglican and Jewish service. Leo had been a great hero and friend, and he had undoubtedly been "the Member for Happiness", changing people's lives for the better by his great social reforms. Between the two of us, by the time I retired, we would have represented the valley in the Commons for nearly 60 years.

In the summer, I took my annual holiday to France, and in September visited Lisbon with my priest friend, Father Bill Redmond – although I had to return to London in the middle of the holiday for a Cabinet meeting.

We visited the great Catholic shrine of Fatima, and really enjoyed the Portuguese capital.

That year's Labour conference was held in Manchester. It was the last one I attended as a Cabinet Minister, and the final one I addressed. I concentrated in my speech on how Labour in Cardiff and in Westminster worked together, praising the North Wales Airbus plant as an example of joint enterprise – and apparently, I used the word "socialist" in my speech, to the surprise of some press commentators.

I also paid tribute to Rhodri Morgan, who had announced he was standing down in 2009. He was absent from the conference because he was in the USA collecting the baton for Wales to host the Ryder Cup in Newport in 2010.

The economic situation was becoming increasingly uncertain, and a crisis was growing. Gordon had set up the National Economic Council (NEC), on which I represented Wales, and was in daily contact with Rhodri over the government's £500 million economic rescue plan. I also sat on the Welsh equivalent of the NEC – the Welsh Economic Council.

With a devolved government, Wales could do a fair bit to assist people affected by the economic downturn, with schemes like the so-called Proact, to help keep people in jobs in industries and businesses affected by the crisis. I was asked to explain the scheme to the members of the NEC. When world leaders came to London to discuss the situation, I was deputed to welcome the Japanese and Canadian prime ministers. Gordon had indeed galvanised the world's governments into tackling the worldwide crisis.

Elsewhere, in October, I addressed the Oxford Union. In late November, I gave a talk to an audience of 500 in Westminster Cathedral on Elgar's oratorio *The Apostles*, which was being performed by the parliamentary choir. And, two days later, I attended a Cabinet meeting in Leeds, after which I flew to Paris to celebrate my 60th birthday with Stuart, Pam, Don and Jen.

In December, there was an article titled "Defeating Disadvantage" in the magazine *GC: Government Computing* which discussed my role as Digital Inclusion Minister. This ministerial role turned out to be much more interesting than I had anticipated; 17 million people in the UK were not digitally literate and, though I was not the greatest expert on the subject, I could see how important digital prowess could be. Old and young alike would lose out if they could not use the Internet, and I spent a good part of my time on this job visiting schools, community centres and OAP schemes to see how people adapted to the new skills.

I talked about the digital divide, especially between the old and the young, but also between the rich and the poor and between the educated and the less-educated. I also made the point that raising people's digital skills helped business and our economy. Although an unlikely candidate for this job, I came to realise that people's lives could be much better if they were able to use computers and the Internet, and I took the message to conferences across the UK.

The government decided to appoint a Digital Inclusion Champion, and I offered the job to Martha Lane-Fox, founder of *lastminute.com*, who was to become the youngest female member of the House of Lords.

The economy, however, was dominating our lives. In January 2009, Gordon Brown visited Wales, and Rhodri Morgan and I were able to explain to him the different initiatives the Welsh Government was pursuing in order to try to ride the financial storm.

In the Commons, at both Welsh Questions and the annual Welsh Day debate, the economic and financial issues facing our country were again the main debating points.

A pleasant interlude to an otherwise gloomy winter came when I was made an Honorary Fellow of Glyndŵr University, Wrexham, in February. This was in recognition of my "major contribution to Government in Wales and the United Kingdom". I had known and admired the work of the vice-chancellor Professor Michael Scott for a number of years, and I was particularly pleased to have been awarded the Fellowship by Lord Barry Jones, my old friend and former boss!

After visiting Ireland and talking to the British–Irish inter-parliamentary body, I attended the Labour Party annual Welsh conference during April in Swansea. I introduced Gordon to the conference, and he was given a fantastic reception. Gordon's wife, Sarah, kindly wrote later to thank me for my welcome to the Prime Minister.

The European elections in Wales and throughout the UK were poor for Labour. In Wales, we ended up with only one MEP, Derek Vaughan, and UKIP gained one – a far cry from the days when Labour held all four Welsh seats in the European Parliament.

Labour had done poorly the previous year at the Welsh local government elections. In Torfaen, we had lost a number of seats, including that of my friend, Stuart Cameron, and were no longer in overall control of the council. Gordon had been reluctant to report the Welsh result in Cabinet, even though the overall outcome in Wales could have been worse – the 10p tax charge had gone down badly, and had hit a large number of our traditional voters.

We were heading for electoral defeat in 2010; I am still convinced that, had Gordon called an election in 2007, Labour would have won.

In the summer of 2009, the so-called expenses scandal erupted, and practically all of us were caught up in it. The problem was that successive governments, Labour and Conservative, had been reluctant to raise the salaries of MPs, opting instead to increase expenses and allowances. The regime was poor; it was too loose and, in reality, we should have had a simple overnight allowance scheme, which is what happens in most other European countries. Instead, we were able to claim for all sorts of things under the catch-all of "accommodation" – including the interest on mortgages. It was a daft system, and it was bound, eventually, to cause problems.

When *The Daily Telegraph* received a stolen CD of all MPs' expenses, the balloon went up. For me, the problem was that Cabinet members' expenses were the first to be exposed. The main issue that I was criticised for was claiming for a replacement boiler in my London flat; the "boiler" was in fact a water-tank, and in my amateur and untechnical letter to the Finance Department I had not really correctly described the reason for replacing the tank. The newspapers made fun of the water being "too hot", but, in fact, the temperature could not be regulated and the 44-year-old tank was faulty and dangerous. But it was useless trying to explain; it was a good story and the media were running with it.

I was defended by Libby Purves in *The Times*, who wrote: "Some of the expenses are fine. I accept that the poor Welsh Secretary should not be poached, like an egg on his national rarebit, by a defective boiler 145 miles from home."

Gordon initially tried to introduce an overnight allowance claim system, but it never happened, and IPSA was set up to deal with MPs' allowances. It was a terrible time, and I am still not sure we have the right solution.

In June, I ended my second stint as Secretary of State for Wales. There had been a half-hearted coup against Gordon, which amounted to nothing, and he continued as Prime Minister for another year.

Gordon wrote to me on 5 June, thanking me for my work as Welsh Secretary and as Minister for Digital Inclusion, and for overseeing devolution. He said:

> I was pleased to welcome you back to the Government . . . Your work with the Welsh Assembly Government has been exemplary, not least in helping the response to the economic downturn, and guiding the ideas on the future for devolution in Wales.

I had known from the beginning that my renewed tenure of the job was to be time-limited, but I enjoyed my second term in the role. I received letters of thanks and appreciation from many people – UK Ministers, MPs, Welsh Government Ministers, AMs and top civil servants. Rhodri wrote:

I know that I speak for the whole Cabinet in saying that your experience, wisdom and sheer practical common sense contributed enormously to developing a sound working relationship between the Wales Office and the Welsh Assembly Government – you will be sorely missed.

Peter Hain replaced me. Again, another swap! Gordon also asked if I would be interested in becoming the British Ambassador to the Holy See, which was a tempting offer for me as a Catholic, but I felt my age was against me. I was too old to learn Italian. There was also the issue that, although all the indications were that a future Conservative government would honour a commitment from Gordon, this could not be guaranteed. In the end, I decided to remain in the Commons.

In the Chamber, I continued to speak on Welsh affairs, care for the elderly, and on the ISC. In February and March 2010, I made special references to my close friends Don Touhig and Kim Howells, who were both retiring from the House. The General Election was held on 6 May, and I was elected for Torfaen in my 23rd year as an MP, with a respectable majority of 9,306, despite a swing to the Tories. The *Free Press* headline read: "Evergreen Murphy re-elected in Torfaen". But we had lost the country, and David Cameron became Prime Minister.

Rhodri Morgan had stepped down from his position in Wales as First Minister in January 2010. He wrote to me on that occasion, saying "I don't think we ever had a cross word together, even though we had originated on different sides of the devolution argument."

I had backed Edwina Hart to succeed Rhodri as First Minister, but she was beaten by Carwyn Jones, for whom I had a considerable regard.

We were now in a new era. A new government, a new First Minister, and I was returning to parliament as an opposition backbencher for the first time in 22 years.

2010 and after

I REALISED THAT AFTER the 2010 election, I would remain on the back benches. I had been on the front bench for two decades, and during that time my priorities were determined by my various jobs. In my new situation, constituency matters would, as always, be a special concern; but apart from such issues, it would be entirely up to me to decide how best to use my time and I would have to ensure that I did so wisely.

The first major decision I had to resolve concerned who I should support in the new race for the Labour Party leadership. Gordon Brown had resigned immediately at the election defeat; personally, I thought he should have remained until his successor had been chosen. I understood his feelings, however, and I had to make up my mind on his successor. It was going to be a choice between one or other of the Miliband brothers and Ed Balls. Individually, they were all very able people, but in the end I decided in favour of Ed Miliband. I had sat next to him in the Cabinet, and I liked him a lot. Importantly, I also thought he could be the best unifying leader. His brother David was very distant toward me because of my decision – but that's politics, you have to do what you think is right. I had a great deal of time for David, and I was sorry to see him leave British public life.

I continued to be heavily involved in the British–Irish parliamentary assembly, but now as vice-chair, since the governing party always takes the chair. Plenary sessions were held in Cavan, in Swansea, and on the Isle of Man. The Irish co-chair of the assembly was Niall Blaney, and I was pleased to meet up with Brian Cowen (by now Prime Minister of Ireland) in Cavan, and with Gerry Adams in Swansea.

I still made speeches in the Commons, of course, on matters ranging from Severn Bridge tolls to IPSA (the body dealing with MPs' expenses), and I questioned the Prime Minister David Cameron on the Saville inquiry, and spoke in the subsequent debate on Bloody Sunday. Much of my time in the

Chamber was taken up with opposing the government's intended legislation to reform the House of Lords and to reduce the number of MPs.

I had never been in favour of an elected Upper House; I believed it would be a rival to the Commons, and I thought the severe reduction in the numbers of Welsh MPs (which was part of the proposed overall UK cut from 650 to 600) was wrong and threatened the union. The Welsh Secretary, Cheryl Gillan (whom I trusted and admired), refused to call a Welsh Grand Committee on the boundary issue, and non-Tory Welsh MPs convened the "Welsh Parliamentary Party" consisting of all MPs for Welsh constituencies, which had not met for many years. Three former Welsh Secretaries – Peter Hain, Alun Michael and I – wrote to David Cameron complaining about the poor provision that had been made for parliamentary discussion of the proposals, but to no avail. The government was determined to change the boundaries, reduce the numbers of Welsh MPs, and thereby lessen Welsh influence in the Commons.

Contrasting with this contentious matter, one of the highlights of the year turned out to be the address by Pope Benedict XVI to both Houses in Westminster Hall on 17 September. The following month, in mid-October, I led a Commonwealth parliamentary association visit to Sri Lanka. I have already described how, at Tony Blair's request, I visited the country in 2006 to explain the potential lessons to be learned in Sri Lanka from the Northern Ireland peace process. But, unfortunately and tragically, it was the military solution proposed by the Sri Lankan army that was adopted, rather than the Northern Ireland model. A terrible civil war followed, with thousands of Tamil deaths, and we were now visiting to view the current state of the country.

The cross-party delegation, including Stephen Hammond MP as the senior Conservative, benefited from the experience of the CPA UK branch secretary Andrew Tuggey. We covered an extensive programme, meeting President Mahinda Rajapaksa as well as other ministers, and the speaker of the Sri Lankan parliament.

We took the opportunity to visit the north of Sri Lanka and meet refugees in the re-settlements at Jaffna and Trincomalee. I was able to undertake a good deal of media work, and stressed that the UK would do all that it could to help reform Sri Lanka, and return peace and stability to the country.

There was still much reconstruction work to be done, not to mention the need to restore democracy at all levels and in all parts of the country – which has partly happened in subsequent years. In 2010, it appeared to us that the country was becoming more authoritarian, but this was to change with the election of the new president, Maithripala Sirisena, in 2015.

Despite the fact that Sri Lanka didn't choose the same route as Northern Ireland to resolve its conflict, we can only hope that stability, peace and prosperity can be achieved. I never regretted trying to help the people of this wonderful country.

There were some staff changes in my office during this time. Dave Roberts, a highly gifted young man who was to receive a doctorate in Architecture and Social Studies at University College London, joined the team – although he only worked part-time due to his academic commitments. Dave had a fine mind and sound judgement, and enjoyed the additional advantage that his father's family was Welsh!

I had employed interns from the Catholic Bishops' Conference for some years, very gifted young people who were paid, and who worked for a year with parliamentarians. Andrew Duncan joined me, having studied History at both Oxford and Cambridge. His mother was English, and his father was an Anglo-Indian ear, nose and throat consultant at Noble's Hospital on the Isle of Man. After his year was over Andrew remained with me for a further year until he decided to train as a teacher. A very courteous and pleasant man, he was to prove invaluable when I researched the issue of Oxbridge entrance from Wales.

When Dave left, I recruited Briony Robinson, another researcher, who had studied politics at Wadham College, Oxford, and at Sheffield University. She had also worked as a pub manager, and had fought an election as a Labour candidate in a very difficult ward in Derbyshire. Briony was an extremely bright and committed person who also gave me a great deal of help on the Oxbridge project, and eventually worked for my successor as MP before joining Channel 4. I really was blessed with a fantastic team: Anthony, Sian and Pam in Torfaen, and Briony and Andrew in London.

Constitutional issues still dominated 2011, with continuing rows over the proposed new parliamentary boundaries and the mooted reduction in the numbers of Welsh MPs. I managed to win a debate in Westminster Hall on the so-called West Lothian question, which related to the reduced status that Welsh, Scottish and Northern Ireland MPs would have, post-devolution. Popularly characterised as the issue of "English Votes for English Laws", EVEL had always been the war-cry of the Tories, but again I considered it as a danger to the union. In my view, an MP for a Welsh constituency should have precisely the same status as any other UK MP, and I argued for this in the debate. The government, however, refused to concede on the matter. The planned change was introduced, and MPs for constituencies in Wales, Northern Ireland and Scotland were no longer allowed to vote on specifically English issues.

I continued in my role as vice-chair of the British–Irish parliamentary assembly, and in 2011 the assembly met in Cork and in Brighton.

On 3 March, a referendum was held in Wales on legislative powers for the Welsh Assembly. I had gradually changed my mind on devolution, to which I had originally been opposed, but the Thatcher years had guided many of us to a different view. My experience as Welsh Secretary now persuaded me that the Welsh Assembly, which had come into being in 1999, should be given primary legislative powers. I was also convinced that there ought to be a referendum before such a change could be introduced.

I took part in the referendum campaign, and the vote produced a decent majority in favour of new powers for the Assembly. It was an important moment in the history of devolution, and the Assembly was now very much part of the lives of Welsh people.

I spoke in the Commons on the Silk Commission, which was going to look into the function and financing of the Assembly, and on Northern Ireland matters, as well as the ISC, Lords reform, fuel costs and the Severn Bridge tolls.

In July, I was asked by the Foreign Office to travel to the Philippines to see if our experience in Northern Ireland could help resolve a continuing conflict, a sort of civil war among the communists, and a separate conflict between Christians and Muslims in the southern Philippines. I had five days of intense discussions and meetings, first in Mindanao in the south, and then in the capital, Manila. I met religious leaders, business people, senior politicians and the various negotiating panels set up by the Philippine government. Some time after my visit, the government hosted meetings with David Trimble, Lord John Alderdice and Robert Hannigan.

As had been the case with Sri Lanka, I emphasised that while no two peace processes were the same, lessons could certainly be learned from Northern Ireland as far as the importance of independent international arbitration, the constant attention to detail, proper dialogue and parity of esteem of all parties were concerned. My message to the peace parties was that "Peace doesn't happen overnight but if there's a will then eventually it will. You can't negotiate peace part time."

It was especially important that I met with the Moro Islamic Liberation Front, in addition to government and security agencies. I was even asked if I was willing to "do a George Mitchell", and become their international arbitrator.

The visit went well and, happily, the Filipinos decided to apply the Northern Ireland peace process as a basis for their talks. Ultimately their own peace process, involving the Moro Islamic Liberation Front, was successful.

During 2012, I continued to speak regularly in the Commons on matters such as the alleged exploitation of tenant landlords by pub companies, rural bank closures in Wales, jobs and growth, Internet evidence in court, the North Wales child abuse inquiry, and even women bishops.

The BIPA met in Dublin and in Glasgow, where there was much talk of the forthcoming referendum on Scottish independence.

The Parliamentary Boundary Committee for Wales reported in January. Under its proposals, the Torfaen Constituency was to be enlarged to take in Croesyceiliog, Llanyrafon, Llanfrechfa and Ponthir (all of which were already in the Torfaen County Borough area) – a sensible idea. Not so obvious was the justification for including Caerleon (currently in the Newport West constituency). As it turned out, the Liberal Democrats opposed the boundary changes (because the Conservatives had failed to support proposals for reform of the House of Lords – an issue that had featured in the 2010 coalition agreement), and my successor was to fight the 2015 election on the old boundaries.

In July my niece Rachel graduated in Law from Swansea University. My nephew Daniel had completed his degree in Information Technology at Cardiff University two years previously. Both have given me great happiness.

I had kept in touch with an old Oriel friend, Peter Gross, over the years, and we got together frequently. Peter's wife Ruth, and his two sons George and Ed, were charming and intelligent, as was Peter himself – who was to become a High Court Judge (and Senior Presiding Judge for England and Wales), and a Lord Justice of Appeal. He almost became Lord Chief Justice too, and would have made an excellent one!

Jonathan Phillips was another old friend with whom I kept in contact. He became Warden of Keble College, Oxford, and I have been so pleased to be able to stay with him and his lovely wife Amanda on many occasions in the college.

Even though I was now a thoroughgoing back bencher, I was still kept very busy. The vice-chairmanship of BIPA took me to Letterkenny in Donegal in March, while the assembly met also in London in October. I continued to speak regularly in the Commons Chamber and in Westminster Hall on such diverse subjects as the so-called bedroom tax, the powers of the ISC, scams on older people, food banks and Northern Ireland.

Tragically, during this period my old friend Ernest Nicholson, former Provost of Oriel College, was diagnosed with terminal liver cancer. He wrote his last letter to me in August 2012, and we met for the final time in September at the annual Oriel Society dinner. Ernest died the following year. He had made a huge contribution to the college and to the study of the Old Testament. Ernest came from a Northern Ireland working class background, and had always been committed to widening access to Oxford. I became extremely involved in this subject, partly because my colleague David Lammy MP had looked at all black and minority ethnic entrants to Oxbridge, and I decided to investigate the issue of access to Oxbridge by students from Wales.

I asked my researcher Andrew to work with me on this project, and I produced a report in the spring of 2013 entitled *Oxbridge Access and Wales – Challenges and Solutions*. Students from the Welsh valleys, I discovered, were five times less likely to apply to Oxbridge than were students who lived in Hertfordshire, and ten times less likely to receive an offer. I concluded that among the key factors leading to this distortion were attainment levels in Wales; attitudes to and awareness of Oxford and Cambridge among teachers in Wales; and Welsh educational policies concerning the Welsh Baccalaureate, and the release of data to university admissions tutors.

I also concluded that teachers were key to improving the chances of students applying to and entering Oxbridge by encouraging applications, giving good advice, and by encouraging aspiration and attainment. The Welsh Government should support shared academic enrichment activities between schools; the new "Teach First" system should be introduced to Wales; promotion of Oxbridge should start early in schools; Oxbridge alumni and alumnae should be linked up to schools and act as "ambassadors"; schools and teachers should publicise Oxbridge "outreach" events, and potential students should understand that Oxford and Cambridge are not more expensive than other universities.

As part of the research, I made a special visit to Gower College in Swansea. The college had a very good record in sending students to Oxford and particularly Cambridge, where Jonathan Padley from Churchill College was a major force. His mother taught in Gower College, and they both visited me in the Commons together with the college's principal Nick Bennett (who was a former colleague of mine at Ebbw Vale College, and also a very good friend). They gave me useful ideas and suggestions, which I went on to incorporate into my initial report.

I felt strongly about the issue because in the late 1960s I had myself been given the chance to go to Oxford – a working class boy from the valleys, and the first of my family to go to university. Over the intervening years, fewer and fewer young people from Wales had been applying for entrance to Oxbridge, and I felt the time had come to change this.

The press was very interested in the project, and I wrote an article in the *Western Mail* entitled: "It shouldn't be a bridge too far for our brightest students." I emphasised that I had absolutely nothing against our own universities in Wales, but argued that Welsh students should also have the opportunity to study at Oxford and Cambridge, two institutions with worldwide reputations and histories.

I discussed my report and my conclusions with Leighton Andrews, the Welsh Education Minister, and to my astonishment he asked me to become the Welsh Oxbridge Ambassador, announcing it in a speech on 18 March:

> I have heard it said that certain universities are not for the likes of us. Again I can't accept that. I didn't go to Oxbridge and I don't believe that Oxbridge is the be all and end all of higher education. But I have recently seen evidence which suggests there has been a decline in the number of young people from Wales securing places at these two world-class universities. I want our young people to aim high and not be put off because they have been given the impression that they would not be welcome. So I am delighted to announce that Paul Murphy will act as our Oxbridge Ambassador.

I was very pleased and honoured by this, and soon got down to work. Rowan Williams, the former Archbishop of Canterbury, and Master of Magdalene College, Cambridge, was hugely supportive, as was Richard Partington, senior tutor at Churchill College Cambridge. Professor Andrew Hamilton, vice-chancellor of Oxford, said: "We are delighted to be working with Paul Murphy to encourage all Welsh students with the required grades and a passion for their subject to consider applying to Oxford."

The project had good support in the Welsh Assembly – although Plaid Cymru's Education spokesman wondered why we didn't aim to get students to Harvard.

The Welsh Government supplied me with an excellent team headed by Nia Jones, and Jonathan Padley and Sinead Gallagher were seconded from Cambridge and Oxford respectively. My own staff – especially Anthony, Briony and Andrew – were also heavily involved.

Over the next year, I was to travel to schools and colleges all over Wales, meeting hundreds of teachers and students. I also spent a great deal of time in the two universities, talking to their staff and visiting individual colleges, as well as interviewing current Welsh students in both cities. I also had sessions with alumni and alumnae in Cardiff and in the House of Commons – with Andrew Dilnot, Warden of Nuffield College, chairing the London session. I thoroughly enjoyed working on this project, and it quite rightly occupied a fair proportion of my time.

I published my report at a press conference in Cardiff in June 2014, presided over by the new Education Minister Huw Lewis – a friend for many years, and husband of my excellent Assembly colleague for Torfaen, Lynne Neagle. Lynne had become Torfaen's AM in the first Assembly elections in 1999, and she and I held common political views and worked together very closely over the years. We became good friends.

I opened my *Final Report of the Oxbridge Ambassador for Wales* by saying:

> I present my report to the Minister for Education and Skills with every confidence that by working in partnership we can implement these recommendations for the good of every one of our young people ... We sometimes have a habit in Wales of talking ourselves down. I will have none of that. The Welsh pupils and students I have met over the course of my study are as bright as anywhere else.

My team had done a brilliant job in compiling the report. Among other things, it argued that Welsh students (and some teachers) had a perception of Oxbridge that was long out of date; that the proportion of students with high-grade "A" Level attainment in Welsh schools and colleges was below that in the UK as a whole, and should be improved; that there was some evidence of a lack of aspiration among young Welsh people; and that Oxford and Cambridge should target their outreach programmes to engage with a wider audience.

We compared Wales with the north-east of England partly because a far higher proportion of Oxbridge applicants from the north-east were offered a place compared with those from Wales, despite the two areas being socio-economically similar. But there was also the peculiar and special Welsh aspect that education was a devolved matter in Wales.

In Oxford, St Peter's College, Lady Margaret Hall, and naturally Jesus College (with its long-established Welsh links, beginning with the appointment of an Abergavenny man as its first principal) all had access policies for Wales, as did Churchill and Magdalene colleges in Cambridge. The admissions offices of both universities were very active in promoting those policies. Even so, something new had to be tried, and I came to the conclusion that what was happening in Gower College should be replicated throughout Wales. The report suggested therefore that hubs should be set up where Dons from the two universities would be available to give expert advice on how to apply to Oxbridge, on how to approach interviews, on how to prepare for any admission tests, and so on. Sessions on individual subjects would be arranged so that students could engage with some of the finest brains in their areas of interest, and even if they were ultimately unsuccessful in their Oxbridge applications, the hub experience would make it more likely that they would be accepted at another Russell Group university.

The Welsh Government was quick to implement this main recommendation, and set up the so-called Seren network all over Wales (*seren* is Welsh for "star"). The whole experience of researching and compiling the report, and sensing the enthusiasm and commitment of so many that we had talked to, had been very rewarding.

Even in these early years of the Seren scheme, much has been achieved, and I hope that it will continue to develop and expand, so that more and more young people from Wales will be able to benefit from the kind of opportunity that I was given in the 1960s.

As usual, my speeches in the Commons covered many topics – including pub companies; a tribute to my friend Paul Goggins MP, who had died early and tragically; housing benefits; Severn Bridge tolls; devolution; Northern Ireland; and the increasing problems of so-called legal highs. The BIPA took me to Dublin and to Ypres, and to the First World War battlefields, where both Irish and British TDs and MPs paid tribute to their brave countrymen at a ceremony to mark the centenary of the start of that terrible conflict.

On 17 July, I was privileged to be made an Honorary Doctor of the University by the University of South Wales, at an impressive graduation ceremony at Pontypridd. A fortnight later, my nephew Daniel married Katie Walsh in the Catholic Church at Potters Bar.

In September 2014, I represented the leader of the opposition at the memorial service for the late Ian Paisley, held at the Ulster Hall, Belfast. It was a reflection of how times had changed that a Catholic former Northern Ireland Secretary would now attend such a service, and take part in it. Ian had worked hard to make peace in Ulster, and his unique relationship with Martin McGuinness had been admired the world over.

Tragedy, however, dominated the end of the year. Don Touhig's wife Jennifer, whom I had known for 50 years, died after a long and painful battle with cancer. I had been best man at their wedding, and was godfather to their children, and her death was a terrible blow. I was privileged to give the eulogy at the funeral at St Alban's Catholic Church in Pontypool, the same church where Don and Jen had been married.

The day after Jen's funeral I heard that my good friend Canon Bill Redmond had died. Reflecting on my Oxford days, I have already spoken of Bill's remarkable qualities, of the enduring nature of our friendship, and of his memorable funeral service. He was buried on 19 December at his former parish church of St Oswald, King and Martyr, in Warrington. The principal celebrant was the Archbishop of Liverpool, the Most Reverend Malcolm McMahon. With Bill's passing, I lost a fine, kind and intelligent friend.

I had by now decided that I would stand down from parliament at the General Election in May 2015. It was not an easy decision. I had been in the Commons for nearly three decades. Politics was my life, and I knew I would miss parliament, but I was now an OAP and finding the work of an MP more demanding.

It was at the meeting of the Torfaen Constituency Labour Party on 30 January 2015 that I announced my intention to retire. I told the members that a new five-year term in the Commons would be too much of a challenge, and that the valley needed a younger person to represent them.

One of the first to respond publicly to the news was Ed Miliband, who said:

> Paul Murphy is one of the most respected and liked MPs and his departure will leave a big hole in the House of Commons. He will be most remembered for his role in negotiating the Good Friday Agreement.

Other tributes were made by shadow Welsh Secretary Owen Smith MP, and by First Minister of Wales Carwyn Jones. Gordon Brown and many others wrote me some lovely and moving letters, and the newspapers were very generous in their comments – the editorial in the *Western Mail* was particularly kind. Headed "Murphy's example is one to follow", it observed that "Mr Murphy has proved it is possible to combine conviction with courtesy, [he] articulated deeply-held opinions without slandering the character of those who disagreed. His intellectual clout was only enhanced by his personal graciousness." I could not have asked for better.

Mark Durkan MP, one-time leader of the SDLP, was kind enough to write some appreciative comments about me in the Northern Ireland press, a gesture that I found very moving.

The Torfaen party had to select my successor as Labour candidate for the constituency, and it took them little time or persuasion to choose Nick Thomas-Symonds. Nick was originally from Blaenavon, though later a resident of Abersychan. He went to St Alban's School, Pontypool, and St Edmund Hall, Oxford, where he had been a lecturer in Politics as well as a practising barrister. A fine historian, Nick had published two considerable biographies – one on Attlee and one on Aneurin Bevan – and he had done some work experience with me in the late 1990s before eventually becoming the secretary of the constituency Labour Party. In a way, his career paralleled my own.

We had feared that Nick might have been excluded from consideration if an all-woman shortlist had been imposed on the local party. But everyone, from the leader's office to the trade unions, could see that he would be an outstanding MP, as is already proving to be the case.

I made my final speech in the House of Commons on 5 March 2015 at the annual Welsh Day debate. I reminded the House once more that it was not the feast day of St David, but of St Caron of Tregaron, a third-century Cardiganshire saint. I observed that I had spoken first in a Welsh Day debate 27 years before, and reflected on the changes that had taken place since then. I told the House that, in my view, the office of Welsh Secretary should not be abandoned, and I concluded:

> I have had the great privilege of representing my constituency for nearly three decades. I have represented the good people of the Eastern Valley of Gwent. I hope that whoever succeeds me will have the same duties, responsibilities, privileges and rights. I have been the Member for Torfaen but also a Member of Parliament of this United Kingdom like any other member. If we do not maintain that, not only the House but our Union will be in danger.

Members from all sides of the House wished me a happy retirement, and I duly gave up my seat on 7 May when a new parliament and a new MP for Torfaen were elected.

A fortnight later, my friend Stuart's mother, Yvonne, died. She was 98 and had been physically and mentally active right to the end. I was privileged to deliver the eulogy at her funeral at St Gabriel's Church, Cwmbran. Despite her great age it was still a great sadness that she had left us. I told the congregation that Yvonne was "a gentle woman, full of fun and love and with an engaging and marvellous smile". She would be missed by all her family and friends, and especially by her daughter Sue, who had looked after her for so many years.

In the summer of 2015, Ed Miliband phoned me at home and said that he had nominated me for a peerage. It was formally announced at the end of August. The *Western Mail* issue for the 28th of that month headed its front page with "Hain and Murphy now appointed to the Lords", and I took my seat on 26 November 2015. It was the day after my 67th birthday, and my title was Lord Murphy of Torfaen, and Abersychan in the County of Gwent. Thus did I include the name of my former constituency and of the village where I had grown up. Unfortunately, I had broken my left wrist in a fall the week before, which required an operation at St Thomas's hospital. I was given marvellous treatment there, but it meant that for my introduction to the Upper House I entered the Chamber with my forearm and wrist in plaster and my arm in a sling – which made it quite difficult to manage the ermine robes.

I had scarcely even had time to notice that the carpets had changed colour from green to red when I was contacted by Theresa May, then still Home Secretary, asking me to chair the joint committee on the draft Investigatory Powers Bill. The legislation was designed to regularise and strengthen the power of the police and the intelligence agencies. I entirely agreed with its aim because of new threats to our people but achieving a balance between the liberty of the citizen and the need to protect ourselves against terrorism was critical. There had to be proper means of access to the new world of digital technology, but we also had to include safeguards to counter the dangers that such technology presents.

The committee consisted of 14 members – seven from each House – and we had very effective contributions from everyone. The members were the Bishop of Chester, Lord Robin Butler, David Hanson MP, Baroness Angela Browning, Lord Henley, Victoria Atkins MP, Lord Hart, Lord Strasburger, Suella Fernandez MP, Shabana Mahmood MP, Stuart C. MacDonald MP, Dr Andrew Murrison MP, and Matt Warman MP. As our clerk, we had the hugely able and effective Duncan Sagar.

The joint committee eventually made over 80 recommendations to change the bill, which the government accepted, and the whole process, that we undertook over two months, was both fascinating and enjoyable – despite my broken wrist!

During November, the Catholic Archbishop of Cardiff George Stark told me that I was to be made a Knight Commander of the Royal Order of St Gregory. In December, ITV Wales nominated me for the Lifetime Achievement Award at the 2015 Welsh Politician of the Year Awards. I was very touched by both honours, and I was also pleased to agree to become honorary president of the Pontypool branch of the Royal Welsh Regiment Association. I had a long connection with the association, and with its leading members Dave Thomas and Captain Lewis Freeman. My grandfather had been in the Monmouthshire Militia, and my uncle in the South Wales Borderers, so it was fitting that I followed in their footsteps – in a purely non-military sense.

I made my (second!) maiden speech on 11 February 2016, during the Armed Forces Bill debate. I referred to Don and to John McFall (who had been my sponsors when I was introduced into the Lords), and to Torfaen, as well as to my time as an MP. I also praised my successor, Nick Thomas-Symonds, and told the House that Nick was the latest – the seventh – from the Abersychan production line for Labour MPs.

Speaking in the Lords was different, never heckled or shouted down, and interventions were fewer. It was, above all else, a quieter chamber than the Commons. There is a huge amount of experience in the Lords, especially among the crossbenchers, and someone told me that whatever subject you might choose there was someone in the Lords who would know more than you did.

Lord Reg Empey of the UUP – an old friend – spoke after me, and made some very kind remarks, especially about my time in Northern Ireland.

I chose to contribute to debates on varied subjects, but mainly about those areas for which I had held either Ministerial or committee responsibilities. So I spoke on the Investigatory Powers Bill, the Northern Ireland Bill and the Wales Bill, but I also contributed in the Chamber on the Trade Union Bill and on church schools. I spoke, too, on the Access to Medical Treatments (Innovation) Bill: Nick Thomas-Symonds had successfully proposed a number of amendments to this legislation, reflecting aspects of his own private member's bill, the Off-Patent Drugs Bill, which had been talked out in the Commons.

I went to the opening of the Welsh Assembly by the Queen in June, and around this time I was asked by the Education Minister Huw Lewis AM to undertake an inquiry into the Royal Welsh College of Music and Drama, based in Cardiff, looking particularly at its financing and relationship with the University of South Wales. John Myerscough, an acknowledged expert on conservatoires amongst other things, was to join with me to compile the report. When I was Welsh Secretary, I had had some influence in obtaining Royal patronage for the college, which played a pivotal role in the cultural life of Wales and indeed of the UK. The college produced many famous musicians and actors, and was a major Welsh national institution. The college president, Lord David Rowe-Beddoe, a good friend, has played a significant part in its success – David had been the chair of the Welsh Development Agency, has had a major role in the development of the Welsh economy, and is a great public servant.

That June, the UK voted to leave the European Union – in my view, a disastrous decision. In Torfaen, where I canvassed for remain, 60 per cent voted for Brexit, despite many Eastern Valley jobs being dependent on Britain's membership of the EU. To judge from comments on the doorstep, immigration, especially from Eastern Europe, seemed to be the main reason why local people voted to leave – even though there were hardly any immigrants in the valley. In the wake of the overall referendum result, David Cameron resigned as Prime Minister and Theresa May assumed the role in July 2016, on becoming the new leader of her party.

As I was approaching my 68th birthday in November 2016, I experienced a couple of blackouts and, a few months later in March 2017, I collapsed after a PLP meeting. I was rushed to St Thomas's hospital, and had to have a pacemaker fitted. It was a timely reminder that I was no longer a young man.

I was elected, unopposed, to the parliamentary committee (the executive committee of the PLP) by the Labour peers, which meant I had to attend its weekly meeting with the party leader and deputy leader.

Much of the autumn and winter of 2016 was taken up with the Investigatory Powers Bill and the Wales Bill, as was the beginning of 2017. The big issue now, of course, was Brexit. I spoke in the Chamber, sometimes as a guest from the front bench, on the implications for Wales and for Northern Ireland – the border was a major concern in the debate, as was the Good Friday Agreement, which had been negotiated originally in the context of British–Irish membership of the European Union. The people of Northern Ireland had voted to remain in the EU, while Wales had voted to leave. The whole thing was a real political dilemma for me.

In February 2017, my former researcher Anthony Hunt was elected leader of Torfaen County Borough Council. It was a very good appointment – Anthony's relative youth and vast political experience, particularly as a special adviser at the Welsh Office, stood him in good stead for this important position. Taking up his new role at the age of 36, he was the youngest council leader in Wales.

Some months later in June, another great friend of mine, Phyllis Roberts, achieved something similarly noteworthy for a person of her age. She became the oldest mayor in the country at the age of 93! Phyllis had been chair of Blaenavon urban district council 47 years earlier, and she was now back in the job as mayor of Blaenavon.

Having repeatedly insisted that the 2015 parliament would run its full five-year course, Theresa May called the General Election for 8 June 2017, and resumed office with no overall majority, while Jeremy Corbyn unexpectedly returned an increased number of Labour MPs. For my own part, I was pleased to be once more on the British–Irish parliamentary assembly, which gave me the opportunity to renew my friendships with Irish politicians.

It was during the election campaign that my friend Rhodri Morgan died suddenly at the age of 77. His death was a great blow to his family and friends, and to Wales. I was privileged to speak at his funeral service, a celebration of his life, which was held at the Senedd in Cardiff Bay on 31 May. It was the nearest we have had in Wales to a state funeral, and Rhodri deserved it. He was the father of devolution, and in many ways of the nation, and I was deeply moved by the commemoration and the tributes paid to him. The world seemed strange without Rhodri, who had been a close friend for 35 years.

In the Lords, I spoke on issues ranging from the Battle of Passchendaele to digital television, and I defended faith schools at the annual Archbishop of Canterbury's debate.

The following year, 2018, was to be dominated by the Brexit negotiation, and much of my time was devoted to this. More happy for me was the twentieth anniversary of the signing of the Good Friday Agreement on 10 April, and I returned to Belfast for a number of wonderful events to mark the occasion. Bill Clinton, Tony Blair, Bertie Ahern and all the major players were in town, and the Class of '98 (including me) was much photographed! The SDLP awarded the new John Hume Medal to Bertie Ahern, Seamus Mallon, Mark Durkan and me, for our contributions to the peace process; the individual medals were presented to us by John's wife, Pat.

That year is a fitting point at which to conclude this brief memoir. Throughout my career, both before and during my time in parliament, I have been blessed with extraordinary opportunities. I have been able to spend my working life doing what I enjoy and value. The values that I learned from my parents and my faith shaped my political views, and the Labour way has been my way for 54 years. The stalwarts I met at the Abersychan ward Labour Party meeting in 1964 held principles that I share and that I have sought to uphold as a councillor, Minister, Secretary of State, MP and peer.

In many ways, Wales and Northern Ireland have dominated my parliamentary career. I have seen great changes in the way Wales is governed, and I have played a part in shaping those changes over the past 32 years. I am privileged to have contributed to the peace process in Northern Ireland; and the making of the Good Friday Agreement will always be the highlight of my political and ministerial career.

Yet, none of that would have been possible without the support of the good people of the Eastern Valley, and it is to them that I owe my greatest political debt. They sent me to the House of Commons in 1987, and they provided the moral and political bedrock that has sustained me for three decades.

Index